International Screen Industries

Series Editors:
Michael Curtin, University of Wisconsin-Madison and Paul McDonald,
University of Portsmouth

This unique series provides original profiles of film, television and digital media
industries in a variety of countries and regions throughout the world. It also analyses how transnational flows of goods, services, talent and capital are shaping the
increasingly interconnected global media economy.

Published titles:
European Film Industries *Anne Jäckel*
European Television Industries *Petros Iosifidis, Jeanette Steemers and Mark Wheeler*
Global Television Marketplace *Timothy Havens*
Video and DVD Industries *Paul McDonald*
East Asian Screen Industries *Darrell Davis and Emilie Yueh-yu Yeh*

Forthcoming:
Arab Television Industries *Marwan M. Kraidy and Joe F. Khalil*
The Global Videogames Industry *Randy Nichols*
The Indian Film Industry *Nitin Govil and Ranjani Mazumdar*
Television in India *Shehina Fazal*
Television in Greater China *Joseph Chan*
Latin American Film Industries *Tamara Falicov*

The American Television Industry

Michael Curtin and Jane Shattuc

A BFI book published by Palgrave Macmillan

First published in 2009 by
PALGRAVE MACMILLAN

on behalf of the

BRITISH FILM INSTITUTE
21 Stephen Street, London W1T 1LN
www.bfi.org.uk

There's more to discover about film and television through the BFI. Our world-renowned archive, cinemas, festivals, films, publications and learning resources are here to inspire you.

Palgrave Macmillan in the UK is an imprint of Macmillan Publishers Limited, registered in England, company number 785998, of Houndmills, Basingstoke, Hampshire RG21 6XS. Palgrave Macmillan in the US is a division of St Martin's Press LLC, 175 Fifth Avenue, New York, NY 10010. Palgrave Macmillan is the global academic imprint of the above companies and has companies and representatives throughout the world. Palgrave® and Macmillan® are registered trademarks in the United States, the United Kingdom, Europe and other countries.

Cover image: (front) *30 Rock* (2006–, Broadway Video/NBC Universal Television);
(back) *Lost* (2004–, Bad Robot/Touchstone Television/Grass Skirt Productions/ABC Studios).
Printed in Great Britain by MPG Books Group, Bodmin & King's Lynn

This book is printed on paper suitable for recycling and made from fully managed and sustained forest sources. Logging, pulping and manufacturing processes are expected to conform to the environmental regulations of the country of origin.

British Library Cataloguing-in-Publication Data
A catalogue record for this book is available from the British Library

ISBN 978–1–84457–337–0 (pbk)
ISBN 978–1–84457–338–7 (hbk)

Contents

Introduction   1
1 Key Players   5
2 Audiences and Advertising   34
3 Television Programming   58
4 Making TV on the Broadcast Networks   88
5 Branded Cable Networks   119
6 The New Economies of TV Information   145
Conclusion   172

Bibliography   185
Index   193

Introduction

Media analysts commonly argue that the future of the American television industry is uncertain, given the growing competition from flashy new rivals, such as YouTube, Halo and iPhone. Yet reports of television's demise are often exaggerated, for it not only remains the pre-eminent communication medium in the United States, it continues to reside at the very centre of everyday life. In the month of May 2008, Americans spent an average of 127 hours viewing television, a six-hour increase over the preceding year. By comparison, they averaged only twenty-six hours on the Internet (Nielsen Company 2008).

Although they sometimes devote undivided attention to favourite TV shows, Americans also tune in while they read, eat, wash dishes, socialise or carry on with other household activities. Television offers nightly news, quirky game shows, big-time sporting events and luscious primetime dramas. Almost every American household owns at least one television set and four out of five homes have more than one. Not only is television a ubiquitous presence in the home, it is also widely available in airports, bus stations, schools, hospitals, restaurants, bars and shopping centres. In a country of 300 million people, 282 million watch television in a given month while only 162 million make use of the Internet (Stelter, 'Whichever Screen', 2008). Even among the computer-savvy population, television is the most widely used medium, comprising more than a third of their media diet. If one includes video and DVD viewing, television represents almost half of their total media use.[1]

Part of the reason television is sometimes described as a troubled medium is that few TV shows today can command the vast mass audiences that were typical during television's heyday. Instead, audiences today are far smaller, since they are dispersed among a growing number of channels. Moreover, as Internet usage grows, many believe it is siphoning away TV audiences. Nevertheless, in a fragmented media universe, the major television networks remain the only services that can bring together substantial national audiences on a regular basis. Popular primetime series still attract more than 10 million viewers. The most popular show, *American Idol* (2002–), averages close to 30 million, almost 10 per cent of the total US population. TV also carries a wide range of popular sporting events and championships, among them, the Superbowl football championship that attracts some 90 million viewers. Television is furthermore a leading source of news and it is the most important mediator of major political events, such as elections, debates, inaugurations and military engagements (Learmonth 2006).

A Nielsen Media Research study conducted in May 2006 found that each of the four major broadcast networks attracted between 157 and 179 million unique viewers. That is, more than half the US population watched each of the four major networks during the month compared to 50 million unique visitors to one the Internet's most popular social networking sites, MySpace. As for cable, the most popular channels drew 20 to 30 million unique visitors. Overall, Nielsen found the television channels that attract the most viewers and hold their attention for the longest periods of time are those with strong narrative content (television series) or event-based programming (sports, games, competitions). Consequently, the major networks continue to be most popular, each of them attracting the attention of viewers for an average of 5.6 to 8.2 hours per month (Lowry 2006).

Television in the United States is a resolutely commercial medium. Its fundamental objective is to attract substantial audiences so that it can sell their attention to advertisers seeking to promote their products and services. Each year, TV stations, networks and cable channels produce tens of thousands of hours of original programming that is funded by more than $72 billion worth of advertising (Fulgoni 2008). Entertainment, advertising and consumerism have operated hand in hand since the very earliest years of the medium.

Yet for all its commercial success, television today is undergoing a period of profound change. For decades, audiences tapped television's vast cultural resources by tuning their sets to particular channels. Increasingly, however, they surf the web as well, making online video the fastest-growing service on the Internet. YouTube (owned by Google) is the leader, distributing more than a third of all videos, much of it amateur content, but the most popular YouTube videos often prove to be clips from popular television shows. Furthermore, the most commercially successful video services online are operated by major television companies, for it turns out that advertisers are much more comfortable sponsoring professionally produced web videos ("NBC" 2008). Advertisers have also taken note of the fact that online viewers tend to prefer professional content and that for every hour they devote to Internet video, they still spend 57 hours watching television (Stelter, 'Whichever Screen', 2008). Thus, the American television industry remains the most significant provider of commercially sponsored video despite the emergence of many new technologies and competitors.

The following chapters explain how the industry operates and how it is adapting to changes in American media and society. Chapter 1 describes the origins and development of the largest and most important television companies, which during their early years of operation were closely regulated by the federal government. Over time, criticisms of the network oligopoly encouraged the introduction of satellite and cable technologies during the 1970s and, as the number of available television channels expanded, the original networks were joined by powerful competitors from related media industries. The first chapter describes the corporate strategies that have shaped the industry and it explains the role that government regulation has played as well.

Chapter 2 explains how audiences are measured and advertising is sold. Since the government provides little direct support to the television industry, virtually all of its activities and programming content relies on funding from advertisers. In order to gauge the value of the commercial time that they sell, television services must demonstrate the size and composition of their audiences. Chapter 2 explains how television ratings are gathered and how ratings services have changed over time. It then shows how advertisers use ratings to design their messages and organise their campaigns. Finally, the chapter describes how the television companies market commercial spots to advertisers, and how the two sides negotiate prices for those spots.

Chapter 3 focuses on programming strategies, showing how network executives develop new programmes and promote them to viewers. It also explains how television schedules are worked out and how that may influence the popularity of particular programmes. Primetime programming on the major networks is discussed in detail but the chapter also explains programming strategies for various parts of the day, such as morning and late-night shows. It furthermore describes the programming strategies of cable channels and independent stations. And it shows how programming strategies for mass-appeal television are different from strategies for channels that target niche audiences. It finishes with a discussion of new media providers, such as video downloading and Internet broadband services.

Chapter 4 outlines the studio production process that has prevailed since the 1950s, featuring a highly rationalised mode of manufacture in which creative responsibilities are divided among craft and creative workers, most of whom are unionised. *Law & Order* (1990–2010) and *Frasier* (1993–2004) serve as models of this highly systematised programme production. The chapter further delineates how the networks have varied this system over the years as they responded to economic and technological changes, including corporate conglomeration, labour activism, home video recording and Internet distribution. Programmes such as *24* (2001–9) and *Survivor* (2000–) suggest the ways in which television programmes increasingly seek to incorporate stylistic and content innovations from new media competitors.

Chapter 5 discusses the niche networks made possible by cable technology. Like broadcast programming, early cable channels catered to general audiences, but as the number of services grew, they began to produce programmes appealing to particular audiences or built around specific genres. This chapter shows, for example, how news channels divided into specific services for liberal and conservative viewers, and even into news channels for sports fans or entertainment buffs. Similarly, A&E began as an arts and entertainment channel that would evolve into a platform of services specifically designed to showcase biographical, historical and military documentaries. Because of the smaller audiences, much of this cable programming is produced on far more modest budgets than programming on the broadcast network. The chapter also examines a key exception to this principle: Home Box Office (HBO), home to some of the most lavish productions on television today, such as *The Sopranos* (1999–2007).

Finally, Chapter 6 looks at television's shift from a preponderance of fictional programming to an increasing amount of informational or unscripted fare. Moreover, by the late 1980s news had become so intertwined with TV entertainment that critics coined the term 'infotainment', a category that embraces much of what's produced for television today. The chapter shows how the Public Broadcasting Service (PBS), which established many of the key genres of informational programming, has since the 1980s experienced growing competition from commercial cable channels that produce home-improvement, cooking and history documentaries, as well as popular music shows.

The Conclusion addresses recent developments and future trends in the television industry. It shows that TV companies are adapting to new media and in turn new media are adopting many of the practices that have governed the television industry for decades. Despite this continuity, the Conclusion points to profound transformations now taking place in the American television industry.

Although the authors collaborated at every stage of the writing process, we allocated the primary writing responsibilities as follows. Chapters 1, 2, 3 and the Conclusion were written by Michael Curtin and Chapters 4, 5, and 6 by Jane Shattuc. The authors would like thank colleagues and students at their respective institutions for supporting this venture and for sharing their ideas and insights. We would also like to express our appreciation to television executives, talent and critics for speaking with us about America's leading media industry.

NOTE

1   This figure excludes computer usage at work (Fulgoni 2008).

1

Key Players

Since the 1980s, television in the United States has undergone a dramatic transformation. Before then, American broadcasting was characterised by a network system that aimed to integrate television stations and audiences nationwide. This model was inherited from the radio era and reached its fullest expression during the 1960s and 1970s when three companies dominated the most popular and powerful mass medium in the history of the United States. Since that time, the power of centralised networks has diminished and the number of competitors has grown. Americans now watch hundreds of channels, access thousands of video titles, and increasingly make use of television outside, as well as inside, the home. Despite these changes, the television industry nevertheless remains very centralised with a few firms exercising significant market power. Instead of three networks, six conglomerates now dominate the industry, operating hundreds of channels and services that bring television to audiences throughout the US and around the world. This chapter traces key trends that have shaped the industry throughout its history and describes the operations and strategies of some of the most important players in American television.[1]

THE NETWORK ERA

Networking became a prominent part of the American media scene as early as 1926 when one of the leading manufacturers of radio receivers, the Radio Corporation of America (RCA), launched two networks with the aim of promoting sales of its equipment. Prior to that time, radio stations broadcast their signals within specific geographic locales that were defined by the distance that radio waves could travel from a station's transmitter, usually thirty to sixty miles. Most radio stations were local services in part because of technological limitations. Networking changed this by interconnecting a group of transmitters via telephone lines so that a programme produced in Chicago could, for example, be made available to audiences tuned to stations in Cincinnati and Detroit, as well. The National Broadcasting Company (NBC), which was owned by RCA, employed the technology to establish regular programming schedules aimed at a nationwide audience via dozens of local stations that came to be known as affiliates. Networking also afforded new business opportunities, since affiliates not only shared NBC's programming, they also shared a brand identity and they worked together to promote their services to advertisers. Radio networking mirrored the increasing influence of chainstores in the American economy, such as Sears department stores, Rexall drugstores and A&P grocery stores. Indeed, radio industry publications and government documents of the period often used the term 'chain broadcasting' when referring to companies such as NBC.

The concept of radio networking also drew precedents from live theatre. Vaudeville, for example, was enormously popular during the late nineteenth and early twentieth century, offering variety shows featuring performers who travelled around a circuit of theatres organised by booking agencies and theatre alliances. These circuits were established so that managers could rotate fresh talent into their local theatres on a regular basis. Circuits also allowed performers the opportunity to gain wide public exposure and gave them a chance to learn from other performers they encountered along the way. As a result, vaudeville entertainers developed genres and performance styles that could gain acceptance in many different locales, a precedent that radio would follow. Popular vaudeville performers also provided core talent for radio, as many were lured away to the new medium.

Although the radio industry developed many of the practices that would come to be associated with broadcast networking, these practices would not reach full maturity until the mid-1950s when television became America's leading vehicle of entertainment and advertising, and shortly thereafter the leader in news and information as well. Yet the triumph of national networking was not without controversy and periodic reversals. Rural and smalltown residents were often suspicious of the big networks because they arguably posed a threat to local businesses, social groups and cultural norms. Many politicians wanted radio stations to represent their local communities and to take into account local values and attitudes. In fact, localism has been a core principle of American media regulation since the 1920s, aiming to ensure that community voices would not be drowned out by powerful interests from afar (Kirkpatrick 2006). This principle was emblematic of political attitudes embraced by urban liberals as well as rural conservatives, both of them suspicious of large corporations headquartered in big cities. Broadcasting networks like NBC tried to address such concerns by acceding to the local ownership of most stations, while at the same time forging contracts with local affiliates that turned over large portions of their airtime to network programming.

As a result, radio and television stations in the US were licensed and regulated on a local basis, but they were nevertheless dominated from the very beginning by national networks. The three major networks prevailed most powerfully from the mid-1950s to the mid-1980s, when they controlled key elements of television production, distribution and exhibition. Historian Michele Hilmes (2007) refers to this period as the classical network era, when more than 90 per cent of primetime television viewers tuned into NBC and its counterparts, the Columbia Broadcasting System (CBS) and the American Broadcasting Company (ABC). Aiming their programmes at vast national audiences, these three networks earned most of their revenue from the sale of advertising time to providers of consumer goods and services. They were therefore central institutions of an economy that was modelled on the principles of mass production and consumption with television supplying the means to stimulate and manage consumer demand.

During the classical network era television programmes strove for widespread popularity, but just as importantly they sought to avoid giving offence to any particular group, an approach known as least offensive programming (LOP). Critics claimed that this often resulted in bland content, but audiences expressed enthusiasm for the medium, with the vast majority of homes tuning in on a regular basis. Viewers would adjust personal and household schedules to set aside time for favourite programmes, bringing families and friends together around the TV set on a regular basis. This meant that television viewing was a synchronous experience, for shows generally played only once and would therefore gather nationwide audiences at appointed times.

The popularity of the medium and the growing demand for television advertising fostered consistent growth throughout the network era. This encouraged television companies to extend their core business from national distribution (networking) towards a more robust investment in programme production and local exhibition (station ownership), a process known as vertical integration.[2] Such expansion was largely limited to the broadcasting industry, for networks rarely sought to extend their reach into related media such as publishing, movies or amusement parks. Instead, they tended to pursue medium-specific strategies in part because of government regulations and in part because the television industry was growing so consistently that it encouraged the networks to internalise profits from related sectors of the TV industry rather than expand into other media where network executives had less expertise. The industry also sought opportunities overseas, becoming the world's largest exporter of television shows, but this remained an ancillary enterprise, for the core strategy of each company centred on its US advertisers and audiences.

A brief history of the Columbia Broadcasting System provides a useful example of how the major American networks developed over time. Founded in 1927 by a talent agent as a showcase for vaudeville theatre performers, CBS didn't begin to turn a profit until it came under the leadership of William Paley, the son of a cigar manufacturer and an early enthusiast of radio advertising. The company's main competitor was NBC, which ran two networks, one that tended towards popular programming while the other favoured upscale cultural and informational fare. Owned by RCA, the leading US radio manufacturer, NBC used its networks to promote the sale of radios and to keep politicians and opinion leaders happy with what was quickly becoming America's favourite pastime. NBC also solicited the support of commercial sponsors, but that was only part of a larger picture, for the network's strategies largely revolved around the sale of radio receivers and equipment. CBS, by comparison, relied primarily on sponsorship revenue from advertisers and therefore paid careful attention to the popularity of its programming. Paley displayed a knack for attracting fresh talent, cultivating sponsors and promoting public-service programming that also had popular appeal, such as news.

After World War II, CBS and NBC both became pioneering forces in the development of television and they carried over business practices, programme genres and popular performers from radio to the new medium. Yet television also required a significant amount of innovation as the cost of television production and operations was roughly ten times greater than radio. As a result, CBS and its competitors all spent much of the 1950s experimenting with programming and advertising formats. Most notably, the conditions of production shifted dramatically during the 1950s. When the decade began, more than 90 per cent of the evening schedule was telecast live from New York City, but by 1960 the proportion reversed with the vast majority of shows recorded on telefilm in Hollywood studios for later transmission across the national network. CBS was a leading innovator of telefilm working in conjunction with one of its comedy stars, Lucille Ball. Telefilm not only provided production flexibility, it also helped to contain costs. Perhaps most importantly, however, the recorded programmes could be used for retransmission (summer reruns) or sold to local stations and overseas broadcasters after their network run, a practice known as syndication (Schatz 1993 and Kompare 2004).

Control over programming development and decision-making also changed significantly during the 1950s. Initially, advertising agencies, working in conjunction with programme sponsors, made most of the creative decisions associated with television production. Sponsors funded the shows and agencies managed most aspects of production. Networks provided them with airtime, but due to the tremendous costs of TV production, networks played a relatively minor role in the creative end of the business, preferring to emphasise their role as a distributor. Yet as the industry grew more prosperous, networks took a growing interest in programme production and syndication. They eventually snatched creative control from the agencies and restricted sponsors to the pur-

Lucille Ball and Desi Arnaz pioneered the production of telefilm recordings of their show, *I Love Lucy*, which was syndicated to stations throughout the world

chase of commercial minutes, effectively shutting them out of the production business. Networks then built partnerships with Hollywood studios and became producers in their own right. Just as importantly, networks took an ownership interest in each show, allowing them to earn additional revenue by distributing 'off-network' reruns to stations in the US and overseas. CBS assembled an impressive syndication catalogue filled with durable ratings performers such as *I Love Lucy* (1951–61), *The Beverly Hillbillies* (1962–71) and *The Andy Griffith Show* (1960–8). If network programming seemed bland because it was aimed at a mass primetime audience and sought to avoid giving offence, then telefilm programming exacerbated this tendency, since it strove for validity in many different scheduling contexts: on a wide variety of stations and at different times of the day. Consequently, syndication became a very important and profitable aspect of the television business in the United States.

CBS avidly pursued expansion in the exhibition end of the business as well. Although the Federal Communications Commission (FCC) initially restricted each network to the ownership of only five stations, CBS and its competitors secured licences in the biggest markets, including New York, Philadelphia, Chicago and Los Angeles. Over time, as the population in the US shifted and as FCC regulation allowed the ownership of more stations, CBS would manoeuvre to ensure control over stations in the very largest and most lucrative local markets. The reasoning behind this strategy was that the network itself was only modestly profitable, since it incurred the costs of programme production, which was not only expensive but also risky. On the other hand, its owned and operated stations generated fabulous profit because they produced little more than local news and talk shows, taking most of their programming from the network. They therefore ran few risks and incurred few expenses, yet regularly generated strong advertising sales revenues. Big-city stations were also important because their audiences played a major role in national audience ratings and it was therefore important for the networks to control scheduling and promotion of their programmes in these major markets.

By the mid-1960s, CBS was unquestionably the most successful television network with a string of primetime hits, a strong syndication catalogue and a group of very profitable local stations in the very largest TV markets. It had systematically created a vertically integrated television enterprise that controlled every aspect of the creation, marketing and exhibition of TV entertainment and information. CBS and its network competitors built a truly mass medium that would endure for close to three decades.

This network system came under fire during the 1980s, however, as many viewers shifted their attention to new forms of cable, satellite and video programming. Some analysts claim this signalled the end of broadcasting and the transition to a post-network era. Yet it is important to recognise that the three major networks are still very much with us, albeit in new configurations, and that the concept of networking is still quite prevalent in US media, albeit with traces of the old and the new alongside each other. That is, media companies still employ technology to interconnect media operations. While earlier networks linked together broadcast transmitters, today they connect broadcasting, cable, satellite and wi-fi technologies to bring together geographically dispersed exhibition devices, everything from plasma TVs to mobile phones to laptop computers. Television companies also continue to emphasise the importance of national advertising and the aggregation of large numbers of viewers, even if those viewers are not necessarily tuned to the same show at the same time.

If network television sought to build a flow of programmes that would attract audiences for an entire evening of programming, television today aims to facilitate the flow of viewers' attention across networks of content. Television today operates through conglomeration, cross-promotion, flexible marketing and multiple technologies. Increasingly important are the programmes around which these strategies are organised. Whereas during the classical network era the big three television companies could manage audience access to programming through their centralised control of transmission technology, today networks must compete with a growing number of television services using a variety of delivery techniques. Instead of a networked broadcasting model, television today is a leading component of a media matrix that is comprised of broadcast services (push technologies) as well as a large and growing number of media services available via the Internet and other telecommunication technologies. The latter are often referred to as pull technologies, since viewers actively seek out programmes to download from the web or view online, or they watch shows on their mobile phones or rent them from video providers, both online and in local shops. Viewers are no longer restricted to three channel options, so networks now must rely ever more crucially on the attractions of their software. Today they need to produce shows that audiences will actively pursue among the thousands of viewing options available to them at any time. This has profoundly changed the television business, but the major networks still remain an enduring presence and new competitors emulate many of the practices of their larger counterparts. This is not the end of network television but rather its reinvention in the matrix era using many of the same principles and relationships that governed the industry's early development.

NEW COMPETITORS AND NEW TECHNOLOGIES

Technology is commonly seen as the most important factor in bringing about the decline of the classical network system. According to this view, cable, cassette and satellite technologies transformed American media, society and culture. That is, new technologies *caused* social and economic change. Such notions of 'technological determination' are fairly widespread in popular news accounts and criticism, but they can be enriched by pointing to a host of other factors that prompted the development of these new technologies. This alternative perspective turns technological determination on its head, showing instead how the complex interactions of individuals, institutions and social interests shaped the development of communication technologies, which in turn influenced society. Socio-cultural determination in the realm of television might best be appreciated by recalling the development of another technology, space travel.

Many commentators have suggested that the invention of rocketry pushed society into the space age. Yet rockets were first developed in ancient China and were adapted to modern uses by the Nazi war machine during World War II. After the war, the major superpowers competed ferociously in a space race for military and scientific supremacy as part of the Cold War. Rocket technology certainly would not have developed as quickly as it did during the twentieth century if not for massive investments made by governments and corporations, each with their own agendas. Moreover, popular fantasies of space travel helped to fuel support for rocket research as President Kennedy invoked the mythology of America's frontier to describe the challenges that lay ahead in outer space. In a 1961 speech, the President explicitly challenged Americans to put astronauts on the moon before the end of the decade, a feat that captured the imagination of people around the world. Thus, individuals, institutions and political interests shaped the conditions under which rocket technology emerged and established the terms by which it would be popularly imagined and socially deployed. Material, scientific and engineering factors certainly played a role as well, but these too were shaped by socio-cultural forces.

One must therefore wonder: Did rocketry change society during the twentieth century? Or did various groups align themselves behind the 'invention' of space technologies in pursuit of their own diverse interests? Socio-cultural determination directs our attention to powerful actors and institutional imperatives as well as flights of popular imagination and technological genius. It resists explanations that suggest technology itself acts as an autonomous, singular and determining influence on society.[3]

Similarly, new media technologies played an important role in the transformation of television during the 1970s and 1980s, but the technologies were developed and deployed by various social actors with complicated and often conflicting ambitions. For example, cable-television technology was enthusiastically promoted by the Nixon administration in large part because President Nixon and many conservatives resented what they perceived as the power of the major networks to shape public opinion. Nor were they alone in expressing such concerns, many groups on the opposite end of the political spectrum also questioned the influence of the major networks, including antiwar, environmental and women's organisations. All of them pressed the FCC to relax restrictions on cable technology in hopes that cable would open up hundreds of new television channels. Proponents of cable waxed enthusiastic about the diversity of perspectives that cable might offer. In books, magazines and speeches from the period one can find heady speculation about the vast array of opportunities that would open up on the new cable frontier, much of it comparable to the optimistic conjecture during the early days of the Internet (Streeter 1987). Such speculation should not be seen as empty chatter; it should rather be understood as one of the ways in which various interests align themselves behind particular agendas that shape the development of a new technology.

Another group seeking alternatives to the network oligopoly during the 1970s comprised advertisers, many of them frustrated with the limited number of commercial minutes available for sale. These limitations consistently drove up the cost of television ad spots and helped to generate fabulous profits for the major television companies. This inspired resentment but also envy, especially among companies seeking to expand their role in the TV business. Movie studios (e.g., Paramount), newspaper companies (e.g., Chicago Tribune) and publishers (e.g., Time-Life) had expressed interest in television from the very earliest days of the medium and now they sought to break up the network oligopoly and contend for their share of the industry. Studios wanted to increase the number of buyers for their movies and television programmes. Independent stations like the Tribune's WGN wanted to expand their geographical reach. Stations with weak signal strength – those using Ultra High Frequency (UHF) technology – wanted to improve and expand the quality of their transmissions. And publishers like Time-Life wanted to build new services for national niche audiences (e.g., Home Box Office).

Although cable technology had been available since the 1950s, it wasn't until the 1970s that the activities of these various interests converged behind an agenda to facilitate the growth of cable. Quite interestingly, cable would also benefit from the space programme, as the government spun off commercial satellite operations that assisted with the interconnection of cable services during the 1970s and in the ensuing decade provided direct-to-home broadcasting satellites (DBS). Rather than cable and satellite technology causing changes in TV and society, we can see that social actors, political interests and industry players shaped the development of these technologies, spurring their deployment during the 1970s and engendering new competitors for the major networks.

Socio-cultural determination also helps to explain the introduction of video cassettes, which allowed consumers to circumvent the programming schedules of the broadcast networks. German companies were the first to develop audio tape recording technology during World War II and in the following decade, video tape recorders were first sold to networks and local TV stations to help facilitate production and distribution of programmes. In the 1960s networks started using them for sports programming as well, allowing instant replay of key

Table 1.1   Adoption of New Technologies by Percentage of Total Households

	Multiset	Cable	DBS	VCR	DVD	Digital TV	PCs
1970	32.2	6.7					
1975	41.4	12.6					
1980	50.1	19.9		1.1			0.0
1985	56.8	42.8		20.9			14.0
1990	65.3	56.4		68.6			22.0
1995	70.9	63.4	>2.0	81.0			36.0
2000	75.6	68.0	9.2	85.1	13.0	>1.0	58.0
2005	79.0	67.5	20.3	90.2	81.0	15.0	73.0

Source: Nielsen Media Research (TVB Online) 2008.

moments during a competition. Nevertheless RCA (the parent company of NBC) had little incentive to market the technology to consumers because that might distract them from purchasing RCA's colour televisions, which were then new to the market.

By the 1970s, however, most US households owned a colour set and the electronics industry was beginning to look for the next big product to bring to market. American manufacturers were also beginning to feel pressure from Japanese competitors who had built their reputations on transistor radios, portable TVs and portable audio recorders. Japanese companies were renowned for scaling down the size and costs of electronic devices, and for making them consumer-friendly. One of these manufacturers, Sony Corporation, developed a new compact technology for industrial video recording, called the U-matic. Not only was it much smaller and more portable than earlier versions, it was also easier to use because the tape was encased in a cassette rather than wound on large, open reels.

Sony then took the logic of miniaturisation one step further by building a consumer-grade version that allowed viewers to record programmes off the air at home or buy cassettes of pre-recorded programming. The new product, called Betamax, served the interests of consumers and the interests of Sony, but it also presented a potential threat to the television networks, since it allowed viewers to time-shift their viewing and skip commercials. It also threatened the Hollywood studios because it made it possible to record, duplicate, share and resell copies of popular TV shows and movies (Epstein 2005).

As socio-cultural determination would suggest, consumer cassette technology did not appear out of thin air. It was developed by a Japanese company in response to competitive pressures in the increasingly globalised electronics industry. Sony sensed correctly that audiences might be looking for alternatives to broadcast television, something that a company like RCA would be less likely to provide since it was the parent company of NBC. As Betamax grew in popularity, American TV companies became anxious about its success and sued Sony to stop the spread of the technology, but ultimately the Supreme Court ruled in favour of video cassettes, saying that consumers have the right to make personal recordings of broadcast material. Consumers not only used the new technology to get around television advertising and network-scheduling regimes, they also embraced it as a means to circumvent network censorship codes, so that audiences could view erotic programming. Consumers furthermore employed the technology to purchase instructional videos, programmes that the networks then considered commercially untenable because they were not targeted at a mass audience. Cassette technology entered the scene through the dynamic interaction of socio-cultural forces spurring the development of a new technology that in turn helped consumers subvert the power of the network oligopoly.

THE RISE OF CABLE TV

When cable first entered the scene during the late 1940s, it was primarily adopted in rural areas that suffered from signal interference due to mountainous terrain. Then referred to as Community Antenna Television (CATV), most services were provided by small operators, such as a local electronics retailer that wanted to encourage the purchase of television sets. CATV assured buyers that they would enjoy good reception even if they lived in valleys or on the other side of the mountain from their local TV station. The FCC limited cable technology to this simple retransmission function for more than twenty years. With the FCC's *Fourth Report and Order* in 1972, however, the commission shifted course and opened the door to new applications of the technology, allowing a significant expansion in the number of TV channels for rural and urban audiences.

The expansion of cable during the 1970s also helped to revive the fortunes of independent stations because most of them were transmitting on UHF, an inferior technology that often suffered from signal interference. Cable systems transmitted all signals with relatively equal quality, indeed, a higher and more consistent quality than one could receive over the air. With better signals, the ratings and advertising sales of independent stations began to rise, helping to expand the number of channel offerings in many locales. Yet the independents still suffered from programming limitations, with most of them airing off-network reruns, old movies, local sports and local news. Some were nevertheless successful with this formula, especially stations that carried local sports programming.

In Atlanta, Georgia, Ted Turner bought a money-losing independent station in 1970 and gradually built its popularity with coverage of local wrestling, baseball and basketball. WCTG then expanded its service in December 1975 by relaying its signal nationwide via Satcom 1, making it the first station to deliver its programming to distant cable systems by satellite. At first only four cable operators picked up the channel, but soon the service mushroomed, especially in the southern United States, driven largely by the popularity of the Atlanta Braves baseball team. In 1978, WGN, a very successful Chicago-based independent, followed suit and again it was the popularity of Chicago sports teams that helped to build the audience for this 'superstation.'

Both services prospered, but the following year Turner grew even more ambitious, renaming his channel WTBS (for Turner Broadcasting System), which reflected the company's strategic transition from an independent superstation to a national cable network. In 1980, the company added a news department, launching the first twenty-four-hour news channel, Cable Network News (CNN). Far smaller than its broadcast competitors, CNN seemed at first a motley operation with thin resources, few news bureaux and a modest journalistic reputation. It largely transmitted interviews, features and analysis, but soon thereafter it added the Headline News channel, which delivered thirty-minute newscasts back to back throughout the day.

With two news channels running non-stop, Turner made cost-effective use of journalists and resources, growing the service consistently throughout the decade and expanding its operations overseas. Its programmes drew small audiences, but research showed that viewers tended to be upscale consumers and included many opinion leaders, both domestically and overseas. The service attracted larger audiences when breaking news events encouraged viewers to check with the channel throughout the day for ongoing updates. During the 1991 Gulf War, CNN's audience and reputation grew dramatically as it supplied continuous and extensive coverage, earning praise as the only American news service to keep reporters in Baghdad throughout the conflict. Its impartial, timely coverage attracted millions of new viewers both domestically and internationally.

Despite success with news and sports, Turner nevertheless lacked a substantial core of drama programming, one of the fundamental strengths of the major networks. Given the costs and risks involved in narrative television production, Turner trod cautiously in this area, preferring instead to invest money in the 1986 purchase of the MGM film library, the largest collection of its kind, including many classics from the vaults of MGM, RKO, Warner Bros. and United Artists. At the time of the deal, old Hollywood movies were considered to be of limited value. Most new feature films premiered in theatres and were then licensed for network exhibition followed by syndication to local television stations around the country. After network exhibition and the first few years of syndication, the value of the films dropped dramatically.

Turner used the vast MGM collection as a core resource for his expanding cable services and in 1988 launched a new channel, Turner Network Television (TNT), with a marquee broadcast of *Gone with the Wind* (Victor Fleming, 1939, US), a film that is reportedly Ted Turner's favourite. TNT has systematically mined the MGM library for programming ever since, a strategy that would act as a model for other cable services and one that would increase the value of film libraries tremendously. Turner's strategy furthermore stimulated reflection throughout the entertainment industry on the importance of creating content libraries that could be repurposed in the multichannel environment over an extended lifespan.

Ted Turner purchased the MGM film library to provide programming for his growing cable operations. He used *Gone with the Wind* as a marquee attraction to launch TNT in 1988

Although none of the Turner channels could individually compete with the major networks for ratings or revenues, Turner's constellation of niche cable services underwritten by cost-efficient programming provided steady streams of income that added up each year to impressive profits. The company never attacked the big networks head-on, instead it cultivated niches that the major broadcast networks ignored due to their focus on mass audiences. Only once did Turner tilt its lance directly at a network foe, when in 1985 the company mounted an audacious offer to buy its much larger competitor, CBS. Although ultimately unsuccessful, Turner's bid sent a jarring message that the supremacy of the three major networks was no longer assured.

Independents weren't the only ones to exploit the opportunities of cable. As mentioned earlier, movie studios had an interest in television from the very early years of the medium, but they found it difficult to secure broadcasting licences from the FCC because of troubles with government antitrust regulators. Overall, the 1950s and 60s were difficult times for the Hollywood studios, and in the late 1960s several studios passed into the hands of larger corporations, Warner Bros. among them. Sold in 1969 to Kinney Services, a collection of non-media enterprises run by Steve Ross, the company was soon transformed into Warner Communication International. One of Ross's first objectives was to expand into cable television by purchasing local cable systems around the country.

During the 1970s, most cable companies were run by local businesses that, in accordance with federal law, had negotiated with city and town governments to secure access to public-utility rights of way. This allowed them to string cables along the same routes utilised for telephone and electrical services. In exchange for such permission, cable operators paid fees to the city and in many cases funded public-access channels that would carry city council meetings, local TV productions and other civic programming. As the promise of cable mush-roomed, some large companies began to purchase numerous local systems, becoming multiple-system operators (MSOs). Warner Communication became one of the most aggressive MSOs, buying up many local systems so that it soon delivered cable service to more than 500,000 homes, most of them in big-city markets. This made Warner one of the most important providers of technolog-ical infrastructure, but it also fuelled the company's interest in the development of cable TV content.

Warner then entered into a joint venture with American Express, called Warner Amex, an early experimenter with niche television services, such as Music Television (MTV, aimed at teenage music fans) and Nickelodeon (aimed at children), and a premium movie service, The Movie Channel. The company was also one of the first to experiment with interactive television, setting up a test service in Columbus, Ohio that allowed audiences to communicate back to their cable provider with programming requests. Warner Amex took advantage of this test market to experiment with a host of information, commercial and financial services – hoping eventually to offer everything from pay-per-view movies to banking services to online shopping. Yet these ventures proved costly and the cable industry in general began to hit a downturn, so in 1983, Warner Amex sold its movie channel to Viacom and two years later sold MTV and Nickelodeon to the same company. Warner hadn't given up on cable programming, however. Shortly thereafter it entered into merger negotiations with Time-Life, a renowned publisher of weekly and monthly magazines, and an investor in various television ventures from the very earliest days of the medium. By the late 1980s Time-Life was the second-largest MSO in the United States and operated the leading movie channel, Home Box Office, as well.

Although Warner Communication came from the world of entertainment and Time-Life from the world of news, the two partners found common ground in cable, which both believed would play a crucial role in delivering future forms of information and entertainment. At the time of the merger in 1989, invest-ment bankers behind the negotiation argued that Time Warner (TW) would combine two sets of complementary enterprises, bringing together movies, music, publishing, television and cable under one roof. It was argued that the value of these enterprises was more than the sum of the parts, since the publishing end of the business could help to promote the movies, while the movie studios could supply products for the cable systems and so on. Although the multichannel environment was undermining the mass audiences of the network era, businesses such as TW would use their multiple enterprises to ensure that core content was leveraged across many delivery platforms, helping it to exploit fully its core intellectual property and guarantee profitability. This principle, referred to as 'synergy', became the foundational premise behind most media mergers and acquisitions during the latter part of the twentieth century. Time Warner became a bellwether of this trend, swallowing up Turner in 1996 and merging with America Online (AOL) in 2000. Indeed, throughout the 1990s, Time Warner was the world's largest media conglomerate, dwarfing its TV network competitors in size and scope.

As one looks back, it seems as if today's leading media enterprises systematically and strategically followed a path to certain success. In fact, however, the path was filled with risks, reversals and dead ends. Clearly the wealth and scale of these enterprises helped them achieve their objectives, but notice Warner's abandonment of its early MTV and Nickelodeon ventures, decisions that might in retrospect seem foolish. Notice too, that at the height of its power and influence, Time Warner made one of the grossest miscalculations in American corporate history when it merged with AOL, a company whose value plummeted during the dotcom collapse that ensued shortly thereafter, costing Time Warner more than $100 billion in losses. Finally, it's important to acknowledge the role of luck and coincidence, and the fact that corporations often succeed because they learn to exploit unexpected developments, not because they sure-footedly engineer profitable innovations. Both Turner and WGN benefited from their experimentation with satellite-cable technology, but it was Turner that continued to exploit this advantage by rolling out new networks, repurposing content and cultivating new programming and new advertising niches. Likewise, Time and Warner experimented with many different technologies and programming services, but it was their determined commitment to cable over the long haul that elevated them to a position of leadership.

THE POWER OF POLICY

Government regulation and policy-making have played an important role throughout the history of television, first by favouring the major radio companies during the transition to television and then by favouring the development of a strongly centralised network regime during the 1950s. Only a decade later, however, the FCC reversed course in an attempt to unseat the very oligopoly it had fostered. Cable then became the preferred technology, spurring the growth of new channels and services. The government provided further assistance by

commercialising its satellite technologies, encouraging the national interconnection of cable services. Just as significantly, the FCC forced the major
networks to give up their investments in primetime programming, by adopting
the Financial Interest and Syndication Rules (fin-syn) in 1970, which effectively
shut the networks out of the lucrative production and syndication businesses. It
could be argued that government policy fostered both the rise and the demise
of the major broadcasting networks.

Although policy, like technology, has been very influential, it is not an
autonomous force, but is rather the product of struggles among various interest
groups. Some groups represent segments of the public, but most are stake-
holders in the media industries themselves, each vying for a greater share of the
market. Often the FCC and Congress mediate among the various contenders,
fashioning compromises that are palatable to the companies and to the larger
public. Such 'pie-sharing' exercises also tend to reflect political trends, so that
policies in the 1950s conformed to broader agendas aimed at national integration and the promotion of consumerism, while policies in the 1970s tended to
dovetail with a growing celebration of subcultures, personal expression and
alternative political perspectives. Thus, markets, institutions and cultural change
all play a role in shaping media policy, which helps to explain why government
regulation periodically shifts – or even reverses – course. Such was the case with
policies regarding network involvement in programme production.

The major networks became interested in the risky business of programme
production during the late 1950s as they observed the tremendous revenue
potential in the telefilm syndication market. Previously, they simply paid the
Hollywood studios for broadcasting rights to programmes the studios produced.
The networks received the right to a premiere showing and a summer rerun of
each show, after which the studios were free to syndicate the programmes to
local stations and overseas broadcasters as off-network reruns. For many years,
the income from network exhibition helped studios to cover most of the costs
of production, while syndication gave them an opportunity to turn a profit. Studios therefore established syndication divisions or they worked through
companies that marketed large catalogues of programming for them. Many syndication deals were made at major trade shows where hundreds of syndication
and TV station executives would meet on a regular basis (Kompare 2004 and
Havens 2006).

As syndication grew more lucrative, networks began to negotiate for a financial interest in the shows that they licensed for primetime, reasoning that they
were creative collaborators in the development, financing and promotion of new
shows, and therefore should share the long-term benefits of syndication. The
networks had strong justification for requesting an ownership interest in each

show, but this put the studios in an awkward position: if they refused to make the network a partner, they worried that their show would not be picked up for primetime exhibition and without such exposure, the show would be worthless.

Tensions between the studios and networks intensified until government regulators stepped in to rule that the networks were engaged in anti-competitive practices because they were acting as both buyers and sellers of programming, and were seeking to extend their oligopoly from distribution to the production sector of the industry. The Financial Interest and Syndication Rules (fin-syn) banned networks from ownership of primetime programming with the exception of news and sports, which meant that they could neither produce nor own a share of the primetime programmes they telecast. Around the same time, the FCC also took steps to boost the fortunes of independent producers and to ban the networks from moving into the new terrain of cable television. After favouring the networks for two decades, the government was pressing to expand the number of players in the TV industry.

In response to these rulings, CBS bundled its production, syndication and cable divisions into a company called Viacom and then spun it off as an independent corporation in 1971. Something of a hotchpotch at the outset, Viacom was nevertheless a leading syndicator and a comparatively large MSO in the nascent cable industry. It sustained its cable leadership throughout the 1970s and 80s by adding more local franchises and by laying cable in dozens of communities across the US. It also invested in cable programming ventures, launching Showtime in 1976 as a competitor to HBO and acquiring MTV and Nickelodeon in 1985 from Warner Amex. Up to the mid-80s, cable was generally a money-losing business, yet Viacom remained profitable largely because of its syndication catalogue that included many of the CBS hit series from the 1950s and 60s. Viacom proved much less successful at developing new television programmes, but in the late 1980s, its fortunes began to change as MTV and Nickelodeon started to take off. In part this was due to shrewd programming decisions and in part due to the increasing importance of niche audiences, especially teens and young adults, that were considered attractive markets for many advertisers.

Athough these services flourished, other investments were turning sour for Viacom, making it a target for corporate takeover. It was difficult to sell the company, however, because it owned a small chain of radio and television stations, which made any sale subject to an FCC licensing procedure. Here again, changes in the policy arena would dramatically affect the fortunes of Viacom, as the FCC reversed course and loosened such restrictions in response to influence from the Reagan administration. This opened the door to a flood of station sales during the 1980s and made it much easier to buy and sell media conglomerates, such as Viacom. The deregulation of financial markets during this same period made it possible for companies to borrow money enlisting new types of investment securities. Consequently, low-grade investment bonds, or 'junk-bonds', played a role in the sale of many TV stations and media assets, sparking a fever of speculation and reorganisation in the media industries.

Amid these changes, numerous suitors began to pursue Viacom and after protracted manoeuvring, Sumner Redstone, the owner of a modest New England movie chain called National Amusements, emerged as the winning bidder in the spring of 1986. Using mostly borrowed funds, National Amusements was able to purchase a far larger corporation, a strategy referred to as a leveraged buyout. Such strategies can lead to enormous gains or staggering losses. Indeed, many critics wondered if Viacom's lacklustre performance might ultimately drag its suitor down. Yet the government again proved to be an influential player when it relaxed restrictions on cable fees to consumers. As a result, household cable payments began to rise dramatically and MSO revenues soared, enhancing the value of companies like Viacom. MTV also continued to flourish and by 1989 it was earning 15 per cent of *all* cable advertising revenues. Bolstered by this success and by the emergence of cable-satellite services worldwide, MTV then expanded into Europe, Latin America and Asia. Redstone not only benefited from hard work and good fortune but also from the shifting course of government regulation, which Viacom's high-paid lobbyists in Washington DC helped to nurture.

Despite these successes, the company nevertheless remained an ungainly collection of media enterprises until 1994 when Redstone engineered the takeover of Paramount Pictures, adding one of the leading Hollywood studios to the Viacom family. Later the same year, Viacom purchased Blockbuster Video, then the biggest and most prosperous video-rental company. Shortly thereafter, Redstone glimpsed another opportunity, as the FCC allowed the fin-syn rules to expire, making it possible for the major television networks and the Hollywood production studios to be part of the same conglomerate. The FCC reasoned that unlike 1970, when three networks dominated the television business, audiences during the 1990s could choose from a variety of television channels, video services and Internet resources. Similarly, TV programme producers could market their wares to a diverse array of potential buyers. The government therefore allowed the major television networks to re-enter the production and syndication businesses, a decision that made it possible for Viacom to purchase CBS, the very company from which it was originally spun off!

With the purchase of CBS in 1999, Viacom capped a period of expansion that in only thirteen years catapulted it into the very top rank of media conglomerates. What had at one time been a disparate collection of unrelated enterprises grew into a comprehensive juggernaut spanning film, television, cable and book publishing. It furthermore operated divisions dedicated to production, distribution, exhibition and merchandising, making Viacom a fully integrated media conglomerate. After the acquisition of CBS, Viacom executives proudly pointed out that, despite the proliferation of cable channels and the fragmentation of television audiences, their company could serve audiences in almost every major demographic group. In fact, they crowed, viewers might grow up with Nickelodeon, experience adolescence through MTV, transition to adulthood with UPN and Comedy Central, and then mature as loyal adult viewers of CBS. Although the network era had passed, Viacom claimed that its various TV services reached just as many total viewers as the networks had during the 1960s. Executives also took pride in the fact that Viacom had significant stakes in production, distribution and exhibition across a range of media formats, something the networks never achieved during the 1960s.

Viacom was more powerful and more expansive than CBS had been in its prime. Spun off as an orphan enterprise only thirty years earlier, it came home to CBS as one of the most powerful conglomerates of the era. This stunning corporate turnaround was emblematic of an even more stunning reversal of government policy. Government policy that during the 1970s sought to restrict the major networks and encourage new competitors dramatically changed course during the 1980s and 1990s thereby fostering the growth of huge media conglomerates like Viacom and Time Warner.

FINALLY, A FOURTH NETWORK

Although the Reagan administration was perhaps the most avid and vocal advocate of deregulation, the trend actually began during the Carter administration when influential corporate and political leaders began to argue that regulation of such industries as airlines, telephony and television imposed unnecessary burdens on companies, thereby retarding innovation, restricting competition and undermining the interests of consumers. Better, they argued, to stimulate competition among firms and to lower barriers to market entry by new companies than to attempt to keep a check on industry practices and prices (Horwitz 1991). This philosophy helped to shape the revision of cable regulations during the 1970s, and these changes did indeed bring new companies into the TV business over time, but these new niche services were not direct competitors to the major networks. Try as they might, government policy-makers found it much more difficult to encourage the formation of new broadcasting networks that might directly challenge the majors.

In part this was because such an endeavour would be a massive undertaking. First of all, a new competitor would need to own or purchase a collection of stations in the largest TV markets, including New York, Los Angeles and Chicago. As mentioned earlier, such 'owned and operated' (O&O) stations are the core profit centres for major US television companies, since the networks themselves are only marginally profitable due to high production costs. Big-city O&Os are not only profitable, they generate strong and consistent cash flow, money that can either be returned to stockholders or serve to upgrade and expand network operations. Second, a new competitor would have to line up affiliates across the country, a difficult task since the strongest stations in each market are already spoken for. And third, a new network would have to invest in programme production and promotion, two of the riskiest areas of the tele-vision business yet arguably the most important, since ratings (and advertising revenues) rely on a network's ability to generate shows that attract loyal audi-ences. These barriers to market entry proved so formidable that the three-network oligopoly persisted for more than thirty years.

By the 1980s, cable television had helped to erode one of the most significant barriers by boosting the fortunes of independent television stations thereby making more stations available as potential affiliates for a new network. Recall that many independent stations went bankrupt during the 1950s and 60s because of their comparatively weaker UHF transmission technology. As cable became more common in American homes, it levelled the playing field by trans-mitting independents with equal signal quality to that of network affiliates. This not only boosted the fortunes of independents, it encouraged investment in new stations as well. By the mid-1980s the number of stations had grown substan-tially, so that many more independents were now competing for syndicated programming. This sparked price increases in syndicated fare and it stimulated new production activity. It also stimulated discussion about the potential viabil-ity of a fourth network. With the costs of syndicated programming on the rise, such a network would probably find independents in many markets receptive to the prospect of signing on as an affiliate. A fourth network would nevertheless be an extremely risky and expensive venture.

Around this time, News Corporation, an Australian media conglomerate headed by Rupert Murdoch, started making inroads into the US media market. After taking control of the troubled 20th Century-Fox studio in 1984, News Corp. lured Barry Diller away from the top job at Paramount to run the Fox operation. Diller brought with him a plan for building a fourth television net-work, one that Paramount had rejected as too risky but one that intrigued an ambitious Rupert Murdoch. In 1985, News purchased the Metromedia chain of television stations for $2 billion, what was considered an astounding sum at the time. Much of the purchase was financed with junk bonds, making the invest-ment appear even more daring, but Murdoch reasoned that the Metromedia chain would give him access to major urban markets across the country, providing core O&O stations for his proposed network. Before he could seal the deal, however, Murdoch had to seek FCC approval, since government regulations require station owners to be US citizens.

Hoping to further the prospects of a fourth network, the FCC granted approval contingent on Murdoch changing his citizenship, which he did expeditiously. With its O&Os secured and a studio production facility in hand, News Corp. began to line up affiliates, but again FCC approval would be necessary, since this would result in a vertically integrated media corporation with a studio, a network and a chain of stations under the same corporate umbrella, a practice forbidden by the fin-syn regulations that were still in force during the 1980s. Here again the Reagan-era FCC acquiesced, reasoning that the vertically integrated Fox media empire would actually increase market competition, which was the original intent of the fin-syn rules.

In 1987, the Fox network launched a limited schedule of programming for two nights a week aimed not at a broad mass audience but rather at a young, urban audience. Over the first four seasons, Fox distinguished itself with satirical programmes (*The Simpsons*, 1989–), ribald fare (*Married with Children*, 1987–97), trendy youth drama (*Beverly Hills 90210*, 1990–2000) and reality TV (*America's Most Wanted*, 1988–). The network also made a strong pitch to African American viewers, an audience that the three major networks ordinarily ignored, believing that they would follow the tastes of the mass-market, white audience. The majors furthermore contended that programmes pitched at African American viewers ran the risk of alienating white viewers, so when the networks did include black characters in primetime shows, they were commonly portrayed as either indistinguishable from white characters or as two-dimensional stereotypes. Fox, however, became the first major network to craft programmes specifically aimed at black viewers (Gray 2004 and Zook 1999).

In 1990, Fox commissioned an ensemble variety show written, produced and hosted by Keenan Ivory Wayans and performed by a predominantly black cast. *In Living Color* (1990–4) gleefully skewered the conventions of network television, offering pointed satires of racial stereotypes in mainstream media. Immediately controversial and surprisingly popular, the show became a cornerstone of Fox programming. Although the weekly schedule seemed like a jumble of unrelated shows, Fox succeeded largely because its programmes were edgy and because it attracted viewers that were unhappy with mainstream network fare. It also succeeded because the FCC accommodated Fox at various turns, perhaps most surprisingly by waiving public-service requirements that allowed Fox to operate as the first American network without a daily news programme.

Keenan Ivory Wayans and Damon Wayans spoof television's racial barriers by impersonating the Smothers Brothers in order to get a chance to perform on network primetime. Their show, *In Living Color*, was part of Fox network's attempt to court African American audiences

As it grew, Fox added more nights of programming and aimed to expand its audience, ultimately de-emphasising the niches that helped it prosper during its early years. Today it competes directly with the other major broadcast networks, engaging similar programming strategies and attracting comparable ratings. Although the emergence of Fox has increased the number of network broadcasters to four, its distinctive programming formula has now given way to a mass broadcasting approach very much like its competitors. Interestingly, News Corp.'s initial strategy was later employed by Paramount and Warner Bros. (WB) when they established the United Paramount Network (UPN) and WB networks in 1995. Both secured core O&Os, trolled among independent stations for a roster of affiliates, and rolled out a slate of programming two nights a week. Aiming to attract young viewers and African Americans, both networks also followed Fox's precedent by slowly expanding their schedules and aiming to grow beyond these market niches. Yet UPN and WB faltered early on because they both followed the same strategy, competing in the very same market niches. They merged in 2006 as the CW network, pulling together the strongest stations and the strongest programming into a single entity, and consolidating their audiences in hopes of making them more attractive to national advertisers.

Fox was also a model for the television industry in another way, since it was the first network paired with a major Hollywood studio, a clear transgression of the fin-syn rule. After the adoption of fin-syn in 1970, networks chafed at the rules, repeatedly complaining that they failed to acknowledge the important role networks play in the development of new programmes. As the Reagan administration launched its widespread assault on government regulation during the 1980s, network complaints about fin-syn grew louder and the volume further intensified when the FCC gave Fox a waiver and approved its plan for a fourth network.

The launch of Fox proved to be something of a watershed, since it signalled that the government stance on fin-syn was softening and in 1995 the rule formally lapsed when the agency decided not to renew it. In the decade that followed, all three major networks would align themselves with a Hollywood studio: ABC with Disney (1996), CBS with Paramount (1999) and NBC with Universal (2004). In part this consolidation of networks and studios was driven by a strategic concern about access to programming. What, for example, would NBC do if Fox studios were to decide to produce programmes only for its network partner? Studios were likewise uneasy, for what if Fox television network showed no interest in Paramount's new shows, preferring instead the programmes developed by Fox studios? Historically, studios had hawked their programmes around to all three networks, but the integration of network and studio engendered the prospect of huge media corporations that could produce, distribute and exhibit an entire season of programming on their own. This was an unprecedented possibility, and it furthermore threatened to eliminate the role played by independent studios and producers.

Debates over fin-syn were taking place at the very same time that the US Congress was beginning to deliberate over a rewrite of the 1934 Communication Act. Confronted with the growth of cable and satellite services, the emergence of the Internet and the globalisation of the American economy, Congressional leaders and the Clinton administration worried that the existing framework for media regulation needed a significant overhaul. They began to fashion a vision of media convergence in which all forms of communication would become digitised and intermingled as they travelled along the 'information highway'. The future, they believed, would belong to innovative enterprises that could provide a range of services and compete in international markets. Seeing information, entertainment and communication as increasingly profitable sectors in the global economy, they sought to fashion legislation that would protect and extend the market advantages enjoyed by American firms.

Whereas the 1934 act sought to regulate communication companies in the national public interest, the Telecommunications Act of 1996 sought to unleash media companies to pursue their interests worldwide and with few restraints. Proponents of the act argued that previous policy had been premised on a scarcity of channels, requiring that the government ensure that they not be used in the interests of a few. With only three commercial networks and a handful of channels in any given locality, regulators thought it best to keep a close eye on television companies that were making private use of public airwaves. By the 1990s, however, digital technologies had greatly expanded the available number of television channels, telephony services and Internet offerings. Given the prospect of multiple networks and media plenitude, regulators reasoned that government oversight of the media industries could be relaxed. They furthermore contended that deregulation would spur further innovation and make it possible for American media companies to sustain their global leadership. Companies would grow, but so too would audience opportunities.

This vision suggested that scale and scope were necessary elements for future success. Media companies of the twenty-first century would not only need to be large but would also need to reach across media platforms and across national borders. Like News Corp. they would move beyond their country of origin and beyond their traditional emphasis on film or television or music. They would be multimedia, multinational enterprises, and at the very centre of their corporate structures would be an engine of creativity: a Hollywood studio, spinning out popular content that could be delivered in many different formats to appreciative audiences around the world. This vision not only established a new set of premises for regulatory policy, it also set off another wave of mergers and acquisitions, led by Disney's purchase of ABC the very same year that Congress passed the Telecommunications Act of 1996 (Aufderheide 1999).

CONGLOMERATION AND SYNERGY

By the dawn of the twenty-first century all of the major television companies were subsidiaries of major conglomerates. This was a significant turnaround from the classical network era and it was an especially dramatic transformation for ABC, which had been the weakest of the three major networks throughout the early years of television. This deficit was largely a result of ABC's historical origins. The company was founded in 1943 when government regulators forced NBC to divest itself of one of its two radio networks. NBC executives of course decided to relinquish the weaker of the two, which was then taken over by a candy manufacturer. Consequently, the launch of ABC's television network did not occur until 1948, several years after CBS and NBC. Unfortunately, this was only months before the FCC imposed a freeze on the allocation of new TV licences while it tried to sort out problems with signal interference. That gave CBS and NBC a decided advantage, since they had already lined up the most desirable stations, most of them broadcasting on Very High Frequency (VHF).

ABC therefore found itself rummaging among the weaker UHF outlets in most markets, a pattern that would continue even after the freeze was lifted. While its counterparts enjoyed truly national coverage, ABC had spotty coverage in many parts of the US. The network was nevertheless attractive to Leonard Goldenson, the head of the Paramount Theatre chain, whose company bought a substantial block of ABC stock in 1953. Goldenson's company had recently been spun off from the Paramount Studio as part of an antitrust lawsuit brought by the federal government. Banned from movie production, Paramount Theatres was looking for investment opportunities in other media businesses.

Besides capital, Goldenson brought fresh executive talent to ABC and movie-industry connections, which he quickly put to good use, convincing the Walt Disney Company to launch a weekly show called *Disneyland* (1954–61), aimed at young children and families. The show was enormously successful, but it underlined ABC's second-tier status, since it performed well in major cities, but lagged in the national ratings. NBC easily wooed Disney away in 1961, placing the programme in a marquee time slot on Sunday evenings. The move instantly gave Disney wider national exposure than ABC could hope to provide.

ABC's fortunes finally improved during the 1970s due to the expanding popularity of cable as well as improvements to UHF technology, both of which raised the network's national ratings. A string of hit programmes during the latter part of the decade finally lifted ABC to a fully competitive position. During the 1980s, the government relaxed regulations on TV and financial capital, sparking a wave of buyouts and mergers, among them, the 1985 takeover of ABC by Capital Cities, a company one-tenth its size. As with other such deals during the 1980s, Capital Cities borrowed heavily and at high interest rates in order to secure its prize. Facing a substantial debt burden as a result of the purchase, executives sought to economise by trimming operations and programming budgets, which weakened the company even further.

It was only a matter of years before ABC became a takeover target yet again. Only this time Hollywood studios entered the bidding due to the expiration of the fin-syn rules and passage of the new Telecommunications Act. In 1996, Disney reconnected with ABC as its new corporate owner. Riding high on a string of box-office hits that included *The Little Mermaid* (Ron Clements and John Musker, 1989, US), *Beauty and the Beast* (Gary Trousdale and Kirk Wise, 1991, US), and *The Lion King* (Roger Allers and Rob Minkoff, 1994, US), Disney was renowned for systematic exploitation of its movies through ticket sales, video rental, television syndication, theme parks and merchandising. The company was considered the leading practitioner of corporate synergy, using each film as core content that was then leveraged across media platforms to exact maximum profit (Wasko 2001).

For Disney, the purchase of ABC seemed to make sense since it included a television network, a chain of TV stations and a cable MSO. ABC would provide important new delivery platforms for the studio's products, promising to make Disney an expansive media creator, distributor, exhibitor and merchandiser. Many industry analysts praised the synergies between the various divisions of the company. They saw Disney as a prototype of the twenty-first-century media conglomerate. It not only held an enviable position in established media industries, it was also expanding in new directions, such as the Internet and DVD retail sales.

Yet things didn't work out quite as planned. Disney's Internet portal failed to take off; its baseball team faltered; and its animation unit suffered a number of mishaps at the theatre box office. As for ABC, Disney worked hard to integrate the TV operations under its corporate umbrella, but critics said that Disney CEO Michael Eisner micro-managed the new assets and tried to harness the network too closely to the studio. Instead of production executives touting new programmes around to all the networks, they tried to envision shows that could be kept under the Disney tent. And instead of the network acquiring shows from a host of out-side suppliers, it focused most of its attention on projects from its own studio. In the end, Disney-ABC faltered because the principles of corporate synergy limited the flow of creative ideas. Fox had a similar experience when it tried to tie together its network and studio operations. Although many television executives believed during the 1990s that ABC and Fox synergies were harbingers of the future, by 2003 most agreed that such attempts were largely untenable. Writers and produc-ers have trouble enough satisfying their audiences without having to worry about corporate loyalties or potential synergies. This was a lesson that both ABC and Fox learned the hard way.

The logic of conglomeration faltered on another front as well. In 2001, the col-lapse of the digital media economy caused massive losses for media conglomerates. Nowhere was this failure more apparent than in the AOL merger with Time Warner, but others, such as Disney and Viacom, suffered losses as well. New and old media didn't necessarily mix. In fact, the concept of synergy itself came under fire during the 2000s, as many executives began stepping forward to explain how difficult it is to run a single division of a media company without having to strate-gise in terms of the parent conglomerate.

For example, a music division must be adept at dealing with musical talent, audi-ences and marketing, all of which operate differently from their TV counterparts. Even at times when collaboration does make sense, the music division of a con-glomerate is unlikely to give the TV division favourable terms on, say, theme music, since each must generate profits that are reported separately to the parent corpo-ration. In other words, for a music division to look good in the eyes of its corporate parent, it has to show consistent profit growth, and its quarterly performance is reg-ularly compared to the performance of other divisions. Rather than act as cooperative siblings, the music and television divisions are just as likely to act as jealous rivals that curry the favour of top management. The music division must therefore treat the TV division the same way it would treat any other paying cus-tomer, seeking the best prices and the best contract terms. This means it has to shop its wares around widely, not restricting itself to inside deals. Moreover, actors and singers have occasionally sued companies for insider deals, claiming that their professional interests have been compromised for the greater good of the con-glomerate.

Despite the wave of acquisitions and mergers that took place in the1980s and 90s, media conglomerates have proven to be unwieldy affairs that have yet to prove their synergistic value. As a result, stock prices have sagged as investors have turned their attention to other industrial sectors. In an attempt to restore the confidence of the market, Viacom decided in 2005 to divide its conglomerate in two, one retaining the corporate title and the other reorganising under the moniker of CBS. It was a telling admission that synergy and conglomeration may have their limits.[4]

CONCLUSION

The American television industry first emerged as a network system in which three major corporations ran centralised systems of production and distribution, pushing their programming out to mass audiences who viewed them at approximately the same time. This was an enormously profitable system, yet it concentrated power in the hands of a few and therefore engendered resentment and envy from various political factions and prospective competitors. It also limited the amount of commercial time available to national advertisers. These tensions engendered a search for policy and technological solutions to the network oligopoly. By the mid-1980s, most American homes had gained access to cable, satellite or home video, allowing them to select from an expanding menu of shows and, if they recorded them, to view them at a time of their choosing. Although most programmes were still watched at the time of their original airing, viewing behaviours became increasingly asynchronous and audiences divided into smaller and smaller groups. Programmes with mass audiences and high ratings during the classical network era gave way to an expanding number of channels featuring shows that targeted niche audiences, an era that Amanda Lotz (2007) refers to as the 'multichannel transition'.

Television is now on the cusp of another transition, as Internet and broadband technologies make it possible for viewers to download and otherwise acquire favourite shows, *pulling* content from providers who may be networks, studios, third-party distributors or independents. TiVo, i-Tunes, YouTube, MySpace and Netflix are only a few of the many places that audiences can turn to for video content. Although the major networks still have the power and resources to push and promote particular programmes, audiences increasingly search for content that suits their particular tastes. Instead of centralised networks, we seem to be moving into a multichannel, multimedia and multidimensional environment, one where producers, distributors and consumers all attempt to build linkages, find pleasure and make meaning out of the diverse range of content now available. We might refer to this as the matrix era, a media environment that poses significant challenges to existing television institutions and to the advertisers that have funded the industry since its very inception.

Box 1.1 Major US Television Conglomerates

Walt Disney
ABC Network & Stations
ESPN (80% ownership)
Disney Channel
ABC Family
A&E (37.5%)
Lifetime (50%)
History (37.5%)
E! (39.6%)
SoapNet
Disney Studios

News Corporation
Fox Network & Stations
FX Networks
MyNetwork
Fox News
Fox Sports
Fox Kids
Speed
Golf
National Geographic (67%)
MySpace
Hulu (45%)
20th Century-Fox Studios

NBC Universal
NBC Network & Stations
CNBC
MSNBC
Telemundo
USA
Bravo
Oxygen
SyFy
A&E (25%)
History (25%)
iVillage
Hulu (45%)
NBC Universal Studios

Sony Pictures Entertainment
Sony Pictures Television
Columbia TriStar Pictures
MGM Television

CBS
CBS Network & Stations
UPN
CW (50%)
Showtime
King World
CBS Radio
CBS Outdoor
CBS Paramount TV Studios

Viacom
MTV
VH-1
Country Music Televison
BET
Nickelodeon
Comedy Central
Logo
Spike
Paramount Pictures

Time Warner
Turner Broadcasting
CW (50%)
HBO
CNN
TBS
TNT
Cartoon Network
Turner Classic Movies
Cinemax
AOL
Warner Bros. Studio

NOTES

1. Excellent histories of television institutions include Anderson 1994; Barnouw 1966–70; Baughman 2007; Becker 2006; Boddy 1990; Castleman and Podrazik 2003; Curtin 1995; Douglas 1999; Hilmes 2007; Kompare 2004; Ouellette 2002; Sterling and Kittross 2001.

2. Although the vast majority of network stations were affiliates, the networks were allowed to own only a small number of stations themselves. So, for example, a network might comprise more than 100 stations, of which the FCC would allow them to own five or more, depending on the regulations at the time.

3. For more about the issue of technological determinism, see Williams 2003; Spigel 1992; and Smith and Marx 1994.

4. For more regarding debates over media conglomerates, see Rice 2008 and Barnouw 1997.

2

Audiences and Advertising

Since the very beginning, television networks and stations have relied primarily on advertising income to support their operations and generate profits. Cable and satellite networks depend on advertising as well, but they also generate revenues from the subscription fees they charge to cable system operators. Advertising is absolutely central to the television economy. In fact, some executives facetiously refer to TV shows as filling the black holes between the ads. According to this view, programming is important, but primarily as a means to an end. Shows attract the attention of audiences and that attention is what TV executives sell to advertisers.

Advertisers pay based on the total number of viewers watching each show and based on the demographic composition of the audience. A dishwashing-soap manufacturer is more interested in placing ads on shows that attract parents and householders, while a pop-music company wishes to advertise on shows that attract teenagers and young adults. Some advertisers, such as restaurant chains and beverage companies, still aim at mass audiences, seeking the broadest exposure that television can provide.

Before examining the intricacies of television advertising, it's important first to understand the role that ratings play in the television economy. In the United States approximately 115 million households own at least one television set and each household averages 1.4 viewers. Audiences are measured by rating points on a scale from 0 to 100. Thus a show with a 10 rating attracts 11.5 million households and approximately 16.1 million viewers. Ten is a very high rating for a television show these days, even for primetime shows on the broadcast net-

Table 2.1 Sample Ratings of Primetime Programmes

	#1 rated show	#15 rated show
1955	47.5 The $64,000 Question	31.9 George Gobel Show
1965	31.8 Bonanza	23.8 My Three Sons
1975	30.1 All in the Family	22.9 The Waltons (tie)
1985	33.7 The Cosby Show	19.8 Monday Night Football
1995	22.0 ER	12.9 Coach
2005	17.4 CSI: Crime Scene Investigation	9.5 Extreme Makeover: Home Edition

Source: Brooks and Marsh 2007.

works, but this is much lower than in the classical network era when leading primetime shows enjoyed ratings in the 30s as shown in Table 2.1.

Rating points measure the number of television households that are motivated to tune their sets to a particular show at a specific time. A 10 rating means that 10 per cent of households tuned in as opposed to 90 per cent that watched another show or weren't watching television at all. A programme's popularity is also measured in comparison to other shows telecast at the same time, what is known as its *share*. For example, at eight o'clock, a show may attract a 20 share, which means that of the total number of households then viewing TV, 20 per cent are watching this particular show. All of the other shows on at that time comprise the remaining 80 share. Because they measure different things, ratings and share can vary dramatically. For example, Programme A at two o'clock in the morning may have a rating of 0.5 and enjoy a 20 share, while Programme B in primetime might have a 7 rating and a 10 share. The early-morning show clearly has a much lower rating, but it performs well for its time period. Indeed, it does better in comparison to its peers than Programme B, which enjoys a much higher rating.

Television networks and stations have research departments that gather and analyse data about shows and scheduling blocks. They try to map trends in viewer behaviour and try to compare the performance of their shows against those of competitors. They also try to anticipate how ratings might change if shows were to be moved around in the schedule or if some shows were dropped and others picked up. Yet the most important audience data is not gathered by TV companies themselves, but is rather assembled by independent companies that are considered impartial by both telecasters and advertising agencies. The firm that dominates the ratings business is Nielsen Media Research, which exercises a virtual monopoly over national ratings and also dominates the local ratings business in most major cities.

NIELSEN RATINGS

Nielsen didn't always prevail. Other companies pioneered audience measurement during the radio era using mail-in response cards, telephone surveys and audience diaries. Each of these methods had shortcomings, however. Mail-in samples only generated responses from those attracted to the promotional prize. Telephone surveys required audiences to recall names of shows they watched recently. And diaries allowed viewers to write down shows as they watched, but viewers made their entries sporadically, sometimes going days before they entered the information. Moreover, all three methods relied on self-reporting one's preferences, and researchers found that viewers would often give answers they believed to be socially acceptable rather than reveal their true viewing behaviours.

Such problems created an opening for A. C. Nielsen during the 1950s when it began to attach meters to television sets across the US, automatically recording the time and station to which each set was tuned. Initially, viewers mailed in the recorded data each week, but by the end of the decade Nielsen had developed electronic methods for data collection over telephone lines, so that telecasters and advertising agencies could have access to ratings results by the next morning, what became known as 'the overnights'. Nielsen meters, what they referred to as Audimeters, also eliminated self-reporting errors, since they didn't rely on viewers' recollections of what they watched.

Nielsen supplemented its meter data with viewer diaries that garnered personal viewing information from each member of the household. It also correlated the diary information with the meter data in order to check for accuracy. The Nielsen equipment not only recorded channel tuning on the set, it also incorporated flashing lights and buzzers to prompt participants to make diary entries on a regular basis. Nielsen's patented technology soon became the industry standard and the company grew enormously prosperous selling its data to telecasters and advertising agencies on a subscription basis. By the early 1960s, it so dominated TV ratings that Congress investigated Nielsen for antitrust violations. Nielsen's reputation as a monopolist continues to haunt the firm even today, but the company has never been indicted for antitrust violations nor have its ratings data been successfully challenged by a competitor.

Nielsen prevails largely because telecasters, studios and advertising agencies have to agree on the pricing of commercial time and the scheduling of programmes. Telecasters of course want to charge the highest prices possible for ad time and therefore would prefer audience surveys that showed their programmes attracting huge audiences. Ad agencies take a more critical view, wanting to be sure that the audience figures are in line with what they pay for commercial time on behalf of their clients. If each side were to commission its own audience research, they would probably arrive at very different assessments of audience viewing behaviours. Nielsen, operating as a third party, supplies a standard set of figures that both sides can employ in negotiations. These data represent a common point of reference from which to begin deliberations, even though each side may interpret the data differently. Nielsen ratings also come in handy when network executives negotiate with producers about shows the studio is providing. They use audience measurement to determine which shows to keep on their schedule and which new ones to acquire. They also use it to determine what they will pay in licensing fees. Nielsen makes it possible for media companies to negotiate more efficiently with respect to both advertising and programming.

Media critic Eileen Meehan (2005) has pointed out that, although Nielsen may meet the needs of media companies, it doesn't necessarily meet the needs

Ratings companies try to make vast audiences intelligible and useful for television advertisers and professionals. This is especially challenging with popular shows that have diverse audiences, such as *American Idol*, here featuring a performance by Jennifer Hudson

of audiences.[1] For example, ratings only report audience selections among a fixed set of options, but viewers are not asked to express their actual interests or desires. Telecasters say a show is popular because it scores higher than its competitors, but this leaves unspoken what audiences may have actually preferred to be watching at that time, perhaps something that commercial television does not offer. Ratings also treat viewing as a consumer behaviour, even though audiences tend to use television for information and entertainment, which are not necessarily consumer behaviours. Finally, ratings don't measure intensity of interest or audience satisfaction. For many years television networks offered least offensive programming (LOP), reasoning that mass audiences could only be built by avoiding content that might drive away particular groups of viewers. Critics argued that LOP did indeed generate substantial ratings, but it did so largely because audiences had only two other network options. Audiences may have chosen what was least offensive, but that didn't necessarily mean it was most attractive. Only as the number of channels expanded did industry executives begin to show an interest in viewer satisfaction, hoping to attract and hold onto viewers who now had many choices.

Ratings are furthermore misleading because they suggest that audiences are actual social entities. 'The audience' for *American Idol* averages close to 30 million individuals and is therefore incredibly diverse. It includes viewers from different generations, genders and sexual orientations; from different races and ethnicities; and from different parts of the country. To say that Albert, a black shipyard worker in Birmingham, Alabama, has much in common with Crystal, a Chinese-American teen in San Jose, or Madelyn, a retired insurance clerk in Hartford, is to stretch credulity. Yet ratings data portray them as part of a coherent social entity. The audience is *represented* as a whole, even though it is made up of millions of individuals watching their TV sets in different ways and in different settings.

Social critic Raymond Williams (1983) famously observed, 'There are in fact no masses; there are only ways of seeing people as masses.' With respect to television, this suggests that audiences only exist as *representations* that are conjured into existence by the TV industry. Audiences as conceived by ratings data are useful fictions that are generated by and for the television industry. These images suggest a collective existence among widely scattered viewers who never gather together in one place and will never know one another. Audience research data suggest that the attention of these viewers can be turned into a commodity and sold to advertisers who wish to use that attention for commercial purposes. Representations of the audience therefore tell us more about the industry that makes use of them than they do about the lives and behaviours of actual viewers. And although the methods for audience analysis are sometimes characterised as 'objective', they are in fact the product of ongoing debate and negotiation within the industry.

PEOPLE METERS

Pressure to improve ratings research escalated during the 1980s as the number of viewing options expanded. Having dominated the ratings business for three decades, Nielsen was reluctant to spend money to improve the quality of its data. Although television was undergoing significant changes, Nielsen didn't offer daily ratings for cable channels, reasoning that their audiences were too small and the cost of gathering data too high. This made it difficult for cable channels to promote their services to advertisers and to negotiate advertising rates for particular programmes.

In 1980, 20 per cent of homes subscribed to cable television and by mid-decade the figure grew to 43 per cent and in 1990 to 56 per cent. The number of broadcasting options also expanded through the decade, as Fox launched a fourth network and new independent stations appeared in many local markets. Changes were taking place on other fronts as well. By 1980, more than half of all homes had more than one TV set and by the end of the decade most TVs were equipped with remote controls, which allowed viewers to surf through a host of channels without having to leave the comfort of their sofa. VCR owner-ship also took off in this period, reaching more than two-thirds of all homes by the end of the decade, allowing viewers to timeshift their viewing of favourite programmes (Nielsen Media Research, TVB Online, 2008).

As viewing alternatives increased, the size of network audiences declined, but Nielsen resisted pressure to expand or alter its ratings, arguing that it still served its major clients cost-effectively. Yet advertising agencies grew restless due largely to the fact that the cost of network advertising continued to increase despite a decline in network ratings. Advertisers hoped that cable could furnish them with alternative delivery channels and help to put pressure on the broadcast networks to bring down their rates. In response, Nielsen grudgingly added daily ratings for prominent cable services in 1982, but this failed to address many of the other changes noted above. Of what use was it to know the number of households tuned to a programme if the audiences watched on multiple sets, zipped between channels and recorded programmes for later viewing?

Sensing an opportunity, Audits of Great Britain (AGB) launched a *people meter* service in the Boston area in 1985, hoping to demonstrate its potential locally and then roll it out in other big-city markets, aiming eventually to build a national competitor to Nielsen. AGB installed meters on televisions that were equipped with remote controls. In addition to capturing tuning data, the AGB remotes required viewers to log in and to indicate when viewers left the room or when new ones entered. It also prompted users to check periodically for any changes in the composition of the viewing group. Each individual log-in was associated with demographic information, such as age, gender and income. AGB could therefore report demographic data on a daily basis, whereas Nielsen was still relying on diary tabulations compiled four times each season during 'sweeps' periods in November, February, May and July.

Aware of AGB's success in the UK, Nielsen developed its own people meter using the very same principles and in 1987 it launched a national service effectively short-circuiting the AGB strategy. AGB also encountered a number of technical and marketing problems with its service and, facing a formidable challenge from Nielsen, decided in 1988 to pull out of the US market. Once again the monopo-list, Nielsen offered national people meter ratings on a daily basis, but having vanquished the competition, it slowed the development of local people meters, tak-ing until the late 1990s to introduce them. Without competition, Nielsen had little reason to bear the costs of timely innovation (2002). Today, Nielsen has a sam-ple of 5,100 people meter households gathering data on national programming. It also analyses local television viewing in 210 markets across the country. Of those, Nielsen provides local people meter ratings in fifty-six markets. In the remainder, it relies exclusively on diaries.

Despite these innovations, questions persist about the reliability of Nielsen data. As VCR use escalated, and as DVD and DVR adoption grew, questions about timeshifting mounted. For many years, viewers had recorded programmes on their VCRs, but digital technology made it easier to select and record shows on a DVR (also known as a personal video recorder or PVR). A company called TiVo pioneered an even friendlier recording interface, making it possible to search for and select programmes using only keywords or title phrases. TiVo units made it possible to watch shows without any knowledge of network TV schedules, adjacent programmes or commercial advertisements. Television and cable networks argued that viewers who record shows should be counted as part of the total audience, but advertisers are reluctant to grant this, since they believe that those who view recorded programmes tend to zip past the commercials. In 2005, Nielsen and others began to study timeshifted viewing, providing ratings for the original broadcast and for viewers that watched the show on video recorders within the next three days, what came to be known as 'ratings + 3'. This gave the networks' audience figures a substantial boost and it furthermore showed that not all viewers skipped commercials, since many could recount significant information from TV ads. In fact, much of the industry research seems to suggest that viewers value timeshifting more than commercial zapping (Story 2007 (August)).

In 2007, advertisers agreed to acknowledge audiences included in the ratings + 3 data but in return networks had to agree to ratings of commercial viewing as well as programme viewing. That is, Nielsen now supplies data on the actual audience size during the commercials themselves. Networks may argue for the popularity of their shows, but if the ratings during commercial spots show a significant drop-off, ad agencies can now press for lower rates or other concessions. This compromise, known as C3 ratings gives each side ammunition to argue their respective interests. Ad agencies also continue to press for measures of audience attention, interest and information retention. And they want to know if advertisements have a demonstrable impact on consumer purchasing decisions. Television executives are worried about making concessions to these demands because they are unsure that current technologies can furnish such information reliably.

Another area that generates controversy is Nielsen's continued attention to household viewing as opposed to other forms of television use. Programming and commercials are commonly viewed in airports, hotels, hospitals, stores, offices and college dorms. TV shows are also watched on planes, trains and automobiles, and via computer and other digital devices. In fact, it's estimated that as much as 20 per cent of all viewing takes place outside the home. In response to these concerns, Arbitron, a firm that once competed with Nielsen in the TV ratings business, is developing a new form of measurement called the portable people meter (PPM). The device looks like a pager, a small plastic box that fits on one's belt. Its job is to listen for audio signals that are embedded in TV and radio programming. The signals are beyond the range of human hearing, but the pager records these signals throughout the day and then, at the end of the day, the owner puts the device in a docking station that both recharges the battery and sends the day's data to the Arbitron researchers (Gertner 2005).

At home, the PPM records when a viewer is sitting in the family room watching TV, but it also accompanies the viewer as she heads to the kitchen for a snack, where another TV may be playing another programme. It also goes with the viewer to the shopping mall or the airport, tracking television exposure in each location. And it records timeshifted viewing via DVRs or video cassettes. Most importantly for advertisers, the PPM provides data on each discrete advertisement, showing, for example, if the viewer left the room during an ad or zipped past it on their DVR.

Ideally, Arbitron would like to correlate this data with information about the buying behaviours of its sample. The problem, of course, is compliance. Many people are leery of responding to surveys or having a metering device on their television set. For them, the PPM seems even more intrusive, tracking one's personal behaviours throughout the day. Add to that a recording of all purchases and one can imagine that those willing to participate would amount to a very small segment of the population. Given that the remuneration for participation is quite small, it's difficult to imagine the motivation to participate. Consequently, compliance remains one of the biggest obstacles for audience-measurement technologies.

Table 2.2 Ratings of Leading Network Shows, 12–18 November 2007

	Household rating	Share	18–49
CSI: Crime Scene Investigation (CBS)	13.5	20	6.6
Grey's Anatomy (ABC)	12.8	19	8.6
Desperate Housewives (ABC)	12.8	19	7.8
House M.D. (Fox)	10.7	16	7.4
NBC Sunday Night Football	10.7	16	6.7
Survivor: China (CBS)	9.2	14	5.2
Two and a Half Men (CBS)	8.7	12	5.0
Private Practice (ABC)	7.9	12	4.3
Heroes (NBC)	6.8	10	5.2
The Simpsons (Fox)	6.5	10	5.3
America's Next Top Model (CW)	3.7	6	2.8
Destilando Amor (UV)	3.3	5	3.0
Smallville (CW)	2.9	4	2.0
Cristina (UV)	2.3	4	1.9

Source: 'Weekly Primetime Ratings' 2007.

CONTINUING CHALLENGES

Viewer participation has been a vexing problem since the very early days of audience studies: how does one get a truly representative sample of viewers? During the classical network era, Nielsen was confident that 1,200 families constituted a large enough and diverse enough sample to make generalisations about national viewing behaviours. Many challenged that assumption, but Nielsen held fast to its argument that statistically there was no value in adding more households, and that it would be unnecessarily expensive. Due to the expansion of media choices during the 1980s, Nielsen increased its sample to 5,100 homes, a figure that some critics say is still inadequate. In an attempt to address this concern some companies, like Erin Media and TiVo, are now developing technology to glean viewing data from digital cable boxes and video recorders. Such services could potentially furnish more accurate information about small audiences for niche programming since these devices are installed in more than 40 million homes. Still, it wouldn't account for households without these technologies nor for those viewing outside the home. These new services also raise serious privacy concerns and some legal experts contend that viewers would have to agree to have their viewing patterns analysed.

The challenges facing researchers remind us that the audience does not exist as an objectively observable entity. It is conjured into existence by ratings services whose numbers are then massaged and deployed on behalf of various contending parties. During the height of the network era, it made sense for television companies and advertising agencies to promote the mass audience as an important component of the national economy and politics. With their account revenues rapidly growing, network executives crowed that television was the most powerful communication and advertising medium in American history. Of course, the rise of television occurred at the expense of other media, with radio, magazines and newspapers each seeing their share of the advertising pie diminished by this popular new competitor. Radio had until the 1950s been a prominent national medium, gathering the attention of vast audiences, but after the arrival of television, the radio industry began to shift its attention to local audiences (and mobile audiences) and in the 1970s it began to focus on small segments of the audience. Magazines retained a broader geographical reach, many of them distributing nationally or regionally, but they too began to define their audiences more narrowly as, for example, young mothers, railroad hobbyists or rock-music fans.

While the major networks were promoting the useful fiction of a mass audience, magazine companies began to promote the notion that narrowly targeted media could provide advertisers with more efficient access to especially desirable groups of consumers. Dollar for dollar, they claimed that an advertisement in *Parents* or *Babytalk* would attract the attention of more young mothers and fathers without wasting ad resources on teenagers or retirees. They argued that on a cost-per-thousand (CPM) basis, it was cheaper for a baby-shampoo manufacturer to reach its audience through a niche magazine than it was through television. Moreover, readers of the magazine were more likely to pay attention to the ads because they were more intensively engaged with the editorial content. Adopting *efficiency* and *intensity* as their standards, they suggested that niche media ads outperform their network TV counterparts (Turow 1998).

These arguments gathered force within the context of broader social changes taking place in the US during the 1970s and 80s, including widespread criticism of mass culture, celebration of counter-cultures and uneasiness about the relentless suppression of minority voices on television. Feminism had a powerful impact on American thinking as well. Increasingly, media services began to cater to the diverse interests of female audiences, no longer addressing them solely as teeny-boppers, young brides and stay-at-home moms. Attention to teenage media users also intensified, especially after the fabulous growth of MTV during the 80s. Before then, the baby-boom generation commanded most attention, but increasingly generation X and then generation Y attracted their own distinctive niche services. Media furthermore began to pay more attention to African American and Latino citizens, as magazine, radio and TV services designed for these viewers grew increasingly prosperous. Interestingly, however, not all niches were perceived as equal in the eyes of advertising agencies. Although *Elle* and MTV could charge a premium for their advertising, Latino and African American advertising was sold at a discount.

Still, the fortunes of Latino television improved dramatically over the past few decades and yield an instructive example of the ways in which the visibility of audiences is very much tied to the changing interests of advertisers and television companies.[2] Until the 1980s, Spanish-speaking audiences in the US were served by stations that affiliated with television companies from Mexico or Puerto Rico. Most powerful was Televisa, the Mexican conglomerate that established a network of affiliates (many of them owned by Televisa) that played its popular telenovelas. This arrangement called into question an FCC ownership rule that requires station owners to hold US citizenship. Consequently, Televisa – owned by the Azcarraga family of Mexico City – was forced to sell its stations to Hallmark in 1987, but it maintained a minority interest in the Univision network and established an output deal that supplies the network with its most popular programming, telenovelas. These primetime dramas, all of them produced in Mexico, help to perpetuate Televisa's influence in the US, but since the 1990s, Univision's leadership has been challenged by a number of new competitors, including Telemundo (owned by NBC), MTV, ESPN, Fox and Discovery, each of them creating dedicated Spanish-language services.

This growing interest in Latino audiences is in large part due to the fact that the US now has the fifth largest Spanish-speaking population in the world with 39 million residents claiming Latino or Hispanic heritage according to recent census figures. Population projections indicate that this group will grow significantly over the next few decades, while other segments of the US population will hold steady. Latino purchasing power is also growing, reaching $800 billion in 2006 with expectations that it will top $1 trillion before the end of the decade.

The size of this potential market and the television industry's growing interest in niche advertising not only encourages media companies to pay attention to Latino viewers, but to try to understand the diverse interests and tastes among them. Census estimates say that 59 per cent are of Mexican origin, 10 per cent Puerto Rican, 3.5 per cent Cuban, 5 per cent Central American and 4 per cent South American. Some 18 per cent say they fall outside these categories or are of mixed heritage. Although Televisa had long dominated Spanish-language airwaves with shows aimed primarily at Mexican immigrants and Mexican Americans, many of its new competitors target their efforts at the other 41 per cent and at youth audiences with cross-cultural identities. They counter that together these viewers comprise more than half the Latino audience.

This growing interest in Latinos led companies to press Nielsen for more timely and accurate audience data. In 1992, Nielsen set up the Hispanic Television Index, a small segregated service for specialised clients. Over the next fifteen years, Nielsen expanded its national people meter sample and introduced people meters into local markets, consequently tripling the number of Latino households in its data universe. In 2007, it dropped the Hispanic Television Index and now provides Latino data as part of its mainstream services. With 1,400 families now participating, Latino audience preferences have grown more prominent and many media executives were surprised to find that Univision is not only the leading Hispanic television network but also the fifth most popular network overall, behind NBC but ahead of CW. Meanwhile, ad spending on Latino channels has mushroomed since 1992, growing from $200 million to more than $3 billion in 2007.[3]

As this example suggests, Latino audiences in the United States were largely ignored during the classical network era due to a relentless focus on the mass audience. As new services emerged and as competition intensified, Nielsen was pressed to alter its sampling techniques, which in turn rendered Latino audiences more visible, more valuable and more diverse than previously imagined. Yet despite these changes, ad rates on Latino channels remain lower than those at the major networks and at other niche services. Some say this is because many advertisers still believe that they can reach most Latinos through the major networks and that these viewers will respond like the rest of the mass audience. As shown above, however, it is just as likely that ad rates, like audience data, are shaped by struggles among contending interests within the television industry.

As leading television companies and advertising agencies began to target Latinos, they sought better audience data and tried to portray this data in ways that would benefit their new services. Therefore the growing attraction of niche audiences isn't simply the product of technological change or solely the outcome of dispassionate economic calculation. Throughout the history of television, various actors have sought to shape our understanding of audiences and turn them to their benefit. This is the driving force behind changes in the ways that audiences are measured and the ways in which advertising is sold. But before turning to the actual mechanics of TV ad sales, it would be worthwhile to briefly explain the aims and organisation of advertising agencies.

ADVERTISING AGENCIES

When many of us think of advertising agencies, we conjure up visions of creative personnel crafting eye-grabbing graphics and witty punch lines. This is indeed an important component of the advertising business, but it is a very small part of what ad agencies actually do. What follows is a brief explanation of how the major agencies handle national advertising. At the local level, the scale of agency activities is of course much smaller, but the basic principles are similar. As relates to television, four aspects of agency operations deserve close attention: media planning, creative development, media buying and tracking.

Media planning begins with an evaluation of the client's product or service and an assessment of the audience data that will be needed for the ad campaign. Data are purchased from research firms that provide information about various media and demographic groups. Obviously, the more refined and specific the data, the more expensive it is to gather. Agencies can also acquire customised data, such as information about the lifestyles of particular groups of media users: Where do they vacation? What cars do they drive? What kinds of cosmetics do they tend to choose? Research can furthermore furnish psychographic profiles that attempt to correlate media use with attributes such as aspiring, nurturing or materialistic.

Agencies seek data that help them identify the best channels for their messages and the comparative efficiency of those channels. That is, they want to know what percentage of their target audience can be reached through each specific medium and they want to know the cost per thousand (CPM). With these figures in hand, they then try to make an assessment of the qualitative merits of each medium, especially the environment in which the ads will be situated. For example, if one wanted to advertise a trendy sports coupé, *The Daily Show with Jon Stewart* (1999–) might deliver a substantial percentage of your

Table 2.3 Top TV Ad Categories

Network	Cable	Local spot
Auto	Auto	Auto
Medicine	Medicine	Restaurants
Telecom	Financial	Telecom
Restaurants	Food & Food Products	Car & Truck Dealers
Toiletries & Cosmetics	Toiletries & Cosmetics	Furniture Stores
Financial	Telecom	Insurance & Real Estate
Food & Food Products	Restaurants	Financial
Motion Pictures	Motion Pictures	Government & Organisations
Soft Drinks, Candy, Snacks	Toys, Games, Hobbies	Schools, Colleges, Camps
Audio & Video	Insurance & Real Estate	Leisure Activities & Events

target audience at an efficient price, but you might be better served by a show that attracts car fans, such as *Pimp My Ride* (2004–) or *Trick My Truck* (2006–). These shows are popular with young drivers and the atmosphere surrounding the shows is conducive to fantasising about automobiles. Planners enlist both quantitative and qualitative information to develop a proposal for their client that includes a budget for the creation of ads and the purchase of commercial spots or ad space.

After the proposal is accepted, the creative team begins to craft a set of messages, usually around a single theme. Nike invites consumers to 'Just do it.' Diesel tells them to 'Love [Nature] while it lasts.' And Toyota explains that the Scion is 'what moves you'. Large comprehensive agencies often have design and production departments inhouse. They may nevertheless hire freelancers or smaller creative boutiques to assume particular responsibilities or deliver specific creative services. Some agencies have only a design department and subcontract the production work and some subcontract all of their creative work.

The merit of keeping creative development inhouse is that one can derive profits from these activities and the agency can present itself to clients as a one-stop shop. On the other hand, creative work is very unpredictable and some agencies reason that they can save money and achieve better results by shopping projects around to various subcontractors. Regardless of who does the work, every word, sound, visual and bar of music featured in the ad is meticulously recorded, mixed and sweetened. Every second of every ad is carefully calculated with an eye to attracting the attention of the target demographic and delivering an influential message. Given the thousands of images the average person is exposed to each day, the primary aim of the creative team is to 'cut through the clutter' and present the viewer with a memorable image instantly associated with the client's product.

While the creative team is hard at work on the message, agency media buyers begin to craft their strategy for the placement of ads. Although the original planning team combed through vast amounts of audience data and arrived at cost estimates for ad placement, the actual purchase of advertising time is subject to a great deal of negotiation. This will be discussed in the following section, but for now, it should be observed that media buyers inside the agency often work in teams and often represent more than one client's account or more than one product. Agencies are careful to keep the accounts of competitors separate, but one of the virtues of working with a large advertising firm is that large-scale purchases provide leverage when negotiating with television sales departments. The more one buys, the harder one can negotiate.

One of the main jobs of the buyers is to seek discounts and to come up with creative combinations – or bundles – of purchases. Buyers also press hard for favourable placement of their ads, especially important when firms are competing for spots at particular times of day or on particular programmes. Clearly, big agencies also have an advantage because they develop long-term relationships with national television services so that favours are sometimes remembered and reciprocated. Because package sales and professional relationships are so important, some firms specialise in media buying, normally supplying the service to smaller agencies that don't have the heft to sustain a purchasing operation of their own.

Finally, advertising agencies offer tracking services that make sure the message is delivered as contracted. Ads that get pre-empted by schedule changes or suffer from technical malfunction are obvious candidates for refunds or compensation, but one of the most important responsibilities of the agency is to ensure that broadcast and cable networks deliver an audience that matches the 'minimum guarantee' that was negotiated during the ad sale. If a network says that the 8:30 pm show on Thursday will deliver at least 2 million viewers in the 18–49-year-old age bracket, then the agency must make sure that the ratings confirm that guarantee. If they don't, then the agency asks that the network 'make good' on its guarantee by assigning time on another show to compensate for the deficiency. Make goods are an important part of the business and throughout the season each network holds onto a reserve inventory of slots that can serve this purpose.

Throughout each ad campaign, agencies report back to their clients with information about ad placement and audiences reached. At the request of a client, they may do follow-up surveys or experiments to test audience awareness and recall of the ad campaign's message. And they may report on the performance of advertisements by competitors. Agencies provide a range of creative and marketing services, and they represent their clients in negotiations with television enterprises. The most important bargaining takes place each year during the upfront market.

THE UPFRONT MARKET

In May, after the last rating sweeps of the season, the major broadcasting networks stage lavish extravaganzas in New York City to celebrate their accomplishments and to announce new shows slated for fall premiere. These kick-off presentations mix razzle-dazzle showbusiness with shameless promotion and wry jibes at the competition. Network executives often ask TV stars to make appearances on stage and at receptions, and to have their pictures taken with key clients. Although many network executives attend, the performance is primarily aimed at media buyers and their clients who engage in spirited negotiation with their network counterparts over the ensuing weeks.

Each network presentation marks the beginning of what is known in the industry as the upfront market for advertising time. During the upfronts, networks sell close to 75 per cent of the commercial time available for the coming season, representing some $2 billion of revenue for each of the four majors. This is when some of the biggest package deals are made and the best discounts offered. Negotiations begin immediately after each network presentation and continue until each meets its sales target. Some years, the negotiations wrap up in only a few weeks, which tends to happen when demand for commercial time is high and agencies want to lock in favourable slots quickly. Other years the upfronts can drag on into August, especially when disagreements arise about pricing or audience-measurement data.

Because ad spots are sold in bundles during the upfronts, buyers' perceptions of the various networks are as important as their perceptions of particular shows. Therefore kick-off presentations afford networks an opportunity to promote their brand identity. They do this in two ways. First, each presentation tries to proffer a convincing rationale for network programming decisions, pointing to successes from the preceding season and showing how the network plans to capitalise on such successes with their fall schedule. If the preceding season was disappointing, a network tries to show how it will turn things around, attempting to generate excitement about the fall line-up. Second, each network aims to convince advertisers that its shows are the most appealing place to promote products. During the classical network era, the three majors generally characterised themselves as national mass media, but this began to change as the number of competitors increased.

In the early 1980s, NBC was especially concerned about its brand image because it was then running a distant third in the ratings. Grant Tinker, NBC's newly appointed president, paid particular attention to the fact that cable was growing most rapidly in homes with higher incomes. HBO was especially attractive among adults and MTV was drawing a large and dedicated following among teenagers. NBC executives felt these viewers represented the cream of the TV audience, both because of their purchasing power and because ad agencies were increasingly targeting teens and young adults. Agencies claimed young audiences were more valuable because they were more responsive to ads and more likely to experiment with new brands and products. NBC executives worried not only about its ratings but also about the potential loss of premium viewers.

With its ratings sagging and with new competitors on the horizon, NBC executives began to rebuild the schedule with an emphasis on quality dramas and urban comedies. As new shows such as *Hill Street Blues* (1981–7), *Cheers* (1982–93), and *St. Elsewhere* (1982–8) began to attract audiences and critical acclaim, the network actively capitalised on the attention and sought to fashion it into a brand identity that emphasised quality programming aimed at young audiences and upscale adults. Rather than gross ratings, NBC directed attention to the 18–49 demographic and promoted these ratings as the most significant indices for negotiations with advertisers. Executives argued that advertisers should pay attention to those segments of the audience that made the greatest proportion of purchases (Gitlin 1985).

By the mid-1990s, NBC had become the undisputed leader among 18–49-year-old viewers, but most successful was its Thursday line-up of 'Must See TV': *Seinfeld* (1990–8), *Friends* (1994–2004) and *ER* (1994–2009). Not only did NBC dominate the ratings, it also transformed industry thinking about the value of advertising at that particular time. Network executives contended that Thursday represented the last opportunity to reach young viewers before they abandoned television for the weekend. Advertisers for fast food, beverages and leisure products took notice and began to compete for slots, bidding up the rates for commercial time. Movie studios also became important customers, promoting their new releases for the weekend, and car dealers climbed on board, knowing that most vehicle sales take place over the weekend. NBC's success was based not only on the quality and popularity of its shows but also on the fact that executives were able to shape attitudes in the marketplace to their advantage (Carter 2007).

The exceptional popularity of shows like *Friends* among young audiences made it possible for NBC executives to reshape advertiser attitudes about network ratings

Although most advertising strategies are driven by research data, the television business is also influenced by industry discourse about the hottest shows and the latest audience trends. The attractiveness of particular audiences waxes and wanes, as do perceptions of the most innovative and valuable programmes. Thus pricing for commercial time is affected by talk in the marketplace and by competition for a limited supply of advertising slots.

NBC was so successful at shaping perceptions of its audience that its Thursday ad spots sold for as much as double that of its nearest competitor, CBS, which was widely perceived as catering to mass audiences, including older and supposedly less desirable viewers. In the late 1990s, however, CBS's fortunes began to change and during the ensuing decade it assembled a set of popular procedural dramas, including the *CSI* franchise. This helped to boost the network into an undisputed lead in the overall ratings. The audience still skewed older than those of its competitors, but CBS executives stressed the importance of gross ratings as opposed to target demographics, arguing that the distinctive virtue of network television was its status as a mass advertising medium. TV, they contended, is the last big tent in American showbusiness and CBS is best positioned to take advantage of that distinctive promotional feature. CBS sought to reverse perceptions in the marketplace so it could capitalise on its particular brand of programming.

The shifting fortunes of CBS and NBC are case examples of the role that executives can play in shaping perceptions of their networks. Nevertheless networks often go through cyclical changes that are difficult to control. Leading shows age (*Friends, Frasier*). New contenders don't perform as expected (*Joey*, 2004–6; *The Michael Richards Show*, 2000). And other shows prove surprisingly popular or attractive to critics (*The Office*, 2005–, *My Name Is Earl*, 2005–9). Although network executives try to seem like they are in control of the programme-development process, they are often chasing winners and trying to exploit surprising opportunities, all the while attempting to shape the advertiser's perception of the network's performance. Sometimes a network brand seems remarkably coherent and it's easy for an advertiser to envision the audience. At other times, the weekly schedule seems like a collection of odd bedfellows. Such was the case with Fox during the 2007 season: its blockbuster success, *American Idol*, had little in common with the paranoid intensity of *24* or the droll slacker sensibility of *Family Guy* (1999–). How could such different shows be part of a unified programming strategy? What exactly was the Fox brand and who was its audience?

ADVERTISING SALES

During the upfront selling season, advertising agencies are most interested in securing ad spots at times when most of their target audience is watching. They

Table 2.4 Cost of a Thirty-second Spot on Leading Network Shows, Fall 2007

Grey's Anatomy (ABC)	$419,000
NBC Sunday Night Football	358,000
The Simpsons (Fox)	315,000
Heroes (NBC)	296,000
House M.D. (Fox)	294,000
Desperate Housewives (ABC)	270,000
CSI: Crime Scene Investigation (CBS)	248,000
Two and a Half Men (CBS)	231,000
Survivor: China (CBS)	208,000
Private Practice (ABC)	208,000

Source: Steinberg 2007.[4]

may also want to place ads with particular shows, but since each show has a limited number of spots and since popular shows often attract a great deal of interest, network sales departments try to accommodate their clients' wishes while also directing their attention to other shows and times that may be compatible as well. In other words, networks will present their clients with a bundle of ad spots that include the requested shows as well as others with similar audience characteristics. Ad spots on popular programmes often act as colourful bows that wrap the bundle. They may help to attract buyers, but the primary focus of most negotiations is the total reach of the advertisement. Networks generally offer a minimum guarantee that ads will be seen by a specific number of viewers within the target demographic. Shows that carry over from the preceding season usually hold their audience and hit their guarantees. Shows that slide in the ratings or new shows that don't perform well require a 'make good' offering of extra time slots. These are provided from the inventory of spots that networks set aside for scatter market sales during the season.

Scatter-market sales are made throughout the television season. Sometimes the cost of a scatter-market ad may be twice as high as a purchase during the upfronts. On the other hand, poor performance by a show or a network may drive down the value of spots. Scatter-market prices are also affected by other factors in the economy, such as consumer demand and seasonal cycles. The winter holiday season is, for example, a period when companies jockey for advertising slots, raising the price of commercial time. Scatter-market prices can also be affected by broader trends in the economy. Prices may fall due to sluggish growth, rising unemployment or high interest rates. At such times companies may trim their advertising budgets in an attempt to cut costs. Thus, supply and demand have a strong effect on ad sales during the season and even though networks can usually command higher prices in the scatter market, they

Table 2.5 Comparison of Broadcast and Cable Advertising Rates

PT ad rates by CPM	2001	2004
Broadcast Networks	19.71	24.47
General Cable*	9.04	9.63
Young Cable**	14.17	18.14
Upscale Cable***	20.19	23.80

* TNT, USA, Lifetime
**MTV, Comedy Central, E!
***Discovery, History

Source: 'Networks Thrive' 2004.

try to sell most of their inventory in bundles during the upfronts so as to smooth out demand cycles and reduce transaction costs.

Smaller networks (such as Univision and CW) and cable networks also engage in upfront negotiations that usually follow immediately after the majors. Cable networks sell roughly 50 per cent of their inventory during the upfronts. Most channels would like to sell more of their inventory upfront, but demand is weak. This weakness is also reflected in the scatter market where cable ads sell at a discount rather than at a premium. In fact, many cable channels fail to sell all of their spots. Industry experts say that even though cable's share of the audience is rising, there are simply too many channels and too many ad spots competing for buyers. Supply far outstrips demand. Interestingly, between 2000 and 2004, cable's combined share of the audience rose from 39 to 48 per cent, while the majors' share dropped from 56 to 50 per cent. Nevertheless ad rates at the broadcast networks rose more quickly than their cable peers. For every thousand viewers that the broadcasters delivered, they charged close to $25, a figure more than double the price at general cable channels such as TNT, USA and Lifetime.

This disparity can be explained in part by the fact that broadcast networks are few in number, but they also attract advertisers because each network averages close to 10 million viewers, while audiences for top ten cable channels range between 1.2 to 2.6 million viewers. Moreover, it takes two weeks to reach the same number of original viewers through a cable channel as it does through one night of network exposure. Low ratings and low revenues also make it difficult for cable channels to develop original programming. Those that rely on a heavy rotation of off-network reruns find it difficult to distinguish their brand. As indicated in Table 2.5, cable channels that fare best have strong brand identities and audience demographics that point towards high levels of personal consumption. General cable channels suffer by comparison due to the fact that they lack distinctive audiences and distinctive identities, pitting them as pale comparisons to their network counterparts.

Table 2.6 TV Ad Volume Distribution (in millions)

Year	Network	National spot	Local spot	Syndicated	Cable
1950	85	31	55		
1955	550	260	225		
1960	820	527	280		
1965	1,237	892	386		
1970	1,658	1,234	704		
1975	2,306	1,623	1,334		
1980	5,130	3,269	2,967	50	72
1985	8,060	6,004	5,714	520	989
1990	9,863	7,788	7,856	1,109	2,631
1995	11,600	9,119	9,985	2,016	6,166
2000	15,888	12,264	13,542	3,108	15,455
2005	16,128	10,040	14,260	3,865	23,654

Source: Universal McCann 2008.

Although broadcast and cable networks command most of the revenue from national ad sales, many viewers are reached via spot sales. In these cases a media buyer specialises in securing ad spots around the country so as to give the advertiser national exposure through local stations and cable services. The buying agency pieces together a national mosaic of ad opportunities and negotiates purchases on behalf of the client. National audiences can also be reached by syndication or barter sales. When shows such as *The Oprah Winfrey Show* (1986–) and *Wheel of Fortune* (1983–) are sold to stations around the country, the syndicator holds back several spots in each show for sale to national advertisers. To compensate, the syndicator makes the show available to local stations at lower cost. This barter arrangement helps to make the show more attractive to local programming executives and it allows the syndicator (and often the producer) to benefit from the popularity of the show through direct ad sales. Barter sales attract major national advertisers even though the programme may be scheduled for different times on a variety of channels across the country.

As for local TV stations, they sell ads using many of the principles outlined above. Affiliates receive marketing support and advice from their networks, and they develop distinctive marketing tools for their local productions, especially news, sports and talk shows. They sell all of the spots on local shows, and during the network feed, affiliates are allowed to sell several minutes of each hour. Local stations also use syndicated programming, both original shows and reruns, during the hours when they aren't transmitting the network feed or showing one of their own productions. Ad spots during these shows are also sold at the local level, with the exception of the minutes withheld in a barter deal. Independent stations don't have the benefit of a national feed and so their schedules are made up of local productions and syndicated fare. They sell spots for all of these shows, again, with the exception of barter spots. Finally, local cable operators retain the right to insert spots in the programming they carry from national cable networks. Many cable networks charge the local operators a subscriber fee for their service and at the time they negotiate these fees, they also reach agreement on the number of spots available to the local operator.

FUTURE TRENDS

As mentioned earlier, Nielsen now provides ratings data for commercials as well as programmes. Ad agencies had for years pressed for this information, arguing that audiences may watch programmes, but not the ads. Moreover, advertisers worry that even if audiences watch the ads, they may not be paying attention. Distractions in the home have always been a factor, but increasingly advertisers worry that multitasking is becoming a common mode of media use. Of particular concern is competition from the Internet.

One study observed 400 people of various age groups and found that over the course of a day they averaged nine hours of media use, much of it devoted to television. Interestingly, however, a third of the time they were juggling more than one form of media, commonly surfing the net while watching TV. Another study reports that of those who access the Internet and TV simultaneously 11 per cent say they pay the greatest attention to TV, 61 per cent to the net and 28 per cent divide their attention equally (Waxman 2006). Such trends are obviously worrisome to advertisers, since they suggest that television exposure is not sufficient to ensure audience attention and, most importantly, recall. Studies are now underway to try to discern whether viewers actually retain information and imagery from TV ad campaigns.

Another important development is the growing presence of the digital video recorder in the home. As of 2009, an estimated 32 per cent of TV homes had at least one DVR. TiVo, the leading innovator, offers viewers a programming interface that makes it easy for them to record their favourite shows without having to pay attention to network schedules. Instead, they let TiVo manage the recording chores and each night they sit down to a menu of offerings. This not only allows them to timeshift their viewing, it also makes it easy for them to skip through commercials. Yet research shows that many viewers still watch the ads and others register key imagery as they zip on through. Advertisers and network executives are pressing Nielsen for more research in this area and they are debating how much weight to attach to DVR viewing of television shows. With DVR penetration rising, some worry that the current model of television advertising could be endangered.

One way to counter the effects of DVRs is to integrate advertising with the programmes. During much of the radio era, sponsors hosted an entire show and their products were often integrated into the plots of the programmes. After television came along, this pattern persisted into the 1950s, so, for example, George Burns and Gracie Allen always took time in their show for a glass of Carnation milk and the boys from Texaco oil sang the introduction for variety host Milton Berle. During the classical network era, such sponsorship disappeared as television migrated to a magazine format, whereby the networks produced the programmes and then sold clusters of spots to multiple advertisers. The networks, like magazines, took control of the editorial content, selling ad adjacencies to their clients. DVRs may reverse this trend somewhat. Although networks are likely to maintain control over programming and ad spots, they are also offering opportunities for sponsors to integrate their products into the programme.

Brand integration first began with the practice of programme producers and prop departments securing products to dress the set. Hoping to save the cost of actually purchasing a car or a sofa, they would turn to auto manufacturers or furniture makers to supply products to appear on camera. Sensing an opportunity for inexpensive publicity, manufacturers were often happy to oblige, but unlike the era of sponsored programming, performers did not specifically mention products on air. The negotiation of these deals was often informal and the impact of the placements was imagined, but never actually studied. Now product placement is seen as an important channel for exposing audiences to one's brand. During the 2004–5 season, the major networks included more than 100,000 placements valued at $1.88 billion, up 28 per cent over the preceding season. Advertisers may pay a fee for the placement or provide an in-kind service (Manly 2005). In many cases the placement is bundled with the purchase of ad spots for the same programme.

Brand integration seems like a win-win situation, but complications do arise. For example, advertisers want their products to appear in a positive, uncontroversial environment, but drama is nourished by tension and controversy. Would Ford be unhappy if the villain drove a Mustang? Should such sponsors have influence over the selection and use of props? Moreover, would the writers for a show find it difficult to write particular products into the script? Should they be hamstrung or distracted by such commercial concerns? Would placements make the shows more timid, so as to foster a positive commercial environment? Crafting a popular show is difficult enough without having to negotiate the intricacies of such matters and many artists, writers and producers have expressed concern about the trend. On the other hand, network executives say they have little choice, pointing to rapidly changing conditions in the television ad market.

CONCLUSION

Audience measurement and advertising sales are central components of the television economy and yet they both rely on useful fictions regarding the television audience. Since audiences don't gather in one place and since most viewing happens in the privacy of the home, 'audiences' are in fact intangible entities that must be conjured into existence so that the industry is able to function. Ratings and other forms of research construct representations of audiences that help in the negotiation of advertising rates. Nielsen Media Research monopolised the ratings business throughout much of the network era, establishing an agreed-upon standard for such negotiations. Yet Nielsen ratings are now subject to criticism due to the growing number of channels and the increasing complexity of media-use patterns. Most homes now have multiple televisions equipped with remote controls and television recording devices. Viewers can timeshift, channel-surf, and zip through programmes. They also watch television in public places and most recently have begun to view video on the go, via iPods and other devices. Audience research companies are trying to keep up with these changes and with the demands of advertising agencies seeking ever-more precise measures of television use.

Although audience measurement plays an important role in the TV market-place, the data are subject to various interpretations and TV executives work hard to put a positive spin on them. Consequently, market demand and industry perceptions are just as important as the figures themselves. Indeed, ad rates at the major networks have continued to rise despite a persistent decline in ratings since the 1980s. Throughout this period, television executives have done a masterful job of massaging audience data and promoting their brands. Whether they will continue to succeed into the future will probably depend on their ability to generate distinctive and original programming, a topic to which we now turn.

NOTES

1. Also see Smythe 1981.
2. Television companies face many challenges when they try to define the audiences they aim to reach, especially with respect to what the industry refers to as Hispanic viewers. Hispanic conventionally refers to peoples with ties to the speech, culture and history of Spain and/or Portugal. This of course overlooks the fact that most inhabitants of Latin America have even more significant ties to native cultures and heritage. Latino, which generally refers to people of Latin American descent, affords an alternative, but it still suffers from other shortcomings, among them the fact that there is nothing particularly Latin about these populations. The industry has chosen to use Hispanic and Latino

interchangeably as terms to describe viewers with cultural and linguistic affinities to populations in Latin America and the Iberian Peninsula. Accordingly, we will follow this usage for want of a better alternative.

3. Data on Hispanic television drawn from Downey 2007. Market and audience data from Applebaum 2007; Learmonth 2007; Rincon & Associates 2004.

4. *American Idol* does not appear above because it runs during the spring when it attracts $500–700,000 per minute.

3

Television Programming

Television programming refers to the strategies that television companies use to develop and schedule programmes with the aim of attracting and sustaining the attention of viewers. These strategies are also crucial for defining the brand identity of each service. Television brands help audiences figure out where to turn for information and entertainment. They also influence advertisers' perceptions of where to buy commercial time. Programming first emerged during the radio era and matured during the 1950s and 60s. Programmers paid particular attention to evening primetime, when the networks scheduled their most lavish productions aimed at broad mass audiences. But television companies also paid attention to smaller audience segments, a strategy that would grow more prominent during the cable era when niche viewers became the primary concern for new television services. Today, the vast majority of television programming is aimed at audience segments. Furthermore, programmers increasingly think not only in terms of television but also related media, such as the Internet and other digital services.

NETWORK PRIMETIME

As mentioned in Chapter 1, network radio was initially conceived as a broadcast medium aimed at people from all walks of life. Radio executives lavished attention on the evening schedule because this was when most listeners enjoyed leisure time away from work, school and church activities. Networks fashioned variety shows, music performances and scripted narratives that aimed to gather the entire family around the radio receiver. Television embraced this tradition with even greater success during the classical network era. By the early 1960s, more than 90 per cent of US homes owned a television set and more than 90 per cent of those sets was tuned to the three major networks during primetime.

Network executives imagined their core audience as intergenerational families, most especially nuclear families of parents and their children. Some households included grandparents, but the number of these dwindled during the classical network era. Consequently, television executives strove first of all to provide programming to suburban families whose purchases drove the prosperity of firms that advertised on television. From a strictly commercial perspective, viewers that weren't part of this target audience were less consequential, but network programmers nevertheless tried to accommodate them in hopes of boosting their overall ratings. Government regulations furthermore encouraged a mass-audience approach, since television stations were licensed to serve the 'public interest, convenience, and necessity', a phrase that was repeatedly invoked in regulatory deliberations. Fearing criticism that they were abusing their government licences, networks strove to present themselves as serving the needs of all.

The major television companies therefore produced shows that were suitable for all ages and for a broad range of viewers, even if this constrained creativity or compromised artistic excellence. Executives coined the term least offensive programming (LOP) to describe the principle that guided their primetime programming practices, suggesting that artistic or provocative shows might not be the best choice for primetime. Programmes should be amusing or intriguing, but above all they should be tolerable. They shouldn't provoke passionate responses, but should instead entertain and inform without giving offence to any particular audience segment.

The primetime audiences of the major networks today are nowhere near as large, but the majors still attract tens of millions of viewers, far more than their cable competitors and far more than any other medium. Most people settle in for an evening of real-time viewing. That is, they don't timeshift or download what they watch. Instead, they tune into whatever television has to offer at that time. They may flip between channels and they may do other things while they watch (childcare, dishwashing or homework), but they use television in the same way that it has been used for several decades. These viewers comprise television's synchronous audience. Later this chapter will discuss some of the ways that networks pursue asynchronous and niche audiences, but first it will examine the programming principles that the major networks apply to pursue a broad, primetime audience.

For decades, ratings have played a very substantial role in the development and scheduling of programmes. Radio networks were the first to employ audience studies, but it wasn't until the refinement of the Nielsen Audimeter during the TV era that networks and advertisers began to enjoy regular and timely information about viewer preferences. By the 1960s, Nielsen began to deliver overnight ratings, which encouraged network executives to tinker extensively and often with programme development and placement. Network executives also intensified their involvement with programming decisions because relations between networks and advertisers took a dramatic turn during the 1950s. Until that time, sponsors and advertising agencies played a significant role in the development and production of radio and television programmes, but during the late 1950s network executives took complete charge of network content, arguing that they could improve the quality of shows and enhance the linkages between shows, so that audiences would stay tuned to their particular network throughout the evening. Unlike a sponsor that might prioritise its own show, networks placed emphasis on the entire evening schedule and executives carefully tracked the flow of audiences from one show to the next.

Early evening came to be associated with family viewing and the busy range of household activities that vied for attention. Programmers considered light entertainment – especially situation comedy and variety shows – most appropriate for this time slot. Later in the evening, after young children went to bed, audience composition shifted towards mature viewers who were presumably less distracted by household responsibilities and therefore willing to invest in longer, more complex and perhaps more serious programmes. Thus, programmers learned to think of television in relation to the rhythms of the household and in terms of audience flow. The television industry came to prize executives who could develop an impressive schedule of programmes across the evening and throughout the week. Even today, in the fractious multichannel universe of digital TV, network scheduling provides executives with a chance to interpret the needs and desires of tens of millions of Americans and to respond with a range of programmes that they will hopefully embrace. It is perhaps the most difficult and creative job at the top of the network organisation. It is also the most visible. The upfront presentations delivered by network chieftains each May not only showcase new shows for the upcoming season but they also unveil each network's carefully crafted strategy for attracting and retaining the attention of viewers.

When assigning a show to a particular spot in the schedule, executives begin with an assessment of the intended audience and qualitative characteristics of the programme. *CSI: Crime Scene Investigation* (2000–) is an enormously popular show for CBS, but it would be folly for the network to place it in an early-evening time slot, since episodes often revolve around the investigation of grisly murders. Parents viewing with their children would no doubt turn to a channel with lighter entertainment fare, although these very same parents might watch the show if it were scheduled after their children's bedtime.

Table 3.1 Primetime Audiences of Major Networks, Fall 2007 (in millions)

Network	Total viewers	Adults 18–49	Adults 18–34	Adults 25–54
CBS	11.49	4.23	1.46	5.11
ABC	10.70	4.54	1.84	5.02
Fox	8.55	4.13	1.97	4.19
NBC	8.40	4.09	1.84	4.32
Univision	3.57	2.00	1.11	1.85
CW	2.8	1.48	0.81	1.32

Source: TV by the Numbers, 'Season to Date', 2007.

Conversely, the NBC game show, *Deal or No Deal* (2005–), might be attractive to the whole family early in the evening and it might fit in well with a range of household chores and activities, since one need not pay close attention in order to catch the salient details. Later in the evening, however, the show might have a hard time competing against glossy, high-quality dramas with absorbing and complicated storylines. As a general principle, then, the genre and tone of a show should match the time slot, with early evenings devoted to the broadest range of viewers and late primetime focused on mature audiences.

Although this seems straightforward enough, imagine that you're programming the ABC schedule for the upcoming season and you have an open slot early on Wednesday evenings at 8:00 p.m. You've learned from the industry trade papers that NBC has decided to shift its popular game show, *Deal or No Deal*, from nine to eight o'clock on Wednesday. You've also learned that CBS is planning to premiere a new reality show called *Kid Nation* (2007–8) that features children fending for themselves in a Western frontier town (imagine a cross between *Survivor* and *Lord of the Flies*). Meanwhile, Fox is heavily promoting its new situation comedy directed by James L. Brooks entitled, *Back to You* (2007–8), featuring Kelsey Grammer and Patricia Heaton, formerly stars of the enormously successful sitcoms, *Frasier* and *Everyone Loves Raymond* (1996–2005). As a result, you're facing stiff competition from shows and genres that are well suited to the early-evening hours.[1]

If you have a strong show elsewhere in your weekly schedule that would compete well against these programmes, you might consider moving it to Wednesday at 8:00 pm, but if not, you'll have to put one of your new shows up against this very tough competition. If you schedule a new sitcom, reality or game show,

Table 3.2 Wednesday Primetime, Fall 2007

Network	8:00	8:30	9:00	9:30	10:00	10:30
NBC	Deal or No Deal	Deal or No Deal	Bionic Woman	Bionic Woman	Life	Life
CBS	Kid Nation	Kid Nation	Criminal Minds	Criminal Minds	CSI: NY	CSI: NY
Fox	Back to You	'Til Death	Kitchen Nightmares	Kitchen Nightmares	Local Programme	Local Programme
ABC	Pushing Daisies	Pushing Daisies	Private Practice	Private Practice	Dirty Sexy Money	Dirty Sexy Money
Univision	Amor sin Limites	Amor sin Limites	Destilando Amor	Destilando Amor	Don Francisco	Don Francisco
CW	America's Next Top Model	America's Next Top Model	Gossip Girl	Gossip Girl	Local Programme	Local Programme

audiences might overlook it for shows and actors that they consider more familiar or, in the case of *Kid Nation*, one that has a lot of popular buzz behind it. Instead of taking the competition on directly, you decide to *counterprogramme* with *Pushing Daisies* (2007–9), an off-beat love story about a young pie-maker named Ned who has the ability to bring people back to life with the touch of his hand, including his long-lost first love from childhood, a young woman named Chuck. During its development phase, audience pretesting indicated the show was attractive to adult female viewers and performed reasonably well with the 18–49 demographic overall. *Pushing Daisies* is a light but somewhat cerebral drama that coyly plays on generic conventions to humorous effect and therefore does well with viewers that have a taste for quirky television shows such as *Desperate Housewives* (2004–) or *The Sopranos*. In other words, it's very unlike its competition and therefore might attract a small but devoted following seeking an alternative to the mass-appeal programmes scheduled by the competing networks for early Wednesday evening.

Pushing Daisies is furthermore a good candidate for eight o'clock because the programme that you've chosen for the important 9:00 pm slot is *Private Practice* (2007–). The latter is expected to be one of the strongest dramas of the week for ABC and therefore acts as a *lead-out* for *Pushing Daisies*. That is, viewers who tune into *Private Practice* will probably want to catch the beginning of the show, so they may tune in early, in which case they would run across the ongoing saga of Ned and Chuck. Hopefully, they will sample an entire episode of *Pushing Daisies* at some point in the season, since it too is a romantic comedy like its lead-out. One of the ways to encourage this sampling is to *hot-switch* between the two shows by shortening the credit sequence at the end of *Pushing Daisies* and by eliminating the commercial break in between the two programmes. It's also common to *cold roll* into the second show by beginning the action immediately and by burying the opening credits several minutes into the show. These strategies aim to introduce audiences to the adjacent programme and to encourage audiences to flow from one show to the next.

As for *Private Practice*, it's a spin-off of *Grey's Anatomy* (2005–), the most popular drama on your schedule. Spin-offs are shows built around a particular actor or television character that moves from one show to another. Network executives believe that television audiences become strongly attached to characters and actors, and are therefore likely to follow an actor when she or he moves to another programme, even if the role in the new show is slightly different. Thus, *The Mary Tyler Moore Show* (1970–7) begat *Rhoda* (1974–8) and *Lou Grant* (1977–82). *Cheers* begat *Frasier*, which in turn begat, *Back to You*. In 2007, ABC executives decided that Kate Walsh, who plays Dr Addison Montgomery in *Grey's*, could be spun off to another series and carry with her some of the fans from the original show.

Kate Walsh plays Dr Addison Montgomery, a character spun off from *Grey's Anatomy* to take the lead role in *Private Practice*

Private Practice is not simply a character spin-off, however, it is also a copy of *Grey's* original formula, which focuses on the love lives of interns and doctors in the emergency room of Seattle Grace Hospital. *Private Practice* is similarly concerned with the lives (especially the love lives) of medical professionals, but it moves Dr Addison Montgomery from a big-city emergency room in the rainy, caffeinated northwest to a wealthy, private medical clinic in sunny Los Angeles. It also tilts the focus more decidedly towards sex rather than sutures.

To capitalise on the formulaic similarities, ABC heavily promoted the fact that Shonda Rhimes, the award-winning writer and executive producer of *Grey's*, is the creative force behind the new series. Viewers could therefore expect the copy to be faithfully executed with respect to plot, dialogue and romantic sensibilities. Spin-offs and copies are not guarantees of success, but network executives believe they help to reduce the uncertainty and risk that surround the development of new programmes. Since more than 90 per cent of all new shows will fail, it is important for executives to take advantage of every opportunity to improve a programme's chances for success.

As an ABC programme executive, you're well aware of these risks but you nevertheless have high expectations for *Private Practice* and want to give it a prominent place on your weekly schedule. Since your most popular Wednesday show, *Lost* (2004–), has gone on hiatus until the second half of the season, you've decided to rebuild the Wednesday schedule by using *Private Practice* as the *tentpole*. That is, you believe the star, producer and formula are strong enough to gather audiences under the ABC tent and in doing so, attract attention to other shows on the same night. It therefore makes sense that the show would act as a lead-out for *Pushing Daisies* but also that it would act as a lead-in for the ten o'clock show, a provocative new drama called *Dirty Sexy Money* (2007–9). Starring Peter Krause, formerly of HBO's critically acclaimed *Six Feet Under* (2001–5), this programme offers a titillating backstage drama about a wealthy, powerful family of morally challenged characters. Krause plays an outsider who is drawn into the intrigues of patriarch Tripp Darling (Donald Sutherland), his socialite spouse, Letitia (Jill Clayburgh) and their five flawed children.

Table 3.3 ABC's Top Primetime Shows, 12–18 November 2007

Show	Viewers in millions
Dancing with the Stars – Monday	21.8
Grey's Anatomy	19.6
Dancing with the Stars – Tuesday	17.6
Samantha Who?	13.7
American Music Awards	11.8
Private Practice	11.5
Boston Legal	11.4
Ugly Betty	10.7
The Bachelor	9.0
Women's Murder Club	8.9
Pushing Daisies	8.8
Dirty Sexy Money	7.9

Source: TV by the Numbers, 'Top ABC Primetime Shows', 2007.

Although similar to the *Dynasty* (1981–9)/*Dallas* (1978–91) formula from the early 1980s, *Dirty*'s chances for success are uncertain, since it will compete against CBS's powerful CSI franchise. Nevertheless you're hoping that the show will be able to hold onto the audience of its lead-in. In fact, television executives usually judge new programmes both by their ratings and by how well they are able to sustain momentum from their lead-in. A new programme may enjoy a strong 6.1 rating, but if it gives up 2 points from its lead-in, then programmers might question its value. Is the show actually driving viewers away rather than attracting them? Ultimately, the value of a show, as well as its fortunes, rely to a significant extent on its placement in the schedule.

These concepts – spin-off, copy, tent-pole, lead-in, hot-switch and counter-programme – are fundamental tools employed by network executives when building a schedule. The aim is of course to attract viewers, but just as importantly it is to hold onto them as long as possible. The vice-president of programming is the creative force behind the overall schedule and she or he confronts a complex set of choices at every turn. For one must take into account the quality of each particular show and its immediate competition, as well as the impact any one decision might have on adjacent shows and other parts of the schedule.

During the 2007 season, ABC created a block of Wednesday shows each of which resonates well with the others and is likely to attract highly prized female audiences. *Block programming* enhances the value of each particular programme by pairing it with others that aim at similar audiences. Yet this strength is also a limitation, since ABC may be driving some viewers away because it is catering to the tastes of adult women. Yet ABC executives counter that this attentiveness to female viewers helps to distinguish it from competitors and that its strategy is in keeping with the brand identity built by ABC over several seasons. This distinctive brand serves as a tool for attracting particular groups of advertisers.

Besides lavishing attention on each evening's schedule, executives are also alert to rhythms and patterns across the week. Sunday night begins the cycle, as audiences return to TV after a weekend engaged in other social and entertainment activities. In fact, Saturday is considered such a low point of the weekly schedule that CBS and NBC now use it for reruns of weekday dramas. Sunday, on the other hand, brings large audiences back to television. Many have spent the day watching sports events and stay tuned through the evening hours while others turn to Sunday-night television as an opportunity to relax before returning to work.

At the other end of the weekly TV schedule is Thursday which, as mentioned in Chapter 2 is an important night for advertisers wishing to reach viewers headed into the weekend. During the 2006–7 season, ABC experienced notable success by pairing *Grey's Anatomy* with *Ugly Betty* (2006–), a campy, telenovela-inspired dramedy. In 2007, ABC programmers may have looked at the general mix of ABC shows earlier in the week and decided to build towards their strength on Thursday. By developing the Wednesday programme block, ABC would now offer two consecutive evenings aimed at female audiences. Advertisers wishing to reach this important demographic before the weekend would do well to consider ABC as an important showcase for their messages. In an increasingly fragmented and competitive television universe, ABC's strategy seems plausible, even if it somewhat compromises the mass-audience rationale of the major networks.

CBS, by comparison, emphasises mass appeal above all else in its weekly schedule. During the first decade of the twenty-first century, CBS has focused on procedural dramas (primarily police dramas) that appeal to viewers of all ages, including those in the over-50 age bracket, a group not generally prized by advertisers. Some have criticised this strategy, saying that CBS's audiences skew older and that its ratings lag behind its competitors in the 18–49 age demographic. Yet CBS makes no apologies for the broad appeal of its shows and points proudly to its solid ratings across the week.

CBS built its schedule around the success of *CSI: Crime Scene Investigation*, a series that recounts the adventures of forensic investigators using the tools of cutting-edge science to capture murderers and other malefactors. The show's special effects and lavish production values embellish the taut plotlines that lead inexorably to a climactic arrest of the villain. So successful was the original series when it launched in 2000 that CBS executives, creator Anthony Zuiker and producer Jerry Bruckheimer decided to expand the series into a franchise. In 2002,

William Petersen plays the lead investigator on the flagship series of the *CSI* franchise, which is produced by Jerry Bruckheimer for CBS

they added *CSI: Miami* and in 2004 they launched *CSI: NY*. A *franchise* is a constellation of copies operating under a single brand name. In this case, the formula for CSI is adapted to the particularities of each locale (Las Vegas, Miami, New York) and to the character dynamics of each show's cast. Zuiker and Bruckheimer oversaw the development of all three shows, but additional creative staff was hired to manage each series. They aimed both to spread their success across the CBS primetime schedule and to develop a collection of episodes that would play well in syndication. Each episode offers a stand-alone formulaic narrative that can be rerun on many different channels and in many different time slots, but each also benefits from its association with the franchise as a whole.

CBS executives further exploited *CSI*'s success by embracing procedural dramas as emblematic of the network's primetime brand, adding such shows as *NCIS* (2003–), *Cold Case* (2003–) and *Criminal Minds* (2005–). On each of the five weekdays that form the core of the CBS schedule, viewers can rest assured that a procedural drama is one of their viewing options. Even on Friday nights, viewers can find a fresh procedural drama (*Numbers*, 2005–) and on Saturday the network reruns episodes from the week during its 'Crimetime' programming block from eight to ten o'clock.

Table 3.4 CBS's Top Primetime Shows, 12–18 November 2007

Show	Viewers in millions
CSI: Crime Scene Investigation	21.4
NCIS	17.4
Criminal Minds	15.7
CSI: Miami	15.5
Survivor: China	14.7
60 Minutes	14.6
Without a Trace	14.4
Cold Case	14.1
Two and a Half Men	14.1
CSI: NY	13.1

Source: TV by the Numbers, 'Top CBS Primetime Shows', 2007.

Clearly, CBS aims to attract viewers and hold their attention by fostering a distinctive brand identity that stretches across the weekly schedule. In a cluttered and fragmented television landscape, audiences understand that tuning to CBS is comparable to choosing Holiday Inn for a hotel or the Outback Steakhouse for an evening meal. One associates the brand with a set of expectations regarding performance and outcomes. Regardless of when or where one might be, the brand presents itself as a recognisable and reliable option. The challenge for CBS is to diversify its schedule as a hedge against the likely prospect that these shows (and the procedural genre) will lose favour as they age and as popular tastes change.

Network programmers realise it's important for them to capitalise on distinctive and successful formulas, and to strive to hold onto to their audiences with consistent fare. Nevertheless they must also compete with a proliferating number of entertainment options, many of them targeted at niche audiences comprised of passionate fans. These viewers won't stay tuned to shows that are merely tolerable and inoffensive. Instead, they graze, search, download and record programmes they truly enjoy. Although the principles of audience flow may continue to guide the calculations of network programmers, they must also think in terms of distinctive shows that appeal to enthusiastic audiences. These viewers will follow a show they truly admire regardless of when it is scheduled. They reserve time in their personal schedules or set their video recorders for shows that executives refer to as *appointment television*. Such programmes distinguish themselves from the norm, engender intensive viewer loyalties and often expand their reach beyond television to the Internet where video downloads, fan forums and dedicated web sites provide a rich array of narrative resources and pleasures.

ABC's *Lost*, NBC's *Heroes* (2006–), and Fox's *24* are successful examples of appointment TV from the 2007 season. Their sprawling and complex narratives demand an intensive investment of energy and attention from audiences (Jenkins 2006; Mittell 2006; and Newman 2006). A missed episode can undermine one's grasp of key plot points, so viewers loyally make appointments to view each show. Networks see themselves as especially suited to deliver such programming, since they have the talent, track record and production resources necessary to produce top-notch television drama. Yet fans and critics notice that some of the very best of such series eventually get diluted over time as networks encourage writers and producers to simplify plotlines in hopes of expanding the appeal of each series. One can see this as cynical commercialism, but it's important to point out that network executives are constantly under pressure to enhance the profitability of their successes. They certainly don't wish to crush the creative spirit that engenders these hits, but they nevertheless feel pressed to capitalise on each hit series, especially given the fact that failures in TV programming outnumber triumphs by almost ten to one. Many critics and fans, however, believe it is this very attitude that drives audiences away from television to other technologies and other modes of entertainment. They claim the very best television isn't to be found on the networks, but instead tends to come from niche media services. Before turning to a discussion of those services, it's important to observe the ways in which networks have for some time tried to accommodate subsets of the national mass audience.

NETWORK DAY PARTS

Less than a decade after the launch of the first radio networks, programming executives began to pay particular attention to the listening habits of daytime audiences, especially home-makers. By the mid-1930s, serial drama had become the most prominent form of programming, attracting loyal listeners who followed the fortunes of their favourite characters on a daily basis. Most shows were produced by advertising agencies operating on behalf of their clients, many of them manufacturers of household products, such as Lever Brothers and Procter and Gamble. As a result, programme producers paid special attention to home-makers, which made *soap operas* the first demographically targeted programming in American broadcast history (Allen 1985; Wang 2006). During the 1970s, however, the genre began to expand its address, as teenagers and college students of both sexes became devoted fans. This surge of popularity in turn encouraged primetime programmers to adopt many of the conventions of soaps, such as a continuing storyline, intensified melodrama and a complex universe of characters and relationships. Some even adopted the genre in its entirety, as CBS launched *Dallas* into primetime in 1978 and ABC followed with *Dynasty* three years later. From there the soap-opera genre dispersed its magic through-out the universe of television, influencing a range of shows and genres.

Interestingly, the diffusion of soap-opera influences helped to undermine the popularity of daytime shows, since they no longer seemed so distinctive (Seiter and Wilson 2005). Soaps also suffered a ratings decline as the percentage of women in the workforce began to climb steadily. This undermined the value of daytime TV to advertisers, many of whom now believe that the most desirable female consumers are away from home during the working day. What remains of the daytime audience, according to research firms, is comprised of stay-at-home moms, retirees and the underemployed. Advertisers of food and house-hold staples still see this as a viable audience, since nearly everyone buys potato chips and dish soap, but it is not as valuable as it once was. This has depressed advertising rates and as a result, TV networks now serve daytime viewers primarily with talk and game shows, genres that are less costly to produce than drama.

Another part of day with a more narrowly focused audience profile is the early morning. NBC president Pat Weaver, introduced the first network morning show in 1952, as a mix of talk, news, weather and celebrity interviews. The *Today* show was inexpensive to produce because it made use of NBC's existing news operation and featured guests who appeared for free in order to promote their latest book, movie or Broadway show. NBC paid only for hosts, crew and stu-dio rental. With its low costs and strong ratings, the show has been a major income generator for the network throughout its history. Moreover, *Today* has been the ratings leader among the early-morning shows since 1995 (Arango 2008). Recent estimates say that the show nets $250 million per year, making it one of the most profitable programmes on television.

Today's dominance during the 1990s was partly attributable to shrewd cross-promotional strategies. Producers regularly showed video previews from popular primetime shows such as *Friends* and *Seinfeld*, encouraging viewers to tune to NBC's 'Must-See' Thursday-night schedule. Then on Friday mornings they showed outtakes from the previous night's show in order to draw audiences back to *Today*. These promotional clips were accompanied by exclusive inter-views with stars from the NBC evening line-up. By linking the morning show to the primetime schedule, *Today*'s producers assisted with network promotion and they benefited from privileged access to some of NBC's leading shows and talent.

Other networks have followed similar strategies. Indeed, ABC's *Good Morn-ing America* (1975–) came close to snatching the lead in morning ratings by featuring clips from *Lost* and *Desperate Housewives*. The success of early-morning shows also depends on the likeability of their hosts, with top talent such as ABC's Diane Sawyer and NBC's Matt Lauer earning annual salaries in excess of $10 million per year, which puts them in the same league as the highest-paid primetime talent. *Today* and *Good Morning America* each draw approximately 5 million viewers and describe their target audience as between the ages of 25 and 54. Women comprise the largest group of viewers, but in many households *Today* is a part of the family's morning routine, which means that many men and children also see it on a regular basis. Morning shows are renowned for attracting dual-income households, which are seen as especially valuable to advertisers.

Another innovation from the Weaver years at NBC was the *Tonight* show, which premiered in 1954, featuring Steve Allen, his comedy sidekicks and a house orchestra led by Skitch Henderson. The show combined off-beat comedy with celebrity performances and interviews. Allen said at the time that he aimed to be funny but also to be warm and likeable. That formula proved successful for Allen and it also served Johnny Carson well during his record-setting tenure as host from 1962 to 1992. It continues to guide the show to this day, attracting a nightly audience of 5 million, most of them in the highly prized 18–49-year-old age bracket.

Unlike primetime shows, *Tonight* draws few young or old viewers and therefore is seen as a cost-efficient vehicle for advertisers who prize the upscale purchasing power of its audience. Although NBC doesn't break out official profit figures for *Tonight*, its net income is estimated to be more than $150 million per year (Carter 2004). Almost as profitable is CBS's *Late Show with David Letterman* (1993–), which draws a smaller audience of roughly 4 million viewers, but is widely praised by critics. It is renowned for attracting a younger, hipper audience, and it brings in close to $100 million in yearly profits for CBS (Carter 2003). Both shows are cost-efficient productions that appeal to audiences highly prized by advertisers. Like their morning counterparts, they also afford opportunities for cross-promotion of network programmes and performers.

Evening news is yet another segment the networks developed during the 1950s, scheduling their nightly programmes immediately before primetime. Initially, news shows aimed to serve a broad audience and to satisfy government requirements for public-service programming. The *NBC Nightly News* and *CBS Evening News* were innovators that sustained their leadership until the 1980s. During that decade, however, the FCC released the major networks from many of their public-service responsibilities as part of the Reagan administration's deregulation policies. These same policies also made it easier to buy and sell media enterprises and by mid-decade, all three major networks experienced a change of ownership. The new owners immediately put more pressure on news divisions to cut costs and/or spread the costs of the newsgathering infrastructure across an increased range of programming. CBS became renowned for dramatically reducing the number of overseas news bureaux and cutting staff across the board. It also tried to build upon the success of *60 Minutes* (1968–) by rolling out a number of similar news magazine shows. Its competitors followed suit, but NBC distinguished itself by actually expanding the size of its news operation, extending its reach into cable television and Internet media. In 1989, it launched CNBC, a cable channel focused on consumer and business news, and then in 1996 it added MSNBC, a hybrid cable-Internet news service that is a joint venture with microsoft. NBC added a Spanish-language news service when it purchased Telemundo in 2003 and five years later it acquired the Weather Channel, filling out a robust matrix of news services that reach across broadcast, cable and Internet media.

The three largest broadcasting networks – CBS, NBC and ABC – continue to offer nightly newscasts, but the number of viewers has been shrinking by roughly 1 million viewers per year since 1980. In 2007, the total audience for all three shows was 23 million per night with NBC and ABC vying for the lead, each with slightly more than 8 million viewers. The median age of the nightly news audience is 61 and as a result, the programmes tend to feature ads for health and financial products. Once the proud flagships of network news, the nightly programmes now skew towards a fairly narrow audience that tends to be less attractive to many advertisers. By comparison, the audience for network news on the Internet is much younger, averaging 49 years old for CBS.com, but ad revenues are much lower.

Primetime news magazines help to boost the overall income of the news divisions and morning shows contribute as well, but by and large ABC and CBS news generate only modest profits. NBC, on the other hand, spreads the high cost of newsgathering across many channels, programmes and day parts. One study estimates that the cost per hour of NBC news programming dropped by 80 per cent during the 1990s (State of the News Media 2008). Although some NBC news ventures are only modestly profitable, others like CNBC and the *Today* show

Despite the flagging fortunes of *NBC Nightly News with Brian Williams*, the network has significantly enhanced its news operations by launching profitable cable and Internet services, such as MSNBC.com

contribute hundreds of millions of dollars in net income each year. In fact, one report indicated that NBC's news division now contributes one-quarter of the network's total profits (Carter 2009). NBC's multimedia strategy has proven far more profitable and it has allowed the news division to pursue a growth strategy that today supports a far larger newsgathering infrastructure than CBS or ABC.

Network expansion into new time slots and onto cable has also been an important trend with sports programming. During the 1950s networks experimented with various types of sports coverage, but due to technological limitations, they could only telecast events that were staged in daylight or brightly illuminated at night. Wrestling matches telecast during the evening hours proved popular with many viewers, but baseball and football lacked sufficient stadium lighting for nighttime events. Most sports were telecast by local stations, since it was assumed that regional loyalties would play an important role in ratings success. Networks showed some sports events on weekends, but it wasn't until the 1960s that network sports coverage escalated significantly, as CBS and NBC began to compete fiercely for the broadcast rights to National Football League (NFL) games. ABC soon joined the fray by supporting the fledgling American Football League (AFL). It furthermore improved the quality of football coverage by introducing mobile cameras, onscreen graphics, videotape replays and live sound on the field.

Throughout the 1960s the number of hours devoted to football telecasts grew rapidly as did revenues from advertisers. In addition to Sunday games, ABC added *Monday Night Football* in 1970, the same year that the NFL and AFL officially merged. A 'world championship' game was instituted in 1967 and was shortly thereafter renamed the Super Bowl, quickly becoming one of the most popular and lucrative special events in American television.

Among sports shows, football is by far the leading generator of ad revenue and in 2007 the networks collectively paid $3.7 billion for the broadcast rights. Such costs mean that not all network deals with the NFL end up being profitable. Yet network executives justify the expense by pointing to the tremendous promotional opportunities promised by sports events and by noting that sports is the most consistent draw for males in all age groups. TV football coverage supplies advertisers with targeted access to an audience that other parts of the schedule do not. Still, it is important to note that audiences for sports events have declined consistently each year since 1990, a decline caused largely by the growing number of viewing options now available to sports fans. For example, on weekend afternoons during the fall, viewers can tune to more than a dozen different football games, several baseball games, golf, tennis, auto racing and a host of other sports events. Not only do football games compete against other football games, they also compete against an array of niche sporting events.

The diversification of TV sports programming can be traced to innovations instituted by ABC during the 1960s. At that time, the network's weak affiliate line-up and lower profit levels put it at a disadvantage when competing for major sports rights, such as football and baseball. Consequently, ABC countered with the development of a regular Saturday compendium, entitled *The Wide World of Sports* (*WWS*). Instead of one marquee sports event, each show featured as many as four different sporting events, shifting between locations and between live and taped coverage. ABC brought to the screen competitions that were until that time considered commercially untenable, such as tennis, figure skating, auto racing and track and field events. Under the guidance of executive producer Roone Arledge, *WWS* pioneered many technical innovations, such as slow motion, flashy graphics and sophisticated statistical measures of athletic performance. Each show also recounted the personal life stories of athletes with the aim of spinning narratives that revolved around 'the thrill of victory and the agony of defeat', a signature line that encapsulated the *WWS* formula. These elements today are the foundation of all sports programming on US broadcast and cable television.

As this overview suggests, US broadcast networks have since the 1950s sought to strike a balance between mass and niche programming. The development of new day parts and the cultivation of audiences for specialised shows have been driven by each network's desire to increase the number of hours in its schedule, so as to generate income throughout the day and across the week. As they pioneered each new time slot, the networks had to convince local affiliates to surrender airtime in exchange for a share of the income from network fare. In many cases, local stations gave up these time slots reluctantly, since many had developed cost-efficient programming strategies that allowed them to keep all of the advertising revenues to themselves. Yet as competition from independent and cable channels increased (many of them employing similar programming strategies), local stations came to appreciate network offerings, since they helped to distinguish affiliates from their peers.

PROGRAMMING AT LOCAL TV STATIONS

Before the advent of satellite technology, television signals could be broadcast no more than sixty miles from any given locale. In order to achieve nationwide coverage, networks in many parts of the world transmitted their programming via a chain of repeater stations spread across the countryside that existed solely for the purpose of relaying the network signal. In the US, however, television stations were licensed as independent entities that are supposed to serve the interests of their local communities and national networks were limited as to the number of television stations they could own. This meant that the television networks needed to recruit local affiliates in order to achieve truly national coverage. Affiliation contracts allowed networks to broadcast their programmes over the local airwaves and in exchange, local stations received payments from the networks and a share of the advertising on network programmes.

Today, national programming from ABC, CBS and NBC fills approximately 70 per cent of the airtime on the local affiliates. Affiliates programme the remainder of their schedules with syndicated shows they acquire, such as game shows, talk shows, movies and off-network reruns. Affiliates also produce local shows, mostly news, sports and public affairs. The flagship productions of a local affiliate are the evening newscasts, which immediately precede and follow network primetime. These programmes emphasise local news, features, weather and sports. On average they contribute 40 per cent of the total advertising revenue that a station takes in. Major advertisers tend to be car dealers, furniture stores, restaurants and real-estate brokers. Consequently, local news shows try to establish a tone that is conducive to these ads and they attempt to draw audiences that will be prized by advertisers. During election periods, local stations attract a tremendous amount of advertising from candidates and political groups, which again is one of the reasons local news is considered the flagship programme on most stations, since local political coverage tends to encourage advertising from political candidates.

Affiliates of the Fox and CW networks follow similar programming policies, although they carry fewer hours of network programming, less than 40 per cent of their total airtime. Neither Fox nor CW offer substantial morning, daytime or late-night programming to their affiliates. Even during primetime, CW delivers only thirteen hours of programming and Fox fifteen, compared to twenty-two from the three major networks. Despite these modest numbers, Fox and CW stations see network affiliation as crucial to distinguishing them from competing independents.

Unlike affiliates, independent stations control their entire schedule, enlisting syndicated programmes and local productions to fill their airtime. In other words, they use essentially the same programming resources that the network affiliates use during their non-network programming slots. The scheduling strategies of independents are similar as well, with one significant exception: independents try to counterprogramme the affiliates, especially when the affiliates are showing network fare. For example, networks rarely show sports programming during primetime, yet many independent stations will opt for local sports events, believing this offers a distinctive alternative to network fare. Likewise, when the network affiliates are running dramas, the local independents may choose to schedule comedy reruns.

Both affiliates and independents acquire syndicated shows from distributors, many of them associated with major television studios (such as Warner Bros.) or networks (such as CBS). Distributors market shows produced by their parent com-

Table 3.5 Leading Syndicated Shows, 12–18 November 2007[2]

Show	Viewers (in millions)	Syndicator
Wheel of Fortune	12.6	CBS Television
Jeopardy	10.1	CBS Television
The Oprah Winfrey Show	8.7	CBS Television
Entertainment Tonight	7.4	CBS Television
Two and a Half Men	7.4	Warner Bros.
Family Guy	6.8	Twentieth Television
Judge Judy	6.7	CBS Television
Dr. Phil Show	6.7	CBS Television
Everybody Loves Raymond	6.6	CBS Television
CSI: Miami	5.9	CBS Television
Seinfeld	5.6	Sony Pictures
King of Queens	4.3	Sony Pictures
Friends	4.2	Warner Bros.
George Lopez	4.1	Warner Bros.

Source: TV by the Numbers, 'Top Syndicated Shows', 2007.

pany and they supplement this catalogue with shows that they acquire from other producers or rights holders. When local stations search for shows to fill their schedules, they look for programmes they can *strip* across the weekday schedule, showing them at the same time each day. Programmers believe that stripping enhances viewer awareness of the local station's schedule and it allows stations to get quantity discounts from syndicators. It also helps economise on promotional spots, since a promotion for one show actually serves five programming slots across the week. Because of these considerations, talk shows, such as *The Oprah Winfrey Show* and *The Ellen DeGeneres Show* (2003–), and game shows, *Wheel of Fortune* and *Jeopardy* (1984–), are produced for daily broadcast. Likewise, off-network reruns are sold in packages that allow stripping by local stations (Kompare 2004).

An off-network series is most viable for syndication if more than 100 episodes are available. This makes it possible for a station to run the show every weekday for twenty weeks without repeating a single episode. Such series are also attractive because they have survived at least four seasons in network prime-time, indicating strong ratings, attractive characters and loyal audiences. Situation comedies, such as *Seinfeld*, *Frasier* and *Friends*, have been especially lucrative shows in syndication, generating billions of dollars in sales to local stations. With strong audience followings and only a half hour to each episode, these shows can be placed in many spots in the schedule, building a bridge between a local affiliate's news show and primetime network fare or yielding potent ammunition for an independent station's counterprogramming strategy. Procedural dramas also fare well in syndication, since the genre is familiar and the episodes need not be played in sequence. When purchasing syndicated fare, local stations assess a show's cost and projected audience, as well as its compatibility with other shows on the schedule and its prospects for success against programmes on competing channels.

CABLE PROGRAMMING

Cable programming strategies can be organised into three categories: general interest, genre and demographic. As explained in Chapter 1, some of the first cable networks originated as superstations that were, in essence, independent TV stations seeking to expand their transmission range via satellite. Consequently, their programming strategies were very much shaped by their previous experience as local stations. For example, Turner's WTBS offered viewers a menu of Atlanta sports and news, off-network reruns and old movies. As it grew from a superstation into a general-interest cable network, TBS held to this strategy, casting about for low-cost programming and basing its financial success on its ability to complement advertising income with subscriber fees from cable system operators. By the 1990s, general-interest cable networks (USA, TNT, TBS) enjoyed comparatively substantial cable ratings due to their general appeal, but many advertisers were nevertheless reluctant to use them as outlets for their promotional messages. Advertisers believed that general-interest cable channels lacked distinctive identities and therefore faced competition from local independents as well as other cable services. This forced the channels to offer discounts in order to attract advertisers. Nevertheless their solid ratings performance helped them negotiate with cable system operators, since they could argue that their popularity justified higher subscription fees. General-interest channels succeeded by focusing on cost containment, broad audience appeal and cable subscription revenues.

By comparison, genre channels developed distinctive programming identities from the very outset. HBO (launched in 1975) focused on recent Hollywood feature films, ESPN (1979) on sports, CNN (1980) on news and MTV (1981) on music. In setting their advertising rates, these channels benefited from being able to demonstrate that they appealed to distinctive audiences and were therefore cost-efficient. If, say, an advertiser of acne medicine wanted to reach teenagers, he or she would pay a higher CPM (cost per thousand) to advertise on MTV, knowing that little would be wasted on older viewers. A general-interest channel might offer a lower CPM, but only a fraction of the audience would find the ad relevant.

In an attempt to reach distinctive audiences, genre channels have been willing to invest in original productions, although they deploy various strategies to keep costs in line. MTV, for example, built its early success on the exhibition of music videos provided for free by major record companies. Adapting a variation on the variety/talk-show format, MTV hosts played countdowns of the hits and staged interviews with stars and fans. The network then branched out into inexpensive reality shows, with such path-breaking hits as *The Real World* (1992–), *Cribs* (2000–) and *Pimp My Ride*. ESPN achieved its success by judiciously securing the rights to second- and third-tier sports events, packaging them for viewers in regions and localities where fan loyalties justified the expense.

ESPN has also succeeded by building an extensive and flexible infrastructure that allows it to spread its costs among many different shows, channels and satellite services worldwide. It also developed a host of ancillary enterprises that deliver sports news and highlights via cell phone and the Internet. Now the most comprehensive source of sporting news, ESPN benefits from being the leading media destination for men aged 18–34, a famously elusive but highly prized demographic. ESPN is furthermore favoured by advertisers because most of its programming draws synchronous audiences, since fans prefer live sports coverage, commercials and all. Successful in almost every respect, ESPN's most telling failure was a short-lived attempt to expand its audience by introducing programmes from outside the sports genre.

Demographically driven channels offer a more diverse range of programmes, but they target particular audiences and, like the genre channels, tend to emphasise the cost efficiency of their advertising spots. Nickelodeon (1979) delivers children's programming and child-friendly family shows. Its daytime schedule is devoted to animated, educational and live-action shows (e.g., *Nick News*, 1992– *Zoey 101*, 2005– and *SpongeBob SquarePants*, 1999–). During school hours, the programming mix tilts toward preschoolers and later in the day it opens up to older children and finally to the entire family during evening hours when Nick at Nite showcases 'television classics', a menu of off-network reruns of family situation comedies stretching back to the early years of the medium.

Lifetime (1984) offers a similarly diverse mix of programming (talk, drama, documentary and movies), but the channel's distinctive identity is based on its address to women. Starting first with health and self-help shows, Lifetime successfully expanded into television movies and series drama. In an attempt to serve its audience with distinctive programming, Lifetime's shows pay particular attention to issues such as breast cancer and violence against women. Its success encouraged the launch of two competing channels (We and Oxygen), but Lifetime remains the leader among its demographic and has expanded onto the Internet, offering services that range from dating to fashion to games (Lotz 2006).

BLACK AND LATINO SERVICES

While both the children's and women's audiences have attracted a variety of competing cable channels, it's remarkable that until recently only a single service, Black Entertainment Television (BET), targeted African Americans. Founded by cable executive Robert Johnson in 1980, BET focused on the 18–34-year-old demographic, using music videos, stand-up comedy, reruns and infomercials as its primary programming. Often criticised for telecasting controversial and salacious hip-hop videos, BET nevertheless proved enormously profitable, and in 2000, Johnson sold the channel to Viacom for more than $3 billion, making him the first black billionaire in US history (joined shortly thereafter by Oprah Winfrey).

Many criticisms levelled at BET stemmed from the fact that it dominated its market niche and was therefore perceived as the de facto representative of black cable television. African Americans were especially critical, chastising BET executives for failing to enhance the quality of programming or develop new services. Alert to these criticisms, Viacom executives more than doubled the programming budget shortly after they took charge and in 2005 hired film director Reginald Hudlin (*House Party*, 1990, US and *Boomerang*, 1992, US) to head the entertainment unit. Hudlin initially rolled out reality and game shows, while beginning development on a group of scripted dramas and comedies that began to air in 2008. Meanwhile, music-video programming was pared back significantly, dropping to only 15 per cent of BET airtime (Goetzl 2007 and Deggans and Holloway 2007).

This remarkable turnaround was stimulated by more than corporate citizenship, as BET was beginning to face competition from TV One, a partnership between Comcast (a major cable MSO) and Radio One (the biggest radio company dedicated to serving African American audiences). TV One, following the tradition of its radio counterpart, pitches its programming at a diverse 18–49-year-old African American demographic. From its launch in 2004, TV One rapidly increased its subscriber base to 42 million homes (about half that of BET) and is hoping to make further inroads due to its mass-appeal programming. BET is facing competition from other quarters as well. For example, a comedy block on the CW network attracts a substantial audience of young blacks on Monday evenings and TBS is drawing strong ratings with *House of Payne* (2007), a TV series produced by Tyler Payne, who is currently the most popular movie director among black audiences.

In response, Viacom and BET executives have expanded programme budgets and launched new cable and Internet services. Confronted by sagging ratings and slowing ad sales, BET is angling to sustain its leadership among young audiences and to launch new services and programming aimed at other demographics. Although these efforts are expensive (estimated at more than $100 million annually), BET still generates impressive profits, greater than any other Viacom division, which is perhaps an indication of the unrealised potential of this particular market. Indeed, the buying power of African Americans in 2007 was $845 billion and it's estimated that it will top $1 trillion before 2011 (Goetzl 2007).

As discussed in Chapter 2, the history of Latino television is somewhat similar in that one service, Univision, has dominated its market niche since the network began in the early 1960s. Key to its success are primetime telenovelas, most of them imported from the leading television company in Mexico, Televisa. Univision's news organisation telecasts a popular nightly news show, *Noticiero Univision*, featuring stories from across the US and from Spanish-speaking countries worldwide. Two other shows with broad appeal are the talk show *El Show de Cristina* (1989–) and the weekend variety show, *Sabado Gigante* (1986–). Both shows are relatively inexpensive to produce, so that – other than the news division – Univision has made little investment in programming, believing its key audiences – Mexican immigrants and Mexican Americans – would be satisfied with imported telenovelas, comedies and sports programming.

Univision added the Galavision cable channel in 1979, targeting upscale viewers and in 2002, launched a second broadcast network, Telefutura, which aims at a younger demographic. Nevertheless the content on all three services is comprised of imported Mexican programming, Univision news and inexpensive talk, game and variety shows. Each has performed well in its respective market, but new competitors believe there is room for services that aim at non-Mexican Latinos and younger audiences with cross-cultural affinities.

Univision's most prominent competitor is Telemundo, which grew out of a Puerto Rican chain of television stations bought by NBC-Universal in 2001. Telemundo's programming strategy aims both at the US market and overseas Hispanics. Network studios in Miami have been complemented by new production facilities in Mexico City and Bogota, Colombia. Executives are especially interested in developing dramas that break with the narrative conventions and production practices at Televisa, which is the main supplier to Univision. Telemundo dramas strive for more sophisticated plotting and a more lavish visual style. They also target a younger audience.

Now the number-two producer and exporter of Hispanic programming, Telemundo has scored significant successes with shows sold to stations throughout Latin America, as well as parts of Europe, Asia and Africa. Executives are especially interested in Latin American markets, believing that popularity in these countries will in turn influence the perceptions of US viewers due to their ongoing ties to family and friends in the region. In 2001, Telemundo launched mun2, a cable service that serves up a range of music, games and reality programming. Executives point out that the average age of the Latino population is 26 as compared to the overall US average of 35. Telemundo believes these younger viewers have mixed cultural affinities and that television companies must cater to their cultural preferences as well as their linguistic backgrounds.

MTV executives share this perspective. When they first launched their Latin American channel, they hoped it would prove popular in the US as well, but soon came to understand that they needed to develop a dedicated service to reach stateside Latinos. Initially called MTV en Espanol, the service was rebranded in 2006 as Tr3s. Like mun2, it mixes music videos with a range of games, talk and reality fare. The channel also emphasises cultural mixing, which is common among young Latinos who grew up in the US. This is evident in the frequent recourse to code-switching, when singers, hosts or other talent fluidly mix Spanish and English in conversation and song. Tr3s plays on this sensibility, since it is a combination of the Spanish 'tres' (pronounced, trayce) and the more universal numeric symbol 3. The channel's web site follows the same inspiration by offering links to 'Blogamole', 'Tu Pride', and 'Music My Guey', each a sly mixture of Spanish and English, reflecting the hybrid sensibility of Tr3s's audience.

Sports programming is another popular genre among Latinos, now served by ESPN Deportes and Fox Sports en Espanol. These channels not only supply Spanish-language narration of sporting events, they also select sports coverage based on the distinctive interests of Latino male viewers, providing extensive coverage of soccer, baseball and boxing. Both complement their telecasts with web-site offerings that include up-to-the-minute scores, statistics and feature stories.

Informational and educational programme offerings for Latino audiences have also grown under the leadership of Discovery, which now has three Latino

Table 3.6 Top Cable Channels, 12–18 November 2007

Channel	Viewers (in millions)
Disney Channel	2.85
USA	2.75
ESPN	2.75
TBS	1.86
TNT	1.66
Nick at Nite	1.60
FOX News	1.49
MTV	1.37
SPIKE	1.34
FX	1.30
Hallmark	1.30
Discovery	1.27
A&E	1.27
Court TV	1.21
Lifetime	1.21
CNN	1.18
Cartoon Network	1.17
Sci-Fi	1.15
HGTV	1.06
History	1.04

Source: TV by the Numbers, 'Top Cable Channels', 2007.

services: a general channel, a youth channel, and a travel and lifestyle channel. These services repurpose content from the worldwide Discovery operation, but they also generate a great deal of dedicated programming, aimed specifically at their US Latino subscribers. Although operating as a demographically defined set of services, market growth has multiplied the number of niche opportunities, allowing Latino genre channels and youth services to emerge as well.

CABLE BRANDS

Overall, cable channels tend to generate roughly half their income from ads and half from subscriber fees, but a channel's programming strategy may skew that balance. General-interest cable channels tend to have higher average ratings and therefore can negotiate higher subscriber fees, but they tend to have lower ad rates. On the other hand, genre and demographic channels have lower ratings but they attract specific audiences. Their subscriber revenues may therefore be lower, but they can charge higher ad rates. Some channels, such as ESPN, enjoy both high ratings and high ad rates. Note, however, in ESPN's case, the audiences are large but they are also decidedly male, giving the company a distinctive brand to promote with advertisers and strong leverage with system operators.

Another factor affecting ad rates and subscriber fees is a channel's relation to its corporate parent. Disney, for example, owns ABC, ESPN, ESPN-2, Soap Net and the Disney Channel, as well as partial interests in other cable properties, such as Lifetime (50 per cent) and History Channel (37.5 per cent). In negotiations with cable operators, the popularity of ESPN helps Disney push for higher subscriber fees for its other cable networks. And in negotiations with advertisers, Disney offers bundled packages that may include ad spots on a mix of its broadcast and cable properties. A channel such as Hallmark, which is owned by the greeting-card company and has no companion cable or broadcast

Table 3.7 Cable Subscriber Rates

Channel	Cost per subscriber ($)
ESPN	2.90
TNT	0.89
Disney	0.80
USA	0.60
FOX News	0.60
CNN	0.44
Nickelodeon	0.33
BET	0.15
Cartoon Network	0.08

Source: Higgins 2006.

services, suffers by comparison since it cannot package channels together during negotiations with system operators and advertisers.

The most significant growth in cable television since the 1990s has been with niche channels that develop distinctive brand identities, such as Court TV, SyFy and Lifetime. Success in any particular niche usually attracts new competitors, which can undermine the value of the path-breaking service. For example, Nickelodeon's success with children's programming attracted competition from Disney, Fox and Time Warner. The niche proved too small to be profitable for all, so Disney bought out the Fox Family Network and Time Warner's Cartoon Network shifted its programming focus, redefining itself as a cross-generational animation service.

This tendency towards the subdivision of successful niches has led some companies to pre-emptively develop new services in hopes of keeping competitors at bay and in hopes of building a platform of related services. For example, Discovery Channel subdivided the 'edutainment' genre into a host of services that include Animal Planet, the Learning Channel, the Military Channel and the Science Channel. Each offers a distinctive thematic environment for advertisers and a distinctive audience mix. This provides advantages when negotiating fees with advertisers and system operators, and it offers a host of cross-promotional opportunities.

Yet another reason cable services tend to grow into platforms is the desire to take up channel space on the tuner. Although cable system operators today can deliver far more channels than ever before, technology and cost still limit the number of available channels to roughly 100 per household.[3] If a platform like Discovery increases the number of channels it controls on any given system, it increases the likelihood that viewers will see its programmes and advertisements, and just as importantly its promotions for other Discovery shows. Furthermore, for every channel assignment that Discovery secures on a local cable system, it eliminates one competitor. Therefore, executives for cable platforms battle ferociously to secure carriage for their services and to locate them in the busiest parts of the channel line-up. Broadcast networks remain the highest-rated services and they often receive channel assignments between 2 and 15. The low end of the tuning assignments are therefore seen as highly desirable, as are assignments that tend to cluster one's service with other popular channels. Such considerations encourage cable companies to increase the number of channels they offer.

Finally, the growth of cable platforms is in part attributable to the fact that it is difficult to increase the ratings for any single cable channel. Programmers can invest extensive resources improving the quality of shows on one particular channel and yet experience little change in the ratings. Even when ratings improve, the increase may not be commensurate with the programming costs or the risks. If a channel had an average rating of 1.7, it could cost tens of millions to grow the audience even a small amount. If, however, a cable service adds a second channel and spreads the costs of programming between the two, it could achieve a 0.4 rating for the second channel at relatively reasonable cost. With a composite rating of 2.1, the cable service would also be able to realise some of the advantages mentioned in the preceding paragraph. As a result, many cable companies are tempted to increase the number of channels they offer rather than intensify their programming investment in any one channel. Yet this strategy, which prevailed during the 1990s, has begun to change as the number of available channels has mushroomed.

Today cable programmers are feeling pressed to develop signature dramas that can help distinguish a channel from its many competitors and from the broadcast networks. Lifetime was one of the first cable networks to experiment with original scripted dramas as early as 1989, but it enjoyed uneven success for a variety of reasons, including the fact that cable channels could ill afford the big stars and lavish production budgets that prevail in primetime on the major networks (Meehan and Byars 2000; Lotz 2006). Despite these challenges, Lifetime continued to experiment throughout the 1990s and was joined by such others as TNT, USA and FX. All of these channels felt it important to develop their own series as a way of distinguishing themselves from the growing list of competitors. In 1985, the average television home in the US received 18.8 channels. Ten years later the average increased to 41.1 channels and in 2006 the number of channels available in the average American home exceeded 100 for the very first time (Nielsen Media Research, 'Average', 2008). As a result, cable programmers need to develop signature series that will compete for critical acclaim and for the attention of audiences. They also see original series as an important promotional device, since those searching for a channel's signature series may linger long enough to sample other programmes as well. The growing number of original cable productions became especially apparent in 2007 when more than a dozen channels introduced close to thirty scripted series during the summer season.

Historically, programmers at the major networks considered summers an addendum to the regular season, since audiences decline due to milder weather and longer daylight hours. With this in mind, the majors rerun episodes of their primetime series, gathering additional revenues to help pay for the expensive dramas and comedies they produce. As cable channels began to expand the number of original productions during the early 2000s, they targeted the summer as a window of opportunity, since their shows would not have to compete against the premiere run of the big network dramas. Over time, summers became the core season for original primetime cable programming, drawing substantial audiences and transforming viewer attitudes about the summer season. Although the size of TV audiences slumped by 15 per cent during the summer months of 1975, it was off only 3 per cent in 2007. Programme executives say audiences now watch more TV during the summer because more homes are air-conditioned, more channels are available and more original series are launched each summer.

In 2007, Lifetime rolled out *Army Wives*, FX introduced a legal drama called *Damages*, and TNT premiered a police procedural, *The Closer*. All three drew positive critical reviews and strong ratings. Most noticeable was AMC's very first scripted series, *Mad Men*, a meticulous period drama about the personal and professional lives of Madison Avenue advertising executives and their families during the early 1960s. Produced by a former writer and producer for *The Sopranos*, Matthew Weiner, the series exhibited the polish and sophistication that viewers have come to associate with the major networks or HBO. Interestingly, the major networks and HBO passed on the opportunity to sign the series, giving AMC the chance to snatch it up for a relatively modest licence fee.

When *Mad Men* (2007–) premiered in late July, it drew more than 3 million viewers and pushed AMC to the number-four spot in cable ratings. Not only did the show improve the channel's ratings, it helped to cultivate a passionate fan base and proved to be an effective vehicle for promoting AMC's new programming strategy built around quality movies and original TV series. The summer's most talked about series, *Mad Men* earned a host of award nominations, took home the Emmy for best drama, and began a second successful season the following summer. It's a good example of the ways in which a signature series can boost the fortunes of a cable network.

PROGRAMMING PERSONAL TV

If the cable television revolution of the 1980s and 90s was characterised by a proliferation of channel choices, the current era is characterised by a growing number of technologies that allow viewers even greater discretion as to what they watch and when. The introduction of the video cassette recorder during the 1980s was the early harbinger of this trend, allowing audiences to record and timeshift the viewing of their favourite programmes. Many television executives protested at the time that VCR recordings would erode the size of the broadcast audience and syndicators worried that personal libraries of favourite shows would undermine the value of off-network reruns, which are crucial to the programming strategies of local TV stations and many cable networks. As a result, few distributors were willing to experiment with the sale of pre-recorded cassettes.

Even after the emergence of DVD technology in the 1990s, relatively few television shows were available in the sell-through video market. As late as 2000, TV sales represented only $132 million of the $5 billion DVD market. But as the market for movie DVDs began to mature, sales growth slowed and so Hollywood

Table 3.8 Top-selling TV Series on DVD through 2006

Series	DVD sales in millions
Sex and the City	435.3
Friends	418.1
Seinfeld	372.8
The Simpsons	363.7
The Sopranos	341.2
Family Guy	311.9
24	263.6
Chappelle's Show	218.9
Gilmore Girls	192.5
South Park	183.3

Source: Atkinson 2007.

studios and syndicators began to roll out boxed sets of popular TV shows. Customers responded enthusiastically, quickly making TV series the fastest-growing segment of the video market. Sales exploded to $2.3 billion in 2004 and television producers now see the DVD market as an important revenue stream.

Sales figures seem to indicate that primetime hits fare well, but so too do niche cable offerings with devoted fan bases. Notice among the top sellers, only four were hit shows in network primetime. *Sex and the City* (1998–2004) and *The Sopranos* were pay cable shows that played to a very small subset of the television audience. Likewise *Chapelle's Show* (2003–6) and *South Park* (1997–) aimed for niche audiences on Comedy Central, and *Gilmore Girls* (2000–7) and *Family Guy* enjoyed only limited success during their network runs.

In fact, *Family Guy*, which was launched by Fox in 1999, was cancelled in 2000, revived a year later, and then cancelled again in 2002. Shortly thereafter, strong DVD sales among a devoted core of fans convinced Fox to give the series another try, reviving it yet again in 2005. Although a weak performer on network television, the series nevertheless generated more than $300 million in video sales, making it very profitable overall. Such examples have encouraged television executives to revisit their assumptions about the financing, production and distribution of television series. Where once it was assumed that network primetime was the primary path to profitability, television companies are beginning to explore alternative revenue streams and delivery mechanisms.

DVD viewing habits are also encouraging television executives to question their assumptions about the nature of serial drama. In recent years programmes with complex storylines and character relationships – such as *The Sopranos*, *24* and *Lost* – have received a great deal of attention because of their ability to attract devoted fans who loyally tune into each episode. In an era of channel surfing, timeshifting and fragmented audiences, these fans stand out because of their willingness to watch each episode at the time and date scheduled by the network.

They also participate in online discussions of story points and key characters, and they access Internet resources set up by the networks to promote the series.

Fans tend to become emotionally invested in particular shows and often buy series DVDs soon after they are released. Some purchase them as collector's items, while others acquire them so they can re-view favourite episodes and reflect upon complicated turning points in the storyline. They avidly study character traits and narrative arcs, and speculate about them with other fans online. Interestingly, the buzz among fans is often accompanied by a buzz among critics, and those viewers that missed the first few episodes of an intriguing series will often buy the DVD set so they can catch up to the broadcast version.

Sensing this opportunity to draw in new viewers, television companies have taken to releasing DVDs of the preceding season a couple of months before the premiere of the new season. This allows latecomers to acquaint themselves in time for the season premiere. Just as interesting, DVDs are also popular with those who never follow the broadcast version, preferring instead to watch the series at their own pace, sometimes watching entire seasons during a weekend marathon. HBO reports that even though *The Sopranos* has finished its eight-year run, the series continues to attract new viewers through the DVD box sets.

This passion for particular series and these new modes of viewing have helped to encourage television companies to produce visually lavish and narratively complex series, such as *Lost, Heroes* and *Jericho* (2006–8). Where once television was programmed as a medium that had to capture its audience at first glance, it is increasingly seen by some of its most enthusiastic audiences as an art form that deserves careful attention. DVDs also make it possible for some cancelled series, such as the cult sci-fi classics *Babylon 5* (1993–9) and *Battlestar Galactica* (2004–9), to continue their storylines through an afterlife of new episodes released directly to video.

Other technologies – such as digital video recorders, television web sites and video downloading – are furthermore encouraging a transformation of television distribution and exhibition. Digital video recorders enhance timeshifting capabilities and services like TiVo provide sophisticated search options, so that audiences need not pay attention to the weekly network schedule. In fact, TiVo usage is in many respects similar to web surfing in that the user searches, selects and downloads files to be saved, screened, or put to other uses at their discretion. With DVR penetration at 32 per cent of homes and rising, many of television's most avid viewers are no longer influenced by the sophisticated programming strategies discussed in this chapter.

Audiences have also registered their enthusiasm for online delivery systems such as YouTube, Yahoo, i-Tunes and Mefeedia. Viewers search and select from among millions of amateur and professional video offerings, many of them less than a minute in length. In 2007, Google/YouTube was the industry leader, streaming 1.167 billion videos to more than 50 million users in the month of January alone. Television companies are trying to stake their claim to this growing market, providing their own branded services and battling to control unauthorised use of video clips from their TV programmes. In January 2007, Viacom streamed proprietary versions of its shows, including the popular *Daily Show with Jon Stewart*, to almost 20 million viewers (Story, 'Viacom', 2007). Later that summer, NBC and Fox launched Hulu, a pay service designed to compete directly with YouTube. The site proved so successful that Disney/ABC joined Hulu in 2009, allowing three of the four major networks to deliver high-quality video via a web site that they owned and controlled.

Where once the tools of programming revolved around the principles of mass-audience flow across a restricted schedule of network offerings, television executives today are challenged to think more expansively about ways to inform and guide audiences through the myriad of potential media choices. Programmers increasingly have to think of their shows as part of a multimedia experience that may involve broadcast exposure, web-site enhancements, online forums and sell-through video. They also need to envision ways to make their shows visible to particular groups of viewers and to guide them to related offerings that may be of interest. If television began with broadcasting and matured during the multichannel transition, it now seems to be evolving into the matrix era, where media users select, sample and interconnect a diverse ensemble of technologies, texts and experiences. The challenge for television executives is to ensure that their companies play a role in guiding these experiences. In this new environment the network programmers' job will become more complex and open-ended, and ever more important.

NOTES

1. Although I include the evening schedules for the CW and Univision networks in the chart, our hypothetical ABC programme executive is likely to focus most of her or his attention on major network competitors NBC, CBS and FOX. The four majors compete for broad primetime audiences that range in size from 5 to 20 million. Univision targets Spanish-speaking audiences and CW caters to younger viewers. If ABC were to skew its programming toward either one of these audiences, it would be likely to lose viewers in other audience segments and compromise its broad appeal.

2. The dominance of CBS television distribution grows out of its acquisition of King World in 2006. The latter built a syndication empire based on the enormous success of its signature productions: *Jeopardy*, *Wheel of Fortune* and *Oprah*.

3. The average US household received 104 channels in 2006. See Nielsen Media Research, 'Average', 2008.

4

Making TV on the Broadcast Networks

As discussed in Chapters 1 through 3, American television networks are fading. The products they shaped – programmes – are also shifting. We are moving from a stable system of mass production of the networks to programmes that are informed by the diversification and realignment of the networks. But how different is the multichannel fare of cable, Internet and satellites that defines American TV in the twenty-first century? Five minutes of clicking from channel to channel produces a familiar sense of vast duplication – nothing changed.

However, this initial viewing fails to register how programme-making is more guided today by the fact that its products can be played out on multiple platforms than by adherence to the established rules of the industry. Because television and its content have changed both dramatically and subtly, this chapter chronicles the complexity of that transformation by first establishing the classic mode of the TV production under the networks. With networks and their audiences becoming more diverse and technologically sophisticated by the 1990s, the production process has changed. The broadcast networks have turned to the independent film traditions and foreign formats to infuse their programmes with a cheaper and more varied form and content to compete with cable and premium networks.

This chapter will map that production shift and offer a close analysis of a classic programme (*Law & Order*) and then three programmes (*Survivor*, *24* and *Ugly Betty*) which represent the new breakaway style of network programming in the multichannel era. Most particularly we will chart the establishment of new formats or genres that result from the technologically informed audience of the matrix era. How do you finance and make TV programmes when the experience of them has become personalised?

PREHISTORY OF THE STUDIO SYSTEM

Scripted or fictional programmes have always been the hallmark of the networks. The broadcast networks originally inherited the production style and generic structure of their programming from the dominant entertainment industries of the 1940s: radio, theatre and motion pictures. In the mid-1940s the established radio networks – National Broadcasting Corporation (NBC), Columbia Broadcasting System (CBS) and Dumont – began to go into television broadcasting, though Dumont did not have the financial resources to keep up with the costly prime programming and ceased broadcasting in 1956. The American Broadcasting Corporation (ABC) came to television later, in 1953. These companies had a highly capitalised investment in conventional sound studios and radio technology primarily in New York City. TV was a live broadcast medium from 1947 through the early 1950s, which limited opportunities for visual experimentation. Production was confined to studios and on-location shooting. The main studios for television were network facilities – NBC's Rockefeller Center/Radio City and CBS's Grand Central Terminal – radio studios that were adapted for television. Because the programmes often engaged a live audience, the networks used myriad legitimate theatres in Manhattan. As a result, they initially relied on rather primitive visualisations of their radio programmes and genres to fill the television schedule. They were guided by the concept of a theatrical stage with a proscenium and scenes shot one after another. American television still remains primarily an aural medium with limited visual complexity with dialogue as the prime source of content.

Initially, advertising agencies continued their role as producers as radio transitioned into TV. In their heyday in 1930s they produced 80 per cent of radio programming. For the first five years of their existence, the TV networks could not afford to produce all their programming because of the high costs of the transition to television broadcasting. Instead, the sponsor controlled the production process through the ad agency, often owning the time slot of their programme. Yet businesses willing to advertise on the new medium were hard to find. Often the agencies had to offer extremely low rates, making it uneconomical to produce TV programmes. Nevertheless, ad agencies created some of the most popular early TV in the 1940s such as *The Texaco Star Theater* (1948–56), *Kraft Television Theatre* (1947–58) and General Food's *The Goldbergs* (1949–51). As the number of stations increased, so did the cost of buying airtime. When productions started to escalate in costs, advertising agencies could no longer afford to produce. The quiz scandals of the mid-1950s had also tarnished the image of the all-powerful single sponsor. After 1952, the networks took over production, they moved to a more profitable system of multiple sponsors which still structures network programmes and the agencies shifted their interests to commercials.

Non-scripted variety and game shows were initially the most thriving formats transposed from radio. Radio had changed the once visual medium of theatrical vaudeville into an aural medium of music and verbal comedy called 'variety'. Television returned visual spectacle to the genre as it reinvigorated itself with elaborate dance, sight comedy sketches and elements drawn from circuses (acrobatics, animal tricks and clowning). In 1948 *The Texaco Star Theater* starring Milton Berle – a master of the sight gag – premiered and lasted to 1956. Known as a 'vaudeo' in the industry, the show captured 75 per cent of the viewing audience during its weekly broadcasts. Jack Benny and Burns and Allen, famed radio comedians, made a successful transition to TV variety. Often zany and a bit bawdy, these comedies began the long tradition of TV stand-up comics whose style was based on ethnic and later racial humor. These early variety shows were progenitors to some of the longest-lived programmes: *The Ed Sullivan Show* (1948–71), *The Tonight Show* (1962–) and *Saturday Night Live* (1975–). Game shows also made an easy transition to television as they were carried out in front of live theatrical audiences. For example, The New Yorker Theatre, a former opera house and legitimate theatre, was bought by CBS in 1950 and renamed Studio 52. It was used to produce early shows as *What's My Line?* (1950–75), *The $64,000 Question* (1955–8), *Password* (1961–71), *To Tell the Truth* (1956–2002), *Beat the Clock* (1950–2003), *The Jack Benny Show* (1950–65), *I've Got a Secret* (1952–67), *Ted Mack's Original Amateur Hour* (1948–75) and *Captain Kangaroo* (1955–84) – all programmes owing their origins to vaudeville/variety and theatre with the self-conscious use of the proscenium and audience.

Anthology drama series – single dramatic performances – were the first form of fictional programming and the first network series. Filmed live in studios in New York, these hour-long dramas were self-contained stories that became famed for their quality due to their literary, dramatic and social content. They received prestige through their association with Broadway and off Broadway. Critics have since dubbed this early period of TV drama the 'Golden Age' for its idiosyncratic style and bold social content. Beginning with NBC's *Kraft Television Theatre* in 1947, the genre dominated through the mid-1960s: *Studio One* (1948–58), *Philco Television Playhouse* (1948–55) and *Actors' Studio* (1948–50). Some of the more famed productions were *Marty* (1955), *12 Angry Men* (1957) and *Requiem for a Heavyweight* (1956). As television production moved to Hollywood during the 1950s, these serious dramas began to die out as sponsors wanted more socially neutral works. The audience also seemingly preferred the more action-oriented programmes produced in Los Angeles with higher production values and movie stars. By the mid-1950s 'TV drama' had evolved into the repeated dramatic performance model that we associate with present-day scripted TV.

Radio soap operas evolved on TV as one of the best vehicles for commercial sponsorship as the sponsor's products such as soap became not so subtly woven into the visual *mise en scène* of the drama. Borrowed from nineteenth-century theatrical melodramas, the form (a serialised drama about the domestic conflicts of women and family) continues to this day. The broadcast networks transferred their radio soap operas to the home screen without much difficulty, given their characteristic dependence on music and dialogue. *The Guiding Light* originated on radio in 1937 and moved to CBS TV in 1952 where it ended in 2009 – television's longest-running narrative. The late 1960s was the heyday of soaps when all three networks had multiple successful programmes competing furiously for afternoon hegemony. Although they are less overt in their sponsorship and more stylish and younger in their appeal, present-day soap operas still comprise up to fifty hours of daytime weekday programming.

Another fictional form originating in radio, domestic comedies also dominated early TV. *The Goldbergs* (1949–51), *Amos 'n' Andy* (1951–3) and *The Jack Benny Show* were defined by their limited stories and characterisations on radio. These comedies with their minimal sets were easily recreated in the former radio studios of the networks. However when they shifted to TV, their uncomfortable stereotypes were made even more transparent within a visual medium. For example, *The Goldbergs* premiered on radio in 1928 as the story of a Jewish immigrant family and their struggles to survive in America. Moving to TV in 1948, the programme survived only until the early 1950s due to its wooden portrayals and adverse publicity from the lead actor being branded a Communist by a Senate investigation. Although *The Jack Benny Show* slowly broke through early TV stereotypes with its progressive depiction of the all-knowing black valet, Rochester, the racist *Amos 'n' Andy* (with its minstrelsy of whites playing in blackface) lasted only two years. Sitcoms have always carried the burden of their stereotyping. But the shift to Hollywood allowed TV programmes to become more expensive and less visually simplistic.

HOLLYWOOD AND THE MAJOR TV STUDIOS

Although American television still produces some programmes in New York (primarily soap operas, news and late-night talk shows), 'TV' has become synonymous with Los Angeles to which many refer as 'the industry'. Since the late 1950s TV studios have been mainly subdivisions of the motion-picture companies that dominate the landscape in Hollywood. The business arm of the networks in New York hired studios in LA to make their programmes. What are termed the 'majors' in TV production – Warner Bros., Universal, 20th Century-Fox, Disney and Paramount – are subsidiaries of the major film studios from the 1930s and 1940s. The movie studios became aware of the potential rivalry of TV after they had lost their monopolistic hold on film through the Paramount antitrust suit in 1948. At the outset, the film industry saw television as a conduit for film profit, experimenting with projecting television in movie houses and paying television for their movies. More generally, however, the studios saw TV as an advertising vehicle for their films. Studio-produced programmes were known as telefilms. Many of the initial producers migrated from B-picture studios, bringing with them action genres – detective, science fiction and Western – which evolved into the basic formats of scripted TV.

The studios left their entertainment stamp on television as programmes became more star-driven and more standardised. Warner Bros. began the film studios' shift to TV. Initially, it used its programmes as a medium for advertising its pictures. In 1955 the studio produced *Warner Brothers Presents* (1955–6) for ABC – a programme hosted by the movie actor Gig Young where episodes of three different series would rotate. The plots were loosely based on Warner Bros. movies (*Casablanca*, Michael Curtiz, 1942, US, *King's Row*, Sam Wood, 1942, US and *Cheyenne*, Raoul Walsh, 1947, US).The *Cheyenne* segment was the only one to thrive, airing for eight years and becoming the first successful TV series for a major studio. By 1959, Warner Bros. was the largest producer of network series. It is often credited with defining the narrative style and regularised production process by which the majors created dramatic TV – a returning goal-oriented protagonist who solves a major conflict each week within a three-act hour-long programme.

Simultaneously, the studios began to exhibit their pre-1948 movies on TV. By 1965 this shift had established theatrical films as a staple of TV programming with prime programmes such as NBC's *Saturday Night at the Movies* (1961–78) and ABC's *Sunday Night Movie* (1964–95). A third film-inspired format was the made-for-TV film or the movie of the week (MOW), which became a staple of the industry in the 1970s. When the price of renting feature films in the 1970s skyrocketed, the networks began to make their own films for an average of $750,000 – far below what the motion picture companies charged for renting a film.

Before long, the major studios and networks formed affiliations. MCA and NBC had a strong alliance with the production company MCA-Universal, whose drama series came to dominate the network's schedule well into the 1970s. After introducing movies to primetime with *Saturday Night at the Movies* in 1961, NBC joined with MCA-Universal to develop several long-form programme formats, including the ninety-minute episodic series (*The Virginian*, 1962–71), the made-for-TV movie (debuting with *Fame Is the Name of the Game* in 1966) and the movie series (*The NBC Mystery Movie*, 1971–7), which initially made *Columbo* (1971–90), *McCloud* (1970–7) and *McMillan & Wife* (1971–7) under its umbrella title. ABC, the weak sister network of early TV, made a deal with Walt and Roy Disney in 1954 whereby in exchange for Disney producing a programme for the network, ABC helped finance a theme park – aptly named *Disneyland*.

Box 4.1 Major TV Studios and Selected Productions

20th Century-Fox Television, Television Century City, CA
Crusade in Europe (1949), *My Friend Flicka* (1956–8), *Broken Arrow* (1956–60), *Voyage to the Bottom of the Sea* (1964–8), *Peyton Place* (1964–9), *Daniel Boone* (1964–70), *Batman* (1966–8), *Room 222* (1969–74), *M*A*S*H* (1972–83), *The Paper Chase* (1978–86), *L.A. Law* (1986–94), *The Tracey Ullman Show* (1987–90), *21 Jump Street* (1987–91), *America's Most Wanted* (1988–), *The Simpsons* (1989–present), *COPS* (1989–), *In Living Color* (1990–4), *The X-Files* (1993–2002), *NYPD Blue* (1993–2005), *Buffy the Vampire Slayer* (1997–2003), *Malcolm in the Middle* (2000–6), *Reba* (2001–7), *24* (2001–), *My Name Is Earl* (2005–) and *Prison Break* (2005–).

Paramount Television, Hollywood, CA
The Brady Bunch (1969–74), *Love, American Style* (1969–74), *The Odd Couple* (1970–5), *Happy Days* (1974–84), *Laverne & Shirley* (1976–83), *Mork & Mindy* (1978–82), *Taxi* (1978–83), *Webster* (1983–9), and *MacGyver* (1985–92), *The Andy Griffith Show* (1960–8), *Cheers* (1982–93), the *Star Trek* franchise (1966–2005), *Frasier* (1993–2004), *Girlfriends* (2000–8) and the daily Paramount staple *Entertainment Tonight* (1981–), among others.

Universal-MCA, Universal City, CA
Provided studio services for Jack Webb's Mark VII productions and MCA's Revue Studios, filming such series as *Alfred Hitchcock Presents* (1955–65) and *Leave It to Beaver* (1957–63), *Friday Night Lights* (2006– NBC), *Heroes* (2006– NBC), *House* (2004– Fox), *Las Vegas* (2003–8 NBC, co-production with DreamWorks Television), *Late Night with Conan O'Brien* (1993–2009 NBC), *Law & Order* (1990–2010 NBC), *Law & Order: Criminal Intent* (2001– NBC), *Law & Order: Special Victims Unit* (2009– NBC), *Monk* (2002–9 USA, co-production with ABC Studios), *Psych* (2006– USA, co-production with ABC Studios).

Warner Bros. Television, Burbank, CA
Warner Brothers Presents (1955–6), *Maverick* (1957–62), *77 Sunset Strip* (1958–64), *The F.B.I.* (1965–74), *Alice* (1976–85), *The Dukes of Hazzard* (1979–85), *Night Court* (1984–92), *Growing Pains* (1985–92), *Perfect Strangers* (1986–93), *Full House* (1987–95), *Murphy Brown* (1988–98), *Family Matters* (1989–98), *ER* (1994–2009), *Friends* (1994–2004), *Babylon 5* (1993–9), *The Drew Carey Show* (1995–2004), *The West Wing* (1999–2006), *Gilmore Girls* (2000–7), *The O.C.* (2003–7), *Two and a Half Men* (2003–), *Nip/Tuck* (2003–), *The Tyra Banks Show* (2005–).

RISE OF INDEPENDENT PRODUCERS

By the 1950s the networks licensed, helped finance and scheduled programmes, but rarely did they make them. When the networks wrestled production control from the sponsors, they also saw greater profit could be made by independents shouldering the high costs of production. There was a new breed of independent producers and syndicators who would go on to make the majority of TV until the 1990s. Initially, they numbered in the hundreds. The incentive to create American TV came not from the initial broadcast of the work, where the networks have exclusive rights to air the show and receive advertising revenue. Rather, creators only made back their investment and any potential profit when the series went into syndication and foreign distribution. At that point there were huge profits to be made in post-network distribution by creators. These producers had their own companies made up primarily of offices devoted to pre-production (development, writing and management); they rented soundstages from the major studios where they filmed or taped their work.

There were a few rogue entrepreneurs such as Fred Ziv, who moved from radio to television as a programme syndicator in 1948. Riding the emerging light-entertainment wave of television, Ziv created a number of successful first-run syndicated series such as *The Cisco Kid* (1950–6), *I Led Three Lives* (1953–6), *Highway Patrol* (1955–9) and *Seahunt* (1958–61) and sold them in a piecemeal fashion to local stations, many unconnected to the networks. But it was the independent Desilu production company – responsible for *I Love Lucy* – that became the first producer to film a regular series. The Desilu studios are credited with establishing the American television production process that was later absorbed by the networks – the returning actors/characters, writers/formula and sets/settings each week allowed for a mass production system and the standardised model known as American TV. The company began renting out space at the General Service Studio on Santa Monica Boulevard in 1950. As Lucy succeeded and was sold into syndication, the company began to buy more and more studio space, eventually owning 33 soundstages by 1957. The studio went onto create some of America's most popular TV: *Star Trek* (1966–9), *The Andy Griffith Show*, *Mission: Impossible* (1966–73), *The Untouchables* (1959–63), *I Spy* (1965–8) and *Hogan's Heroes* (1965–71). Desilu remains one of the most successful independent studios.

More typical was Mary Tyler Moore (MTM) Productions in the 1970s. Husband/wife team Grant Tinker and Mary Tyler Moore created their production company when CBS committed to thirteen episodes of their series, *The Mary Tyler Moore Show* (1970–7). Based on the success of its original series, MTM was able to grant its writers a lot of creative freedom. As a result, it went on to be one of the prolific producers of sitcoms in the 1970s. In the 1980s,

Stephen J. Cannell Productions was another highly successful independent with a number of hit shows. In 1979, Cannell left Universal Television, where he had produced a string of successful action-adventure shows (e.g., *The Rockford Files*, 1974–80) and formed his own production company on Hollywood Boulevard. Independently, he went on to make *The A-Team* (1983–7) and *Wiseguy* (1987–90) among other lesser-known shows in the 1980s. He later bought his own soundstage in Vancouver to lower the spiralling costs of working with the large American studios; it was here where his series *21 Jump Street* (1987–91) was filmed – the first hit programme for the new Fox network.

Today, small production companies with one or two successful shows still dot the Hollywood landscape. For example, *America's Funniest Home Videos* (1989–present), a long-lived and popular ABC programme of amateur home-movie clips, is produced by Vin Di Bona Productions in Hollywood. The company rents out a soundstage at the Raleigh Studios in Manhattan Beach to film the programme with a live audience. But all aspects of the programme – development and pre- and post-production – take place at the unassuming offices of Vin Di Bona Productions in Hollywood.

As the networks became more established and production costs grew, they turned their focus towards producing only major successes or 'hits' – which meant working only with independents such as Cannell who had a proven record of success. With the number of studios dwindling across the decade, a group of 'major' independent studios evolved. The majors also rented out their studios and became the production home for a number of known independent producers (e.g., MCA for Revue Productions).

THE TENSION BETWEEN THE NETWORKS AND THE INDEPENDENT PRODUCERS

The notion of 'independent' is a bit of a misnomer in that these companies were never free to produce what they wanted. Given the financial costs of TV production, these shows were always underwritten by either or both the advertisers and the networks. Creative control was highly constrained. Just the ability of a network to fund the pilot and the power of scheduling served as a potent system of control on programme content. Network executives have been notorious for 'giving notes' during the production – written memos offering 'advice' or 'directives' to producers about the content and therefore potential success of the show. (See Box 4.4 The Clockwork Production Process of a Sitcom.) When the Justice Department in 1973 filed an antitrust suit against the three networks, a central issue was how much control they exerted over not only their own but independent productions. Given the intervention of the networks, the lure of independence lay not in opportunities for creativity, but in the huge

Box 4.2 Major Independent Studios and Selected Productions

Desilu Studios   Based on the success of its production of *I Love Lucy*, Desilu went on to become the production headquarters of virtually all the greatest hits of the 1950s and 60s. Its television programmes included *Our Miss Brooks* (1948–57), *Make Room for Daddy* (1953–64), *The Dick Van Dyke Show* (1961–6), *The Untouchables* (1959–63), *Mission: Impossible* (1966–73), *Mannix* (1966–75) and *Star Trek* (1966–9). It hosted a number of independent producers such as Quinn Martin and Danny Thomas. It rivalled the output of the major motion-picture companies.

Filmways   A commercial production house which produced all of Paul Henning's rural sitcoms of the 1960s: *Beverly Hillbillies* (1962–71), *Green Acres* (1965–71) and *Petticoat Junction* (1963–70). Other comedies were *The Addams Family* (1964–6) and *Mr. Ed* (1961–6). The company bought Heatter-Quigley Production, a leading game-show studio, maker of *Hollywood Squares* (1966–2004). In 1981 Orion Pictures acquired Filmways.

MTM Enterprises   Formed in 1969/70 by Grant Tinker and Mary Tyler Moore to produce *The Mary Tyler Moore Show* (1970–7), it was known as a refuge for writer/producers such as James L. Brooks and Allan Burns. It began by producing sitcoms (*The Bob Newhart Show*, 1972–8, *Rhoda*, 1974–8, and *WKRP in Cincinnati*, 1978–82) primarily for CBS. In the late 1970s, it moved into innovative dramas – *Lou Grant* (1977–82), *Hill St. Blues* (1981–7), *Cagney and Lacey* (1982–8) and *St. Elsewhere* (1982–8) – many of which NBC picked up. The company ended operations as it was absorbed by 20th Century-Fox Television in 1998.

Norman Lear and Bud Yorkin's Tandem Productions   Originally formed as a motion-picture production company, Lear and Yorkin's firm went into television production in 1971 with *All in the Family* (1971–9 – a remake of the British sitcom *Till Death Us Do Part*, 1965–75). Known for socially conscious content specifically around class, race and gender, Tandem went on to produce *Maude* (1972–9), *Good Times* (1974–9) and *Sanford and Son* (1972–7). Lear sold Tandem (along with his Embassy Television Company) to Columbia Pictures Television in 1985.

Spelling Television/Spelling-Goldberg Productions   It was the leading independent studio of the 1980s – famed as the most prolific studio in television history. Nicknamed the 'king of pap', Aaron Spelling headed the company from 1969 to 1992 and it was absorbed by Viacom in 1999. His studio is celebrated for primetime soap operas. Its seven series on ABC from 1984 to 1989 made up one-third of the network's schedule. A sample of its output includes: *The Mod Squad* 1968–73), *Starsky and Hutch* (1975–9), *Charlie's Angels* (1976–81), *Family* (1976–80), *The Love Boat* (1977–86), *Fantasy Island* (1981–9), *Dynasty* (1981–9), *Hotel* (1983–8), *Beverly Hills 90210* (1990–2000) and *Melrose Place* (1992–9).

(Other major independent studios are/were Quinn Martin, Carsey-Werner, Lorimar Productions, Stephen J. Cannell Studios and Charles-Burrows-Charles Production Company.)

profits that could be made by syndicating a programme owned by a production company.

The government was aware of the networks' control over the making of TV. As already discussed, the FCC established the lucrative role of syndication when it implemented the Financial Interest and Syndication Rules (fin-syn) in 1971. It prohibited the networks from having a financial interest in the profits of TV programming. The new rules were based on the assumption that, by separating exhibition and distribution from production, there would be greater diversity in the industry. Initially, the rules gave independent producers the chance to see a greater financial return on their programmes. The rules also limited network control over syndication profit. As a result, the networks desire to produce waned when there was no continuing financial incentive. The 1973 antitrust case spoke to how broadcasting (even with the fin-syn ruling) was still controlled by the Big Three. At that time, the networks controlled 90 per cent of the TV audience. By the mid-1980s twenty-five established independent TV production studios were producing three-quarters of programming. The networks filled only about one-quarter of the schedule with their own productions.

The broadcast networks lobbied heavily against the rules throughout the 1980s as they watched their share of the audience dwindle to 65 per cent due to cable and the arrival of the Fox network by 1986. In turn, they were met with fierce opposition from the Hollywood production establishment and even then President Ronald Reagan. The networks' share of profit dropped considerably. But in 1991, noticing the growing trend for deregulation in the US, the FCC began to rescind the Financial Interest and Syndication Rules, encouraging networks to get back into production. The change resulted in a wave of consolidation by the networks, led by Disney's acquisition of ABC in 1995. This shift to inhouse destroyed independent producers. Not only was there less demand for their work, but those companies that had a series with a network (such as Vin Di Bona Productions) also lost a huge amount of their profit in after-network airing.

In 2004, CNN and TNT creator Ted Turner wrote an angry analysis, 'My Beef with Big Media: How Government Protects Big Media – And Shuts Out Upstarts Like Me', of the changes that the end of the fin-syn rules created. He argued that when the original rules were in place, the major broadcast networks – ABC, CBS, NBC and Fox – fully or partially owned just 12.5 per cent of the new series that they aired. A decade later, after the elimination of the rules, this figure had ballooned to 56.3 per cent, and by 2002 it had surged to 77.5 per cent. From 1992 to 2002, the number of primetime hours produced by the network studios per week increased by over double. The hours produced by independents dropped by 63 per cent. By 2000, dramas often cost $1 million

---

Box 4.3 Network Studios

CBS Studio Center, Studio City, CA   Formerly the site of Republic Pictures studio, CBS television took this over in 1963. It functions as a production house for independent producers. *Gunsmoke* (1955–75) the MTM series and many sitcoms including *Seinfeld* (1990–8) and *Will & Grace* (1998–2006) were shot at this network studio.

CBS's 'Television City', Los Angeles, CA   Built in 1952 the studio is where the network tapes soap operas (such as *The Young and the Restless*, 1973–), occasional sitcoms, talk shows such as *The Late Late Show* (1962–) and the game show *The Price Is Right* (1956–65). Historically it housed the production of *The Twilight Zone* (1959–64) (with Rod Serling) and variety shows like *The Smothers Brothers Comedy Hour* (1967–70).

ABC Television Center Studios (formerly Vitagraph Studios), Hollywood, CA   It was acquired by ABC in 1949 as a TV studio. Popular game shows and music/variety shows were taped here including *Let's Make a Deal* (1963–77), *Family Feud* (1976–85), *The Dating Game* (1965–86), *Match Game* (1973–82), *The Newlywed Game* (1966–74), *Password* (1961–75), *Dick Clark's Bandstand*, later *American Bandstand* (1952–89) and *The Lawrence Welk Show* (1951–5). The popular soap opera *General Hospital* (1963–) is also housed here. In 2007 Disney rebranded its television arm under the ABC Television Studios moniker.

NBC Studios, Burbank CA   Formerly the Revue Studio. It produces network variety talk show *The Tonight Show* (1962–2007) and the soap opera *Days of Our Lives* (1965–) in this facility. In 2007 NBC announced that it is moving its studios to Universal City as Universal Media Studio (Universal became NBC's parent company) consolidated its production facilities.

---

per episode – much of this was due to above-the-line costs, as investors wanted bigger stars to offset any chance of failure. By 2002, there were only five substantial production studios: Disney (owning a movie studio, broadcast network – ABC and cable network – ESPN); News Corp. (owning a movie studio, broadcasting network – Fox and cable networks); GE (owning a movie studio – Universal, a broadcast network – NBC and cable USA Network); and Viacom (owning two movie studios – Paramount and DreamWorks, a broadcast network – CBS and a cable property – MTV). This situation represented a return to the vertical integration of the classical movie-studio era. Turner concluded: 'At this late stage, media companies have grown so large and powerful, and their dominance has become so detrimental to the survival of small, emerging companies, that there remains only one alternative: bust up the big conglomerates.' [1]

THE MODEL OF NETWORK ERA PRODUCTION (1950–2000)

Comprehending this millennial shift necessitates an understanding of how television was made in the network era. TV production was a highly regulated system. The process mirrors the movie studio system: a highly rationalised mass-production system of tried and true TV genres where individual programmes serve as variations on a norm (or formula). But what distinguished media production from 1955–2000, whether it was film or TV, was the 'package unit system':

> Rather than an individual company containing the source of labour and materials, the entire industry became a pool for these. A film exec producer organized a project: he or she secured financing and combined the necessary labourers (whose roles had been previously defined by the standardized production structure and subdivision of work categories) and the means of production (the narrative 'property,' the equipment, and the physical sites of production).[2]

The major TV studios conducted three activities in relation to TV: licensing features to TV (which peaked in the late 1970s with the shift to cable); syndication of features, series and other programming to local stations; and the production of made-for-TV movies, series and programmes. The independent studios focused on the production and syndication of individual programmes. The network studio functioned as either facilities to be rented by independent producers or for the production of the networks' inhouse programmes (e.g., soap operas or talk shows).

The studio production process involved a number of different programmes: 'made-fors' (films), series and miniseries. Financing was most often done on a piecemeal basis. One year ahead of broadcasting, the television arm of a major studio and a large independent producer would sift through hundreds of concepts. An executive producer or a development team would present a programme idea as a logline or pitch on paper or at a meeting with network executives. A logline distils the programme's logic into two sentences. For example, *Boomtown*, a 2002–3 series was described as '*Rashomon* set among cops, politicians and E.M.T.s in Los Angeles'.

Two to three dozen of these 'pitches' were chosen to be produced as a pilot by the studios, or a prototype which serves as an introduction to the themes and characters of the prospective series. For producers, it functioned as a blueprint or norm where the series episodes function as a variation on that norm. At this point, advertisers often got a chance to preview the programme (see Chapter 2's discussion of 'upfronts') and offer suggestions if they intended to support it. Given that so much rides on the look and feel of a pilot, the cost of producing one has spiralled over the years and more spectacular and highly produced works have therefore been favoured. In early 1970s, a half-hour pilot cost $250,000. By the 1990s, it was $500,000. A 1990s hour-long pilot had the price tag of $700,000. A decade later, the two-part pilot to *Lost* in 2004 came in at between $12 and 14 million.

Networks operated as contributors and financiers. When a project was greenlighted by a network, it put up some (though not all) of the money needed to create the programme through a system called 'deficit financing'. With this licensing procedure, networks pay a fee of 70–85 per cent of the cost of production to ensure the right to show the finished pilot. The production company foots the other 15–25 per cent of the financing. The producer's costs are recouped through international sales and local-station syndication; the production company does not generally see profit for at least four years if the programme succeeds (typically around its eighty-eighth episode, usually in four to five years). A studio can then receive a million an episode. For example, take a typical one-hour action show in 1990, which cost an average of $1.2 million to produce. A network pays a licence fee of $800,000 to the studio for it. The studio will have to wait several years for its show to go into domestic and foreign syndication to become marketable in off-network markets.

Half of the pilots were chosen as series for either a half- or full-hour programming. Each episode conformed to the necessity of the commercial break every fifteen minutes, whittling down the actual length of a programme to twenty-three and forty-three minutes respectively. Often the networks would commit to thirteen episodes, with an option contract adding nine to eleven episodes if the series proved successful. This allowed the network to fill the season but also gave it the chance to opt out mid-season should the programme be perceived a failure. The network typically paid a third of the promised money at each point in the making and delivery of the product: filming/taping, completion and airing or delivery. Prior to 2000, a programme had to clear the 'standards and practices' departments (censors) before the last payment and airing. These departments were dissolved in the cost cutting of the 1990s, replaced by a rating system.[3] Finally, the networks would add 10 per cent for the rerun of an episode – a form of programming that has become increasingly unpopular and non-profitable since the 1990s. This production process was so standardised that the year was divided into clear periods for each step of the process: the first four months represented pilot season – perhaps the busiest time in Los Angeles. The network made its decisions in May and production began at the end of August. The classical broadcast season ran from September to May, lasting twenty-six weeks.

Box 4.4 The Clockwork Production Process of a Sitcom

Frasier (1993–2004) illustrates the manufacturing roots of television.

Wednesday 10:00 am   The actual production of an episode begins. The production team – a group of highly specialised workers – meets. It includes the producer, director, assistant directors, line producer, unit production manager and technical coordinator. They are introduced to this week's writer and script (one of up to fifteen writers on a sitcom). They go over the script and discuss the needs for the production of this episode – the variations that make this script different from the other twenty-three this season. This input is more about process than creativity. For example, director Lee Shallat Chemel, states: 'Quite often, creative input from the director is neither expected nor desired.'[4] The writer is sent back to change the script based on the mainly technical suggestions, which will allow the episode to adhere to the production process. The executive producer serves most often as the head writer or 'show's runner' where s/he maintains the programme's standards while the writers provide variations on that model for each week.

Friday 1:30 pm   The actors get a revised script and the director conducts a run-through with them.

The weekend   The director blocks the camera shots.

Monday   After a series of rehearsals, a complete run-through is carried out for producers and writers where they critique the episode for its successes and failures. The writers are sent back to clean up the weak spots – unworkable parts in the assembly process. A couple more days of rehearsals and re-blocking ensue.

Tuesday   Production day.

10:00 am up to 6:00 pm   Everyone takes part in a complete run-through and the writer adds 'pages' (new lines) trying to tweak the episode's structure to assure quality control.
6:30 pm   The actors conduct a swift run-through of the dialogue during makeup.
7:00 pm   The ticket-holding audience files into the soundstage to the sounds of jazz. A warm-up comedian keeps up the pleasant tone with jokes. A light-hearted Kelsey Grammer, the programme's star, makes a few humorous comments to the assembled viewers.

The cast is introduced and the production moves directly to filming scene A. The script is filmed in order of its scenes.
9:45 pm   The filming is completed including any 'pick-up' shots necessary to maintain continuity.
10:30 pm   The episode 'wraps' with a new script for the next episode being delivered to the production team the next morning – Wednesday 10:30 am.[5]

PRODUCTION OR MANUFACTURING OF NETWORK PROGRAMMES

To what degree can we call a TV episode a product of mass production? Pro-duction crews like to describe their working relations as 'familial' because of the collective nature of the work. One traditionally defines mass production as 'application of the principles of specialization, division of labour, and standard-ization of parts to the manufacture of goods'.[6] However, TV manufacturing is not the same as detergent; TV is a form of custom production, where episodes are mass produced but each episode is customised to be a variation on the for-mula – much like customising cars.

As one *Frasier* writer describes it: 'As the run-through progresses, cast, crew and directing team move from set to set following the action in sequence with the script.' Other producers portray the method as 'a 'well-oiled machine' and done 'by clockwork' . A director maintains: 'We do not rehearse much. We shoot at a certain time. We want to get out at a certain time.' The executive producer David Lee insists: 'This is television where time is a precious commodity.' [7] Yet even though the language speaks to a regulated system driven by the clock like mass production, television production is still customised because each product – the programme – is a variation on the last. One episode is about Frasier offending his father by insulting his favourite eatery. The next has Frasier in a fight with a newspaper over an unfavourable review of his show. A third has Frasier and his brother suspecting that their father cheated on their mother when they were young. The changes each week serve as one of the central acts of the art or creativity of American TV. The viewer returns to the series weekly, enjoying the play of the familiar with the new. Similar to Home Depot mixing unique colours for paints from the same base, programmes work with set ele-ments – situations, characters, sets, music, length, commercial breaks – and each episode becomes a unique version of prescribed ingredients. The dictates of a commercial system require a smoothly running entertainment machine to which people will return, which is the essential logic of American network TV.

NETWORK MODEL OF SCRIPTED TV

NBC/Universal's *Law & Order* presents a model of a classical network prime-time drama. It stands as the second longest-running network series, surpassed by *Gunsmoke* (1955–75); with 387 episodes as of January 2008/9 it is in its nine-teenth year. It evolved out of two well-known popular genres: detective and courtroom drama. Typical of network scripted programmes, each episode is self-contained with a distinct beginning, middle and end (all narrative lines are closed off at the end of an episode). Centrally, its acts are determined by com-mercial breaks. It is written in LA and filmed on location in New York and at the Chelsea Piers studio in Manhattan. It fits the mould of manufactured TV:

the police procedural as a half-hour unit and the courtroom drama as a half-hour unit. (In fact, creator Dick Wolfe sold it to the networks by emphasising the potential for twice the revenue – each half-hour section could be sold separately in syndication.) The series fits clear generic norms and each episode becomes a variation on that norm. The *Los Angeles Times* describes it thus: 'a drama about cops and lawyers with easily changeable cast – so self-contained that any episode could be watched whenever – would be the perfect formula to feed the ever-hungry TV beast'. So powerful was the formula that it became a franchise with two new programmes: *Law & Order: Criminal Intent* (2001–), which focuses on the detectives and the psychology of crime, and *Law & Order: Special Victims Unit* (1999–), which centres on sex crimes. The series is syndicated on cable through Turner Network Television (TNT) with over forty episodes airing per week during June 2007. Reruns have occasionally drawn more viewers than such original series as FX's *The Shield* (2002–8) and USA's *Monk* (2002–10). In 2006 USA and Bravo paid a robust $1.92 million-per-episode licence fee – a basic-cable high at the time to show *Law & Order: Criminal Intent*. Again, the *Los Angeles Times* describes the series: 'Its rhythms and tight format have been so well established that the viewer can join in while the show is in progress without too much confusion.'[8] It fit the traditional broadcast September to May season and reached closure for every episode.

Box 4.5 The Structure of a *Law & Order* Episode

According to Brian Lowry of the *Los Angeles Times*:

Act 1   Before the first fifteen minutes pass, two homicide detectives … are asking questions and taking down names. In the first segment, the search for suspects has begun, in earnest. Cut to the commercial … .

Act 2   Solving the crime is never easy, and the detectives generally run into some hurdle, some complication, some aggravation (this is drama, after all). At least one visit with the boss … helps clarify things, so by the half-hour, an arrest has been made. Before going to the next break, the 'Law' segment has concluded.

Act 3   It's in the hands of the lawyers now. Executive assistant DA McCoy and assistant DA Southerlyn are preparing for trial. But typically moral or ethical matters need to be resolved. DA Branch sometimes provides the impediment, sometimes the solution. Either way, by the end of the third segment the case seems in jeopardy.

Act 4   Any lingering issues from the previous act are brought to resolution. Perhaps McCoy and the more impulsive Southerlyn are at odds, or there could be something Briscoe/Green did or learned in their investigation … but by now it's time for trial. By the time the hour's over, a judgment has been rendered. 'Order' has been restored.[9]

The conclusion to the pilot *Law & Order* closes as the doctor defendant fails a sobriety test in the courtroom

Deriving many of its techniques from classical Hollywood film, the classical TV drama would usually have two plotlines. Here, the courtroom drama serves as the second 'B' plot which maintains the detectives from the 'A' plot to locate any new evidence to convict the criminal and create closure for the episode. For example, the pilot for the programme has a detective follow the negligent doctor defendant to a bar during a trial break and come back to testify that the doctor had six alcoholic drinks. The programme dramatically ends as the doctor fails a sobriety test given by then District Attorney Ben Stone in the courtroom – proof of guilt/closure.

THE ARRIVAL OF REALITY TELEVISION

The arrival of reality TV at the turn of 2000 initially seemed a simple revival of old programming strategies. The term is an umbrella for a number of diverse formats that involve the chronicling of real people in unscripted situations. The format had been around for years. *Candid Camera* (1960–7), PBS's *An American Family* (1973) and *America's Funniest Videos* were renowned for their unscripted premises. But the unexpected success of *Who Wants to Be a Millionaire* (1999–2002, based on a British format) and *Survivor* (based on a Swedish format) respectively put reality TV back on the map. Not only did these programmes mark a growing genre but they also signified a change in what constituted television. Unscripted programmes were challenging the primacy of scripted TV – the hallmark of network programming.

The format also forces us to rethink normal assumptions about the global stream of TV out of America: the genre had its roots in Europe. Producers there could not compete with American fiction producers who were backed by the deep pockets of the networks. American TV was defined by high production values and expensive stars. American scripted television also had a greater chance of making back its costs and was therefore often able to underbid indigenous European TV programmes. In fact, the success of 'reality programming' can be ascribed to the new market in highly adaptable formats that are sold globally to various countries where producers adapt them to local cultures.

Endemol, a Dutch production company, stands as the most successful producer of reality-format franchises with their *Big Brother* (2000–), *Extreme Makeover: Home Edition* (2003–) and *Fear Factor* (2001–6). These three formats have been sold not only to US production companies but also to those in Africa, Europe, Asia and Latin America. The BBC originally produced *Changing Rooms* (1997–2004) and sold it internationally to a number of English-language countries (renamed as *Trading Spaces*, 2000–8, in the US). Originating in England, *The Apprentice* was remade into an international franchise by Mark Burnett, the British executive producer of the *Survivor* franchise. The programme has shown in the US (2004–) but also in Nigeria, South Africa, Brazil, Finland, India and Turkey to name a few. *Dragon's Den* (2004–) is a Japanese programme franchise owned by Sony and first aired on Nippon Television, featuring young entrepreneurs pitching ideas to venture capitalists, that has been sold to producers in the US, Nigeria, Afghanistan, Israel and Australia. Susan Murray states: 'Believing that a program can be evacuated of its cultural particulars and then refilled with new ones once it arrives in another country, production companies assume that the basics of reality programming maintain a universal appeal.'[10]

Reality successes in America at the turn of the century heralded a major change in the industry as many producers attempted to reproduce these hits with their own variations on 'reality'. Industry executives saw *Who Wants to Be a Millionaire* and *Survivor* in revolutionary terms. Garth Ancier, the president of NBC Entertainment, said, 'What happened with those two shows in being so different is that they broke the stranglehold of story-form television.'[11] In 2000, Tom Werner of the Carsey-Werner Company stated: 'It's going to be a tough year for story-form shows … . "Millionaire" and "Survivor" have made that format vulnerable because nothing performed on Hollywood sound stages in the last five years came close to capturing their viewer interest.'[12] Primetime reality TV began the decline of the signature of the networks: fictional programming.

Reality TV as a US format is admittedly a vague concept. Much of American television strives to be 'realistic' with its use of photographic realism. However, this specific format is marked by its lack of writers and professional actors in its attempt to get at the spontaneity of the moment. Chad Raphael aptly lists its characteristics: 'actuality footage of their subjects' (e.g., police stake-outs), 'reenactments of events', 'a tendency to avoid the studio in favor of on-scene shooting', 'mixing footage shot by unpaid amateur videographers with that of professionals', 'appealing to the conventions of "liveness" and "immediacy" through on-location interviews, subjective camerawork, and synchronized sound' and 'appropriating traditional conventions of news coverage, such as the use of anchors or hosts, remote reporting, and the pretense to spontaneity'.[13] The programmes range in content: real police on patrol (*COPS*, 1989–), 20-somethings living together (*The Real World*), amateur videos (*America's Funniest Home Videos*), game shows with high stakes (*Who Wants to Be A Millionaire*), talent searches (*American Idol*) and talk shows (*The Jerry Springer Show*, 1991–). With all this diversity in form, reality is difficult to categorise as a distinct genre. But the unscripted use of non-actors marks this as a salient shift in US programming.

With interest in repeats waning in the 1990s, the networks started to seek other inexpensive options. The average reality show costs about $500,000 per episode. Its savings lie in non-studio locations and the diminished need for conventional labour – especially actors and writers with their top-heavy salaries. It was also an enticing format for the growing online community, as fans visited listservs and bulletin boards to speculate about the logic and intentions of the participants. Of the seven shows that could be labelled phenomenal hits in the mid-2000s, all but one – CBS's *CSI: Crime Scene Investigation* – were reality shows. Reality shows are particularly popular with teenagers and young adult viewers, an audience that had been leaving the networks in droves. The Fox network, with its youth orientation, spearheaded the success of the genre around 2000 after a period of low ratings. The network was willing to push the potential 'good-taste' boundaries of reality TV beyond where ABC, NBC and CBS were willing to go. The fourth network premiered *Joe Millionaire* (2003) where women competed for the affections of a construction worker posing as a wealthy bachelor, *Temptation Island* (2002–3) where contestants tested their emotional and sexual relationships, *World's Wildest Police Videos* (1998–2000), which was criticised for its sensationalism, and *When Animals Attack!* (1996), a series of specials in the 1990s that consisted solely of footage of animals attacking humans. Perhaps the most notorious Fox venture was *Who Wants to Marry a Multi-Millionaire?* (2002). The final married couple ended up hating each other, and the 'multi-millionaire' at the centre of the show had questionable finances and a violent past.

One of the important differences between reality and fictional TV is that reality TV does not do well in reshowings. One of the central attractions of reality is the surprise factor: who will win? Once the competition has played out, these programmes have lost their attractiveness and have no second market life. However, cable has caused an overabundance of second showings of network scripted programmes (*Law & Order* could be seen twenty times a week in many markets) and DVD sales narrow rebroadcast possibilities. The market conditions that made deficit financing and syndication agreeable to the studios had waned. But the parsimonious price of reality makes up for the need to go into syndication. The producers recoup their costs merely through licensing fees. And a number of non-competitive reality programmes – *America's Funniest Videos*, *COPS* and science programmes – do make considerable profit in international distribution, as producers adopt them as templates for various reality programmes with local casts and locations (e.g., the rights to the *Who Wants to Be a Millionaire* format have been sold to over 170 countries).

From its foundations, reality TV has been fraught with ethical controversy. It has created a debate on authenticity, privacy and industry ethics. The tension between the needs of an entertainment industry for drama and the mundane nature of the lives of ordinary people has led to excessive manipulation of the 'real' in the genre. (See the CBS and *Survivor* case study below.) The 2007–8 Writers Guild negotiators argued that reality TV was as scripted as fictional TV and therefore the producers should be included as 'writers' in their union membership. The guild tried to organise reality producers, arguing that they 'wrote' programmes through their tight control of the action.

CASE STUDY: NETWORK REALITY TV

CBS and **Survivor** (2000–) represents the best-known example of the strategic move of broadcast networks to reality or unscripted TV in response to a downward turn in the ratings in the late 1990s. The *New York Times* described the series as 'an experiment in mixing "Lord of the Flies" with "Gilligan's Island" and "Treasure Island"'.[14] It was initially created in Britain in 1992 but was transformed into the popular Swedish series *Expedition: Robinson* in 1997. Creator Mark Burnett tried to sell the American version, *Survivor*, for years before it was picked up by CBS. The network was so wary of the untried nature of the format that it agreed to 50/50 profit sharing and it forced Burnett to sell the advertising for the programme. Burnett innovated associative marketing for *Survivor*, where eight sponsors (including Reebok, Budweiser and the United States Army) agreed to 'buy into' the programme upfront in return for product placement and a set of commercials. Through these unusual agreements Burnett paid for the production costs – a practice that has become more common in the intervening years.

When *Survivor* first aired in the summer of 2000, it drew an audience that exceeded that of any of CBS's regular season programming for three years. For the finale that summer, the network charged up to $600,000 per commercial. The profit-sharing agreement was an anomaly, breaking from years of deficit financing for the networks. Nevertheless, the programme has not only launched the career of Mark Burnett but rescued CBS from a slow death. The network immediately added *Big Brother* (2000–) that summer. The network then reinforced its revival by placing *Survivor* opposite NBC's successful scripted programming during Thursday primetime. More significantly, it tripled the all-important young audience at a time when the network had the oldest viewership in TV. Because of the show's unprecedented success, Burnett and CBS were able to sell the rights for the first ten seasons to the cable network Outdoor Life/Versus. The episodes were also available at Comcast's web site for 99 cents. All these post-network sales defied the adage that reality had no post-network life. Mark Burnett has gone on to insist on similar unconventional business agreements with later reality programmes: *The Eco-Challenge: Adventure Race* (1995–2002), *The Apprentice* (2004–), *The Restaurant* (2003–4), *Combat Missions* (2004), *The Contender* (2005–), and *Are You Smarter than a Fifth Grader?* (2007–) – all of which are based on a concept of survival of the fittest, whether it be in the workplace, classroom or nature. Nevertheless, these programmes are marked more by their pioneering financing and profit agreements than their content.

Survivor is representative of a subgenre of reality TV – a game show based on elimination. This type of show can be subdivided again into sports (*Survivor*), dating (*Who Wants to Marry a Multi-Millionaire?*, 2000) and job/talent search (*The Apprentice* and *American Idol*, 2002–). Other reality series that fit the elimination formula are the *Big Brother* franchise internationally and *The Weakest Link* (2000–) in Britain. *Survivor* is a game show where sixteen to nineteen individuals are divided up into two to four teams (tribes) on a remote location (normally a tropical island) and told to 'survive'. They vote one contestant off the island for each of the sixteen weeks of the show. Each week is complicated by challenges created by the producers where the teams conduct some feat based on teamwork and endurance. A tribal council finally picks from the final two. He or she wins $1 million and a car from the sponsor. From 2000 to 2007 the series staged its contests in Borneo, the Australian outback, Kenya, Marquesas (French Polynesia), Thailand, the Amazon, the Pearl Islands (off Panama), Vanuatu (Islands of Fire), Palau, Guatemala, Panama, the Cook Islands, Fiji and China. Attempts to produce a British and Australian version failed. The American series has had moderate success in international sales. The show's major expense involves carrying out production in a remote setting, which is still cheaper than studio shooting.

In 2006, *Survivor: Cook Islands* drew heavy criticism for creating teams around racial difference where winning and losing became a sign of racial difference

Controversies have abounded concerning the programme and genre. Starting in the first season on Borneo, a contestant sued the producers, claiming they conspired to have her voted off the island. Contestants have lied about their lives in order to gain sympathy and advantage in the contest. The programme has also used actor stand-ins to help smooth over production gaps. Ideologically, the programme came under attack for a lack of racial diversity. The producers responded by making an effort to add Blacks, Asians and Hispanics to the

Survivor: Cook Islands season in 2006. Unfortunately, the show grouped the tribes by race and set them against each other as a promotional stunt. The tribes' structure produced a firestorm of criticism for inviting viewers to judge the teams' performances based on race and potentially seeing the tribes as representing a race as a whole. Campbell's Soup, Home Depot, Coca-Cola and Procter and Gamble, all long-time sponsors, dropped their sponsorship.

NEW MODELS OF SCRIPTED TV

The decline of the broadcast networks' market share has led to their willingness to experiment with TV storytelling. Several cable networks were eager to experiment with storytelling because of their desire to brand their networks as 'quality' as opposed to the traditional mass-produced or formulaic dramas of network broadcasts. Because of its status as 'paid-for' or 'elective', cable is granted relative freedom (in terms of content, nudity, violence and profanity) compared to what is allowed on the public airwaves of broadcast TV. Further, cable has long been a site of experimentation because it is not held to a network tradition of a season and programme length. Working with much less capital, scripted cable utilises less studio time and fewer well-known actors and thus borrows heavily from the independent cinema and its lower cost. Home Box Office led the way when it moved from a venue for theatrically released films to a production house for original programming in the late 1970s.

Beginning in the 1990s with *The Larry Sanders Show* (1992–8), but more explicitly with *Oz* (1997–2003), *Six Feet Under* and *The Sopranos*, HBO reformed the notion of what constituted American dramatic TV. It shortened the length of a season (e.g., thirteen episodes for *The Larry Sanders Show* and a fourteen-episode season of *The Sopranos*), extended the programme length and expanded the content of programmes into new areas not traditionally tackled on broadcast TV. (See Chapter 5 on HBO and original programming.) HBO's model was followed by Showtime, another subscription network whose original programming became prominent in the 2000s with its gay-themed programmes *Queer as Folk* (2000–1; 2005) and *The L Word* (2004–9). However, non-premium cable networks also experimented with drama. Perhaps the best known is FX ('**F**'ox E'**x**' tended Network), Fox's flagship general-entertainment cable network that began in 1994. With its tagline of 'TV Made Fresh Daily', FX also broke with the season format, having thirteen episodes per season, reducing pressure on the writers to script cumbersome narrative arcs over twenty-some weeks of network drama. FX also produced programmes that broke with traditional content: morally corrupt police (*The Shield*), the psychologically disturbed world of plastic surgery (*Nip/Tuck*, 2003–) and self-destructive post-9/11 firemen (*Rescue Me*, 2004–). Other cable networks such as Turner Network Television, Bravo and USA Network have produced a few original dramas based on the network model in order to attract a range of advertisers.

More importantly, these cable companies spearheaded the return of serious serialised dramas to primetime, or again what Bill Carter of the *New York Times* called 'appointment TV' because of their growing experiment with structure, which demanded unprecedented attention to complex narrative changes.[15] Serialised primetime narratives have always existed: *The Fugitive* (1963–7) and the primetime soaps of the 1980s and 1990s – *Dallas*, *Dynasty* and *Beverly Hills 90210* were the exception rather than the norm. Furthermore, the new dramas took their logic from the art and independent American cinemas, where causal links were loosened and films more dependent on character psychology than linear action. Traditional sitcoms and dramas tended to close off the story each week primarily so they could be shown as reruns and in syndication. With the cable networks needing reruns to fill their schedule and the growing after-market use of DVDs, these programmes do not depend as much on syndication for profit. (See following case study on *24*.)

In response to the success of these cable shows and their own shrinking market, the broadcast networks began experimenting in around 2000 with serial narratives and a shorter season. After fifty years of twenty to twenty-five episodes per season of a forty-three minute length that needed every element resolved weekly, the broadcast networks began to innovate. Fox led the network move in 2001 with *24*, its zigzag spy thriller where plot time parallels real time. Although on multiple levels the plot made no logical sense in its effort to condense actions to a twenty-four-hour clock, the programme succeeded in attracting a devoted weekly audience pulled in by the breath-taking rollercoaster of events across the season. Next came *Lost*, ABC's successful 2004 series, which experimented with flashback and flash-forward to produce complex portrayals of characters, plot motivation and an ambiguous set of potential causal agents ('the others', fate or monsters). By the second season the programme's schedule was split – two semi-seasons with a long hiatus in early winter – an unprecedented network strategy. Interestingly, both of these hit serialised programmes have not succeeded in rerun – a mark of how serialisation depends on surprise and freshness.

By 2006 the broadcast networks were alive with narrative experimentation. After Fox's premiere of *Prison Break* (2005–9) with its escapees careening through a maze of hurdles with little to no closure, CBS and NBC created *Jericho* and *Heroes* respectively in 2006. Both programmes were popular serialised dramas that drew out their plots across the season and/or seasons with a complex sophistication that demanded viewer devotion. Other serial narratives aired but did not often succeed due to convoluted narrative premises which could not be sustained in future seasons. The networks also began to offer episodes on their web sites. To balance out the tease of a suspended season, these 'webisodes' of coming attractions and character profiles air on the Internet – all strategies designed to retain their more migratory viewers.

CASE STUDY: 24

Fox and 24 (2001–) is an example of a new network rewriting the rules of television production. The programme is produced by 20th Century-Fox Television and Imagine Television at a studio in Chatsworth, California right outside Burbank. The story involves antiterrorist agent Jack Bauer and the Counter Terrorist Unit in Los Angeles battling the fictional threats of rogue governments, nuclear bombs and power-hungry corporate executives. The programme is played out in real time where twenty-four signifies a day in the life of our hero. Each episode represents one hour (really forty-three minutes with commercials) of one jam-packed day where Bauer saves America from another major danger only to realise that another is on its way – next season. The real-time format, borrowed from recent film-making, indicates how TV programmes in the 2000s are daring to deviate from the seamless style of traditional network drama. The plots play out on the streets of Los Angeles away from a traditional studio to underline the potential 'real' menace of these terrorist scenarios.

Fox is part of the recent phenomenon of a studio network such as CW (combining the former networks of the WB – Warner Bros. and UPN – Paramount) and ABC/Disney, where production and exhibition rights are owned by the same company. Fox began in 1987 and started with only of fifteen hours of primetime TV. Its leaner offerings allowed for greater profit. (Fox was making 75 per cent of what NBC took in by 1993.) Its status as an upstart has allowed it to break with the traditions of the established networks. Part of its appeal has been its edgy and low-budget youth-oriented programmes such as *Married with Children* (1987–97), *In Living Color* (1990–4), *The Simpsons* (1989–) and *Arrested Development* (2003–6). It has led the networks in taking on reality TV with *COPS* (1989–), *Joe Millionaire* (2003) and *American Idol* (2002–), with its phenomenal 30 million viewers. As a result, it launched Fox Reality Network in 2005. Further, the network brought the successful soapy sagas of *Beverly Hills 90210*, 1990–2000, *Melrose Place*, 1999–9 and *Party of Five*, 1994–2000 to America.

Beyond its innovative serialised and real-time plot, *24* changed the concept of the TV season. The show went into hiatus in 2001 during the baseball playoffs, with Fox having the all-important rights to air these games and World Series. *24* returned midseason in January, which produced good but not great ratings. Then the network decided to start the next run of series midseason which allowed it to run uninterrupted. The unusual scheduling succeeded: ratings for *24* have soared with the non-stop schedule. This triumph motivated the other networks to experiment with the primetime season (e.g., *Lost*, 2004–, *Prison Break*, 2005–9 and *The Shield*, 2002–8). Viewers could no longer depend on the predictability of the traditional schedule. *24* also represents the growing trend towards the return to the single sponsor of the 1940s. Backed by the Ford Motor Company, the programme began and ended with six-minute mini-narrative ads in *24* style featuring Ford autos. In fact, Ford was Jack Bauer's primary auto choice – a piece of product placement so overt so that by the 2008 season a scene often began with a zoom out from a Ford logo on Bauer's car. Ford's sponsorship replaced the role that commercials played in financing the series.

Significantly, *24* has also led the way in the changes in ancillary markets especially the DVD sell-through market for programmes. Its DVDs have generated $200 million since their initial 2002 release. That stands as more profit than is made from international rights and potentially more than from syndication; the profit has gone back into the growing production costs of *24*. According to the *New York Times*: 'the costs of producing a drama like "24" had become so prohibitive that it probably could not be made today without the DVD sales'.[16] As a result writer and producers have fought for a greater portion of the residuals from DVDs, reality TV and the emerging Internet market ('the electronic sellthrough') for TV programmes such as *24* as the rights to syndication become more elusive. Further the multiplatform nature of *24* constitutes an example of *how* matrix TV affects production, with the financial divide between television and film being slowly erased.

Jack tortures his brother in *24*

By 2005 TV DVD sales involved 10 per cent of the overall DVD market. DVDs, along with the show's web site, mobisodes and cell-phone scenes, have allowed the programme and its after-market products to reach the consumer much more quickly than in the broadcast-and-rerun tradition. These new methods have provided new revenues for the producers. Each of the series' 120 episodes has cost just under $2.5 million to craft. Licensing fees from the Fox network are thought to be $1.3 million an episode, for a total of no more than about $156 million. The rights to broadcast the series internationally are calculated to be $1 million or more an episode, to a total of at least $120 million. All in all, its revenue is $276 million (not enough yield to get rid of the deficit and generate a profit). DVD sales, however, have done just that – allowed *24* to be one of the most profitable programmes on American television with revenues of $300 million.

Nevertheless, the programme has received considerable criticism for its depiction of Muslims, torture, and its ultranationalism as Jack enlists whatever means available to save the United States each week. Usually the threat comes from an outside force. The fourth season began with a Muslim American family joining forces with an Islamic-based terrorist group scheming to destroy the US. The Council on American Islamic Relations protested. In response the producers had Kiefer Sutherland, the actor who plays Jack Bauer, deliver a statement to camera before an episode about how the Muslim American community stands behind America in denouncing terrorism. Further, the use of torture on *24* prompted the US army to ask the producers to tone down the violence because US soldiers were mimicking the TV programme in their interrogations of Iraqi and Afghan prisoners.[17] Bauer famously tortures his own brother in one season. The programme's dialogue often hinges on extreme statements ('When I'm finished with you, you're gonna wish that you felt this good again') that could be frightening or humorously overblown depending on how the audience interprets it. Given the programme's popularity across the ideological spectrum and different nations, these lines have crept into the international lexicon as 'arch' comments about military retribution.

CASE STUDY: *UGLY BETTY*

ABC and *Ugly Betty* (2006–) is an example of how network scripted TV has begun to absorb formulas that circulate internationally. Originating in Colombia in 1999 under the title *Betty La Fea*, the telenovela was a hugely successful daily soap opera about a poor and seemingly ugly girl and her secret love for her rich and rapacious boss. Because telenovelas are one of the most pervasive formats in Latin American television, *Betty La Fea* was packaged and aired in all Latin America and Spain. Given its relative export success, the series was repackaged and dubbed to suit the needs of various countries as *La Fea Mas*

Ugly Betty as an American adaptation of the Colombian telenovela *Betty La Fea* attempts to portray a Latino home for the broad network audience

Belle (Televisa in Mexico), *Verleibt in Berlin* (SevenOne International in Germany), *Yo Soy Bea* (Telecinco in Spain), *Lotte* (Tappa in the Netherlands) and *Yo soy Betty, la fea* (Bosnian Federalna Televizija Croatian RTL Televizija, and Serbian Fox Televizija).

With its track record in numerous countries, the series was then adapted for ABC/Disney in 2006 by Reveille and Ventanarosa, a production company formed by the actress Salma Hayek to produce Hispanic topics. The American version was remade into an hour-long comedy drama about the experience of a lower middle-class Latina (with braces) working at high-fashion magazine *Mode* in NYC. Although not publicly marketed as a 'Latino' programme, the series marks the growing awareness of the networks that a move away from all white characters could help to engage the Hispanic American audience. NBC Universal bought Telemundo, the largest Spanish-language network in the US in 2002. By 2004 it created the Telemundo Television Studio in Miami, which is not only making original telenovelas for the US market but is also translating its telenovelas into English. Telenovelas are seen by the networks as intriguing: a popular and low-cost form of scripted TV. NBC network is adapting a Colombian telenovela titled *Without Breasts There Is No Paradise* and CBS have developed two other telenovelas for primetime. MyNetworkTV, a Fox spin-off cable channel, launched two telenovelas in English for less than $500,000 per episode in 2006 as opposed to well over $1 million per episode for *Ugly Betty*.

As a result, *Betty La Fea* has become the most pervasive franchise in television history. And of the various versions, ABC's *Ugly Betty* is the most seen internationally. Weathering out the WGA strike and the loss of two major producers, the programme succeeded in the American market as the lead-in to the popular *Grey's Anatomy* (2005–) on Thursday evening. ABC/Disney International Television exports it to over 130 international markets competing with the original Colombian telenovela as well as over seventy inhouse versions internationally.

In 2007 Sony Entertainment Television began airing the ABC/Disney series in South America. In Colombia it was resoundingly criticised. The leading newspaper *El Tiempo* on 24 January 2007 began its review: 'New behaviors cannot be induced in the United States if the image of the "ethnic" is by definition degrading and discriminatory.'[18] Such cries of media domination are becoming more complicated as global companies import media products and then customise them for local tastes.

CONCLUSION

American television is moving slowly towards an environment of non-scripted programmes in search of cost economies. The multichannel world of cable will never be able to mount the continuous expensive, star-driven, multiyear series of the network era. The once-powerful networks are losing the mass market that they once relied on to financially mount their affluent series. Nevertheless the networks – now backed by huge multimedia conglomerates – will seemingly remain the central source of scripted TV, which may come to represent their branded difference. Television is no longer just the fifty-year old experience of turning on the set in your living room. The broadcast networks have evolved into multiplatform and international producers.

NBC, ABC and CBS are confronted with the independent cinema as the new drama norm first brought to us on cable and premium channels, reality franchises which have re-excited the all-important 18–30-year-old audience about network viewing, and global genres which cater to a new multicultural American audience. As Arsenault and Castells argue:

> global companies are leveraging partnerships and cross-investments with national, regional, and local companies to facilitate market expansion *and* vice versa. Regional players are actively importing global content and localizing it; and global media organizations are pursuing local partners in order to deliver customized content to audiences.[19]

Matrix TV is about hybridity where breaking through national and industry boundaries in search of content and new audiences has become the rule. As a result network TV has become more varied with the influence of film, cable and global producers. But then a new form of TV manufacturing has begun as global franchises create broad templates or international generic concepts and then sell them to the networks to fill in with American content – a variation on the norm that has characterised American commercial TV since its inception in the early 1950s.

NOTES

1. Ted Turner, 'My Beef with Big Media: How Government Protects Big Media – And Shuts Out Upstarts Like Me', *Federal Communications Law Journal* vol. 57 (2005): 233.

2. David Bordwell, Janet Staiger and Kristin Thompson, *The Classical Hollywood Cinema: Film Style & Mode of Production to 1960*, New York: Columbia University, 1985: 330.

3. The TV Parental Guidelines went into effect in 1997: TV-Y (for young children), TV-Y7 or TV-Y7–FV (for children 7 and older), TV-G (for general audiences), TV-PG (parental guidance), TV-14 (for people 14 or older) and TV-MA (for mature audiences).

4. Lisa Mitchell, 'A Conversation with Lee Shallat Chemel', *DGA Monthly* vol. 1 (November 2004). <http://www.directorsguildofamerica.com/news/dgamonthly-1104/evnt_wsc-shallatchemel-1104.php3>.

5. Darrell Hope, '*Frasier*: How the *Frasier* Directing Team Keeps Things Deliciously Friendly and Funny', *DGA Quarterly* vol. 23, no. 5 (January 1999): 54–60.

6. 'Mass Production', *Encyclopædia Britannica*, 2009. *Encyclopædia Britannica Online*, 28 May 2009: <http://www.search.eb.com/eb/article-9106304>.

7. Hope, '*Frasier*': 59.

8. Brian Lowry, 'How *Law & Order* Rewrote the Rules', *Los Angeles Times* 18 May 2003: E-1.

9. Ibid.

10. Susan Murray, 'Reality Television (U.S)', *Encyclopedia of Television*, ed. Horace Newcomb, 2nd edn. New York: Routledge, 2004: 1903.

11. Bill Carter, 'TV Has New Stories to Tell, but Reality Lurks in the Wings', *New York Times* 2 October 2000: <http://www.nytimes.com/2000/10/02/arts/tv-has-new-stories-to-tell-but-reality-lurks-in-the-wings.html>.

12. Ibid.

13. Chad Raphael, 'The Political Economic Origins of Reali-TV', in *Reality TV: Remaking Television Culture*, eds. Susan Murray and Laurie Ouellette. New York: New York University Press, 2004: 120.

14. Bill Carter, 'CBS's *Survivor* Is Winner for Network: Real-life Show Pulls in Younger Viewers', *New York Times* 2 June 2000: C1.

15. Carter, 'TV Has New Stories to Tell'.

16. Jacques Steinberg, 'Digital Media Brings Profits (and Tensions) to TV Studios', *New York Times* 14 May 2006: 3.1.

17. Janet Mayer, 'Letter from Hollywood: Whatever It Takes', *The New Yorker* 19 February 2007: http://www.newyorker.com/reporting/2007/02/19/070219fa_fact_mayer?>.

18. Maria Antonia Garcia, 'New Behaviors Cannot Be Induced in the United States if the Image of the "Ethnic" Is by Definition Degrading and Discriminatory', *El Tiempo* 24 January 2007: <http://www.watchingamerica.com/eltiempo000030.shtml>.

19. Amelia H. Arsenault and Manuel Castells, 'The Structure and Dynamics of Global Multi-media Business Networks', *International Journal of Communication* vol. 2 (2008): 707–48.

5

Branded Cable Networks

The new technologies of the late twentieth century have changed how America manufactures, delivers and understands its television culture. At no time has this been more evident than at the turn of the century, as American TV shifted from the network era into the multichannel era. TV culture has moved from being a mass medium that a nation consumed as a whole to one catering to a series of increasingly specialised interests, a change facilitated by new technologies such as the increased bandwidth of cable, the proliferation of video web sites and video on demand. The viewer has become the scheduler and distributor of a programme through digital video recorders (DVRs), web sites and downloading. We have moved away from TV providing a unified sense of 'American' culture as we move to a post-network era. But this shift has also meant that TV no longer has to please all tastes as it did when the networks reigned. Today, TV is more specific and differentiated and (most importantly) potentially more remarkable than in the network era.

Chris Anderson of *Wired* magazine has christened this trend 'the long tail'.[1] The term, derived from analysis of economic demand, describes the line of the demand curve that reveals that the 'short head' – traditional big media corporations and their blockbusters in television, music, film and books – is slowly dying out into the boundless abundance of niche products in the digital age that will attract somebody, somewhere, at some time. Like obscure categories of books on Amazon.com, web sites promoting niche musicians and cable channels designed to appeal to the narrowest interests, new technologies have allowed the culture to be segmented into even narrower tastes. According to Anderson,

> the long tail describes the shift from mass markets to millions of niches, the low sellers that we traditionally haven't had room for on our shelves, screens and channels, but which we now do have room for thanks to the internet and abundant distribution systems.[2]

The 'long tail' model envisions an increasingly knowing media consumer who will actively seek out his or her own specific interests and recommend that content to acquaintances – the informed consumer. In fact, so powerful is this need for individual connection between product and user that American media has moved towards marketing that creates emotional bonds to create consumer loyalty in this multiplatform environment.

This chapter looks at how the niche and branding have worked to create greater programme diversity in the highly competitive commercial environment of multichannel television. Anderson notes:

> The audience is migrating away from broadcast to the Internet, where niche economics rules. Given greater choice, they are shifting their attention to what they value most – and that turns out *not* to be formulaic fare with lots of commercials.[3]

A niche network must convey its own quality and distinguish itself, and marketing has assumed a much more important role as makers struggle to declare their product's difference in a crowded market. 'Branding' means trying to create a brand familiarity and a positive brand image in order to build brand equity. 'Brand equity occurs when the consumer is familiar with the brand and holds some favorable, strong, and unique associations in memory (i.e. brand image).'[4] The arrival of cable and satellite has created over 300 networks; only through strong brand recognition can a network or a programme succeed in this multichannel clutter. Cable networks are an example of the nexus of culture and industry in that networks are actively categorising themselves based on a genre in order to construct clear lines of product differentiation. The Hollywood studio system classified films based on the Western, musical or the detective content. Now we have entire networks defined by genre (food, soap opera, sports and news). However, new cable and satellite networks have moved beyond simple content differences to a more nuanced and direct connection to the viewer through multimedia interactions such as online posting, games and video exclusives. No longer do we have TV audiences – now, we have brand communities.

In the 1990s American TV began slowly to move away from the 'majors' – large studios appended to major motion-picture companies (e.g., Warner Bros. and Paramount) producing long-term series in Hollywood (e.g., *ER* and *Frasier*) – to young cable networks creating shows inhouse and commissioning independent production companies often located on the East Coast (e.g., Arts and Entertainment is an umbrella company located in Stamford, Connecticut which runs the A&E, History and Discovery cable networks). As Amanda Lotz states: 'Instead of needing to design programming likely to be less objectionable to the entire family, broadcast networks – and particularly cable channels – increasingly developed programming that was more satisfying to specific audience members.'[5] News channels exemplify the emerging logic of narrowcasting, catering to a small portion of viewers and specific consumer interests based on political values and the consequent loss of the appearance of objectivity that the broadcast networks once perpetuated (see Chapter 6).

ARTS AND ENTERTAINMENT NETWORK (A&E)

The Arts and Entertainment Network is also primarily an information-based network but one built around popularising the arts. It initially succeeded by mining the right to broadcast arts events as an inexpensive content source. Since then, it has become one of the biggest networks on cable, with over 40 million viewers watching weekly. As a satellite and cable network, it has gone through three shifts in content: arts, history documentaries and true-crime reality. As it grew and succeeded with one genre, it has spawned a new network devoted to that thriving content. It was able shape a new identity brand – even though it started as a utility brand devoted to 'arts'. First airing in 1984, the network grew out of a combined business venture by Hearst (37.5 per cent), Walt Disney Corp. (37.5 per cent) and NBC Universal (25 per cent) which came to be known as A&E Television Networks (AETN). The joint venture owns a number of networks: A&E, the History Channel, Biography, History Espanol, History International, Military History, and Crime and Investigation Network. Famed for its frugality, A&E initially mixed its offering of opera and ballet with servings of movies and slapstick comedies. In fulfilling its fine arts' aim, it bought as much as 60 per cent of its programming from the BBC in the 1980s. The network was determined to be a more 'entertaining' arts channel than public television. It designed its programming to attract a select and affluent audience; its early audience was primarily upscale women aged 25 to 54.

Originally, A&E created its identity around its most well-known programme: *Biography* – life-story documentaries of well-known individuals. The programme exemplifies how a network is able to construct 'passion or touch points' where an audience identifies strongly (even emotionally) with a programme. Running since 1983, *Biography* was initially a rerun of the popular CBS series of the same title from 1962. In 1987, the network began to produce its own episodes. The programme was augmented with a strong web site which extended the issues and information of the various biographies. The programme garnered 3 million viewers nightly and allowed A&E to branch out with video tapes/DVDs and its own magazine. Slowly the network became what is considered 'a foundational network' with over 8 million viewers. This accomplishment allowed AETN to spin off a network devoted to life stories in 1999: the Biography Channel or simply 'Bio'. The network began a successful shift to the highly sought male audience by showing more historical and military content in the early 1990s. The success of this transition allowed it to spin off the History Channel in 1995.

More recently, A&E has rebranded itself a third time as a 'true-crime' network through numerous documentary series. It moved to producing reality programmes in search of cost economies: *Dog the Bounty Hunter* (real-life bounty hunters, 2004–7), *Growing Up Gotti* (the life of a Gotti crime family member, 2004–5), *Airline* (the day-to-day activity at Southwest Airlines, 2004–5) and *Criss Angel Mindfreak* (illusionism distributed by A&E, 2005–). However, it has been its true-crime series which have garnered the most notice. *American Justice*, hosted by Bill Curtis, has been in operation since 1993 presenting over 250 crimes making it the longest-running justice documentary. Much like a majority of cable documentaries, the production process involves interviews, reenactments, and studio shots of its narrator Bill Curtis as he susses out the clues and enigmas of the crime. It spawned *Cold Case Files* (1999–), an unsolved murder documentary series with the same production methods and narrator. *City Confidential*, (1999–), investigates a crime in a new city each week. And *The First 48* (2004–) revolves around the pressure on detectives to solve a crime in the first two days after the act. Following its reputation for crime series, A&E bought the rights to syndicate *The Sopranos* in 2005. Costing $2.5 million per episode, the deal was a record for syndication, outdoing Bravo/USA Network's deal of $1.9 million for *Law & Order: Criminal Intent* episodes that same year. Given that A&E is advertiser-supported (as opposed to HBO's subscription basis), HBO edited each episode to remove objectionable material. But A&E's own crime shows reveal the slight variations on a norm that characterise the vast majority of commercial TV series.

THE HISTORY CHANNEL

One of A&E's offspring, the History Channel, represents the ever-growing number of nonfictional or informational channels as cable television has come of age in the twenty-first century. It too is part of A&E Networks and evolved into a standard offering on most basic cable packages by 2000. The British version is a joint venture of A&E and British Sky Broadcasting. The History Channel operates in various forms in Australia, India, New Zealand, Spain, Portugal, Italy and Latin America. A joint venture of A&E and Astro All Asia Networks created a version for East and Southeast Asia.

The channel's slogans – 'All the history, all the time', 'Where the past comes alive' and 'This day in history' – speak to its lofty claim to popularise *all* of history. The *New York Times* put the mission as: to take history out of the 'PBS good-for-you realm and into the hurly-burly of commercial television'.[6] In truth, the channel has favoured military history, which is popular with its viewing backbone: affluent white men between 24 and 54. Initially, the channel was dominated by up to forty programming hours a week devoted to World War II, earning it the nickname 'The Hitler Channel'. This success with military history allowed the network to spin off the Military History Channel, which took with it much of the military programming. Nevertheless, the History Channel has come up against real competition with the creation of the Military Channel, a Discovery Group network, in 1999. The popularity of military history shows how much cable depends on inexpensive public-domain footage to fill its programmes as old newsreels from the world wars are resurrected.

Given the pressure of ratings, the History Channel furnishes a limited range of historical programmes or, as one *New York Times* writer describes it: 'sublime and ridiculous, populist and arcane'.[7] Typically, the network will take a historical moment that is topical (9/11, a murder, or a recent film such as *The Da Vinci Code*, Ron Howard, 2006, US) and examine its historical circumstances. Most often, the programme will fall into a classical narrative structure of exposition, conflict and resolution. The stories call on real historians as experts to elucidate a historical issue or clarify links and to give legitimacy to the TV production as 'history'. To lend these retellings of past events commercial power, the programmes often use reenactment – '*You* are there at the Last Supper.' Two tiers of programming have evolved. First, there are serious histories or formal inquiries into the past, programmes such as *A History of Britain* with Simon Schama, co-produced by the BBC (2000) or *The Missouri River: A Journey* with Stephen Ambrose (2004). The next tier is the more commercial (or as one critic describes it as 'kitsch') such as *Jayne Mansfield's Death Car* (2000) and *Hitler's Skull* (2000). Further, the type of histories produced is influenced by what is popular on television as a whole, whether it is reality TV, a current event or popular culture trends such as rock music. A programme such as *Extreme History with Roger Daltrey* (2003) represents what Gary Edgerton and Kyle Nicholas argue is the 'ongoing negotiation between popular programming trends, brand imperatives, and generic changes that is always a part of producing historical programming'.[8]

The channel's dependence on advertising has led to claims of sensationalism and inaccuracy. It received resounding criticism in the press in 1996 for that year's proposed series, *The Spirit of Enterprise*, which was to have been a weekly history of a single corporation to be produced by that week's subject. Not only was the series condemned for lacking documentary objectivity, it sounded much like a disguised infomercial. The channel was also forced to withdraw the documentary *The Men Who Killed Kennedy* (2003), which offered the inflammatory and audience-grabbing claim that Lyndon Johnson ordered the assassination of John F. Kennedy. The commercialism of the network further reared its ugly head in 2002 when producers circulated a memo stating that programmers should choose more 'telegenic' historians who are forty years or younger, and that these younger historians didn't 'have to be the leading academic on the topic'.[9] Such emphasis on entertainment has led one historian to argue:

> When history is broken down into trivialized stories and jumbled together into an entertaining stew, it loses its capacity to speak to larger questions. 'Fun little stories' about our presidents' martini-making skills don't really help us get a handle on our country's past and what it tells us about where we're heading today.[10]

The History Channel has also come under fire for its emphasis on recent history, especially that of America and Western Europe. Critics and viewers were frustrated by its failure to depict non-western cultures. Responding to the criticism, the History Channel spun off History International, a sister network in 1998. As History International with its slogan 'Globalize Yourself!' (1998–2003) began to extend its international reach, the executives entered a series of joint ventures with local producers in order to fill in its schedule. Its web site proclaims:

> With more than 200 hours of original programming from around the world, HISTORY INTERNATIONAL provides viewers with an enriching mix of historical documentaries with a global focus, original short features, interviews with historians, and exclusive programmes made or acquired in conjunction with our international partners. (http://www.historyinternational.com/)

With series such as *Drive thru History: Conquest of America* (2005), *Past Life Investigation* (with CBC, 2006), *Guns of the World* (2006) and *One Hundred Years of Terror* (2000), the network has continued its propensity for broad and sensational subjects, a common pressure for nonfictional programmes in the highly competitive multichannel world of cable. Yet Edgerton and Nicholas maintain that since the channel has a twenty-four-hour, seven-day-a-week schedule, it has also had to solicit foreign documentaries to fill time. This developing world programming has allowed alternative styles and perspectives from Europe, South America and Asia into the world of TV documentaries.

Although informational production draws from the world of documentary for its productions, cable TV looks for neutral entertainers to make its works. According to Charles Maday, the senior vice-president of programming, History's producers are not historians but 'interested' in history. They come out of the reality, news or magazine programmes of commercial TV. They are not political activists; they depend on historians to set the agenda. The History Channel creates the core 'original' idea for its various programmes but it commissions one of about twelve independent production companies to produce the programme. The historical content of the programmes can get lost in the commercial basis of the network: sensational topics and competition with the programmes of other cable channels often supersede historical content.[11] For example, the History Channel commissioned Original Productions to do *Ice Road Truckers* (2007–), a series about truckers who deliver supplies to diamond mines near the Arctic. Original is a small TV production house in Burbank, California run by a husband-and-wife team since 1999. Although the production company films the truckers on location in the Arctic, the vast majority of their production process involves editing down the footage in Los Angeles studios. In the show's first season, it cost $500,000 to produce an hour-long episode – inexpensive programming when compared to the $3 million-per-hour cost of network scripted programming and $1.5 to $2 million for a reality episode. Its final episode garnered 5 million viewers, making it one of the more popular series on cable. Its exceptional popularity marks *Ice Road Truckers* main difference from the other series produced by the company for its main cable outlet, the Discovery Channel (*Monster Garage*, 2002–6, *Monster House*, 2003–6, *Biker Build-Off*, 2002– and the Emmy-nominated *Deadliest Catch*, 2005–). However, this production house exemplifies how nonfiction producers also become 'niched' for their content (e.g., chronicling hazardous or extreme jobs).

The History Channel is distinguished by its successful merchandising, indicating the growing centrality of marketing in the post-network world. It is doing what modern cultural corporations must to ensure exposure of their products – becoming a conglomerate, spreading into every possible market, and branding. It has negotiated numerous agreements with book publishers, and the New York City public-school system is working with the channel. In 1996, the channel ran a college contest where film and TV students were invited to produce a thirty-second advertisement for the channel's *Digging for the Truth*, with the winner receiving $1,000. In addition, that year the channel awarded cash prizes to teachers who introduced local history to enhance history and social studies units in the 2005–6 school year. It also awarded scholarships of up to $5,000 to students who helped document or preserve their local history. In 2007, it piloted two new online courses with the State University of New York–Maritime College. Both courses were based on History Channel series. According to historian Kevin Matson, 'Today, the HC stands as the most visible form of popular history – the couch potato version of popular museums, reconstructed historical towns, and military reenactments.' It can no longer be just a network devoted to history programmes; rather, it also markets itself as part of the community and school systems. Hopefully the History Channel can generate an emotional tie to the network through popularising history at all levels of experience. Ultimately it aims to craft audience loyalty through its overwhelming offerings in cable programming.[12]

CASE STUDY: THE HISTORY CHANNEL and *BEYOND THE DA VINCI CODE* (2005)

Beyond the Da Vinci Code typifies the kind of documentaries produced for the History Channel. The programme explored the alternative Biblical history suggested by Dan Brown's bestselling novel, *The Da Vinci Code* (2003). The film depicted the relationship of Jesus and Mary Magdalene, the Priory of Sion and the medieval church. The documentary attempts to air the 'true story' behind the fiction. In other words, it was part of the History Channel's ongoing attempt to tell the 'truth', to cut through commercial and historical fictions and to create brand loyalty. Noted for its high production values, the Weller/Grossman film exemplified one of many documentaries for cable networks that tried to capitalise on the inflammatory speculation of this novel.

Box 5.1 Documentaries about *The Da Vinci Code* on cable (2003–7)

- *Legend Hunters: The Holy Grail – The Real Story* (Discovery/Travel Channel 2003)
- *In Search of the Holy Grail* (Learning Channel/Discovery Communications/New York Times 2003)
- *Investigating History: The Holy Grail* (History Channel/Kurtis Productions Ltd 2004)
- *Behind the Mysteries: Unlocking Da Vinci's Code – The Full Story* (National Geographic Channel/ABC News Productions 2004)
- *Conspiracies on Trial: The Da Vinci Code* (Discovery Channel/Outline Productions 2005)
- *Da Vinci Declassified* (Learning Channel/Beantown Productions/ Discovery Communications, Inc. 2005)
- *The Templar Code* ('*Decoding the Past*' series on History Channel/ Windworks Media Group, Inc. 2005)
- *Legend Detectives: The Mystery of Rennes-le-Château* (Discovery Channel/IPM TV Ltd 2005)
- *The Secret Bible: Knights Templar – Warriors of God* (National Geographic Channel/Morningstar Entertainment 2006)
- *The Da Vinci Code – Bloodlines* ('Digging for the Truth' series on History Channel/JWM Productions, LLC 2006)
- *Da Vinci's Code* ('*Is It Real?*' series on National Geographic Television & Film Production 2006)
- *Da Vinci: Seeking the Truth* (Time Warner Cable/Contenuti Productions & Media/Rai Trade 2006)
- *The Lost Tomb of Jesus* (Discovery Channel, Vision TV & Channel 4 2007)

Beyond the interviews with scholars, the film is organised around reenactment footage to bring life to the elements of speculation in the book's plot, including the origins of the Knights Templar, early records of the Priory of Sion, Mary Magdalene, theories of the Holy Grail and hidden interpretations in Leonardo Da Vinci's paintings. Commercial documentaries depend on formulas for profit as much as broadcast fictional programmes such as *Law & Order* do. The formula follows classic cable-network logic: it starts with a bestselling novel (often paraliterature or mass-market fiction) that gives the documentary currency and a built-in audience. Its exploration of history involves more style than content. Experts include: Oxford Professor Karen Ralls, religious-history author Timothy Freke and Richard Leigh, the co-author of *Holy Blood, Holy Grail*, and the 1982 book upon which *The Da Vinci Code* based much of its history.

Images of a handsome Jesus kissing Mary Magdalene illustrate the novel's suggestion that the two were romantically involved. The actor Edward Herrmann narrates the film with a strong, authoritative voiceover as the film vouchsafes a speculative history that contradicts mainstream religious history. The programme was exceptional in its expensive production values, shooting in places like Rosslin Chapel in Scotland, the London Temple (built by the Knights Templar), various cities in southern France, and at the Louvre pyramid, all of which are featured in the book. The majority of the reenactments were shot in the Weller/Grossman studios in LA.

Like most cable documentaries, the majority of the film results from post-production as the makers whittled down thousands of feet of footage and created the special effects to make its ninety minutes. Its unusual opulence can

Reenactment scene from *Beyond the Da Vinci Code*

be seen as resulting from the network wanting to employ it as a showcase announcing its move to widescreen, high-definition programming. The film was nominated for two Emmy Awards. The production was also included in the three-DVD commercial release of *The Da Vinci Code* motion picture. It was later reworked by BBC2, cutting its length in half and adding more critical commentary. This repackaging exemplifies the 'repurposing' that cable networks now carry out in order to capitalise on new revenues when cable broadcast advertising profits are not as great as those of the networks.

The film premiered on 16 January 2005 on the History Channel and aired again on 17 January 2005. Weller/Grossman describes itself as 'a leader in reality, service, documentary, informational and entertainment television with the production of more than 9000 shows'.[13] It typifies the new 'independent' documentary company, producing commercially oriented non-scripted programmes. Weller/Grossman Productions is unusually large for an independent production unit and is therefore able to make a range of documentaries: *Healing the Hate* (1996), which garnered the Governor's Emmy Award for Exemplary Programming, *The Turnaround* (2005) for CNN, *BBQ with Bobby Flay* (1996–) for the Food Network, *That's Clever* (2005–) for Home and Garden TV (HGTV); *Decoding the Past: The Prophecies of Israel* (2005) for the History Channel. It made other productions for the Food Network, National Geographic Channel, Sci-Fi Channel, Discovery Health Network, DIY, ESPN, Discovery Channel, TLC, Telemundo, NBC, ABC and Fox Fit TV. But even Weller/Grossman is beginning to feel the pinch as cable begins to establish its own 'Big Three' networks – A&E, History and Discovery – which are increasingly turning to inhouse production.

DISCOVERY CHANNEL

Discovery mirrors A&E in its genesis as a major cable network. It was launched in 1985 as one of that first generation of utility-brand documentary networks. It focused broadly on technology, science and history or what the network calls 'human adventure'. John Hendricks, an educational fundraiser and later a producer of educational documentaries for cable, persuaded a number of broadcast and cable companies (Cox, Newhouse and United) to put up the money with Group W providing satellite access. The network was offered as a basic cable service where three-quarters of its productions were to be new. Hendricks states that 'his decision to specialize in such programs was fortified by the fact that 23 of the 24 highest-rated shows in the history of the Public Broadcasting Service – such as *Sharks*, *Land of the Tiger* and portions of the *Nova* series – have been non-fiction'.[14] The network initially succeeded by offering its schedule to cable companies for free because the programme producers entered a profit-sharing agreement with Discovery which allowed programming to be obtained inexpensively. The British Broadcasting Corporation, the Canadian Broadcasting Corporation and the National Film Unit of New Zealand entered into these agreements and became the major sources of Discovery's offerings.

Within three years of its initiation the channel became the biggest buyer of nonfiction programming in America, launched with slogans such as 'Explore your world' and 'There's no thrill like discovery'. Its prime programming format was to adopt 'anthologies' – series organised around a theme – with broad titles such as 'Challenges', 'Festivals' and 'The Global Village'. These documentaries were more about enjoying the world's diversity than investigating any issue. In 1988, it began 'Shark Week' programming –the first branded stunt in cable that still runs today. And in September 1989 it produced its first original programme: *Ivory Wars*, a documentary investigating the illegal trade in elephant tusks. In 1995 the channel won a series of awards for its six-part *Yugoslavia: Death of a Nation*. However, its greatest successes were with two 2000 hits that broke all-time records for cable ratings: *Raising the Mammoth* in March (the documentary about extracting a preserved mammoth from Siberian ice) and *Walking with Dinosaurs*, a co-production with the BBC in April that featured lifesize animatronics dinosaurs playing out how 155 million years of plate tectonics and climate change affected animal evolution. In 2005 the channel co-produced with the BBC and CBC the eleven-episode *Planet Earth* – a chronicle of the earth subdivided into its different parts (e.g., 'From Pole to Pole', 'Mountains', 'Deep Ocean' and 'Deserts'). It was the most-watched cable programme to date with more than 65 million viewers. Nevertheless, Discovery moved slowly away from science and documentaries towards the more popular true-crime genre.

With its initial emphasis on science and technology, the channel drew an upscale audience which in turn appealed to Apple Computer, Raytheon and AT&T and in 1988 the channel began to show a profit. From 1989 on, Discovery Communications started launching Discovery Channels internationally: UK (1989), Latin America (1994), Asia (1994) and France (2004). In 1998 Discovery en Español became the first Spanish-language channel in the US. In 2005 Discovery Networks US Hispanic Group added Discovery Kids en Español and Discovery Travel & Living (Viajar y Vivir), establishing itself as a major presence in the Spanish-speaking community in the US. By 2001 Discovery Communications announced that 'Discovery Channel' had become the world's most widely distributed television brand with a reach of 400 million households.

Like A&E, Discovery began to spin off and acquire new cable networks. After buying the Learning Channel (TLC) in 1991, Discovery Communications created Animal Planet – the first cable network devoted to animal programmes. In 1999 it launched a series of digital networks: Discovery Science, Discovery Kids,

Discovery Civilization, Discovery Home and Leisure and Discovery Wings (the Military Channel in 2005). It acquired the Travel Channel in 1997. The Discovery Health Channel began in 1999. And in 2007 Discovery Home and Leisure morphed from a home-improvement and cooking channel into Planet Green, 'a global, cross-platform initiative including the first-ever 24-hour eco-lifestyle television network',[15] replete with a web site 'Treehugger.com' dedicated to sustainability. In 2008 Discovery spun off Investigation Discovery – an amalgam of true-crime and crime-related programmes from the main channel and its archives. Discovery Channel returned to its original premise: family-oriented documentaries and reality shows.

Further, Discovery has been savvy about marketing and promotion through partnerships. In 1996 Discovery Communications acquired the Nature Company's 114 retail stores and created the Discovery Channel Store chain to sell promotional goods. In 1999 it partnered with the National Park system to make documentaries about each of the parks as well as start a teaching centre at the Washington Monument. With its focus on science, Discovery Communications began the 'Young Scientist Challenge' – a national science competition for students in grades 5 through 8. In 2008 3M signed on as a partner and it became 'The 3M Young Scientist Challenge'. The contest evolved into a video competition for middle-schoolers to make the best one- to two-minute video on a scientific subject. In 2002 NBC partnered with Discovery Kids and produced a block of Saturday-morning programming called *Discovery Kids on NBC*. The Silverdocs, a leading documentary film festival, premiered in 2003 in collaboration with the American Film Institute.

That year the Times Company (publisher of the *New York Times*) allied with Discovery to create Discovery Times, a channel devoted to long-form investigative journalism featuring staff from the newspaper. When that network did not succeed it was branded as 'Investigation Discovery'. Perhaps the most innovative joint venture remains the Discovery Channel Pro Cycling Team in 2005 with Lance Armstrong (seven-times winner of the Tour de France), which has won numerous races under the Discovery banner. A 2008 collaboration between Discovery Communications, the Siemens Foundation and the National Science Teachers Association highlights the way in which cable information-based TV blurs the line between education and commerce with the start of a K-12 student sustainability education project, called 'Siemens We Can Change the World Challenge'.

Because of its science interest and its resulting advertiser base format of Apple Computer, 3M and Raytheon, Discovery Communications has been at the forefront of the cable's switch to new media platforms. Beyond its rich web site DSC.Discovery.com, the channel and its educational wing began COSMEO, a 2006 online homework help tool that assists in research reports and provides educational games for $9.95 a month. That same year, the company rolled out Discoverymobile.com, a mobile web site that provides short-form versions of Discovery programmes for cell-phone viewing. In fact, Discovery Communications began closing its retail stores in favour of DiscoveryStore.com as a shopping platform in 2007. Later that year, the parent company acquired How-StuffWorks.com, a major online resource of high-quality, impartial and clear accounts of how 'stuff' actually works. In 2008 it announced a deal with Oprah Winfrey and her Harpo.Inc. to create a multiplatform media venture called 'OWN or the Oprah Winfrey Network' merging the Discovery Health Network and Oprah.com. Most importantly in 2008 Discovery Communications became a public company proclaiming it had 1.5 billion global subscribers, was seen in 170 countries and territories, was translated into thirty-five languages, and had created twenty-six network entertainment brands.[16]

ANIMAL PLANET

Animal Planet is indicative not only of the rise of niche networks but also demonstrates how cable has popularised educational shows. The network mixes traditional documentary distance with anthropomorphised animals to intensify audience identification and narrative potential. Discovery Channel and BBC Worldwide launched Animal Planet in 1996 in response to viewer desire for a channel devoted to animals. As its motto proclaims ('All animals all the time') the network markets itself as the only outlet for programming devoted to the interaction between animals and humans. The schedule mixes original programmes with shows purchased from the international market. The success of such a niche – animal programming – was proven by the fact that it was the fastest-growing cable channel in the late 1990s. Animal Planet could be seen in 31.4 million homes, out of a possible 72 million homes wired for cable by 1998. By 2007, the network had 92 million subscribers and was seen in seventy countries. Along with the other channels in the Discovery Network – the Discovery Channel, the Learning Channel, Discovery Kids, Discovery Health, the Travel Channel – it remains one of the strongest niche competitors for the Public Broadcasting Service (PBS). It popularises PBS's more educative nature shows by placing a greater emphasis on drama and violence, often creatively constructing complex animal family narratives replete with named animal characters who think and act like humans (e.g., *Meerkat Manor* 2005–).

Emergency Vets (1998–) and *The Crocodile Hunter* (1997–2004) were initially the network's two biggest hits. The first programme chronicles an animal ER in Denver, Colorado, and it won critical praise for the explicit way that it records the physical trauma to pets and the psychological drama of life-and-death decisions made in an animal ER. The latter programme was famed for its unconventional approach in that the host Steve Irwin would jump onto, hold and grab wild animals, creating a highly dramatic televisual spectacle, as opposed to traditional nature documentaries that would observe (but not interact with) wild animals. The programme garnered international fame and was wildly successful until Irwin was killed by a stingray while filming an unrelated show.

In 1998 Animal Planet began to work with two of the top wildlife documentary units – the BBC and Survival Anglia, and by 2006 began to succeed with more traditional observation documentaries. That year, the network began broadcasting *Meerkat Manor* – a British documentary by Oxford Scientific Film. Quite opposite in style from Steve Irwin's series, the meerkat saga was remarkable for its natural unstaged drama. However, the narrator vocalised the thoughts and established the conflict ('Each day the struggle begins') as rival groups of meerkats with their leaders such as the famed Queen Flower do battle to survive in a style reminiscent of CBS's *Survivor*. It quickly became the network's most popular programme with its premiere drawing 1 million viewers. In 2007, the network introduced a similar series: *Orangutan Island* (2007–), which chronicles an island refuge for orphan orangutans such as Cha Cha ('The Social Butterfly') or Jordan ('The Socially Challenged') learning wilderness survival skills as they and their families work out their day-to-day problems. By turning the actions of animals into something akin to a reality TV survival contest, Animal Planet has found success in the marketplace. Even though the BBC sold its 20 per cent share of the network in 2006, the English corporation maintains its fifty per cent ownership in Animal Planet Europe, Animal Planet Asia and Animal Planet Latin America. The network also produces various versions that are specific to India, Canada and other countries, all involving its trademark of creating an emotional bond between human beings and an animal, whether it be a grizzly, mongoose or python.

ORIGINAL FICTION PROGRAMMING ON CABLE NETWORKS
Cable-produced drama has caused the broadcast networks to rethink how they make scripted TV. As a whole, basic cable networks do not produce fictional programming because it costs so much more to make than informational programmes. The broadcast networks still rule the world of primetime fiction because of their audience size, higher advertising revenues and established production system. Yet original fictional programmes still exist on cable networks whose financial mainstay is made up of reruns, sports or informational programmes. These dramas tend to be lower budget, more rough-hewn and much more closely aligned with independent films. The programmes break TV content taboos, posing socially relevant questions and answering them with sexually explicit and violent stories.

This mix of drama and information creates a branding problem. USA Network (USA) has created a number of original programmes (most recently *Monk*, *Psych*, 2006–10 and *The 4400*, 2004–7). In 2007, the cable network took on the production of original *Law & Order: Criminal Intent* episodes after NBC pulled its support of the programme. Nevertheless, the network remains without a clear brand. It is known for mainly sports (primarily tennis) and network reruns (*Law & Order: Criminal Intent* and *House M.D.*), rather than drama. Turner Network Television (TNT) is a comparable basic cable network with a clearer brand centred on old American films and sports. It has also succeeded with several original programmes (*LA Heat*, 1999, *The Closer*, 2005– and *Saving Grace*, 2007–) but there is no clear logic to their placement in the primetime schedule. Launched in 1992, the Sci-Fi Channel, a sister channel to USA Network, is more closely with associated original programming specifically based on science fiction, horror, occult and the paranormal. Its top programmes have been *Battlestar Galactica*, *Farscape* (1999–2003), *Stargate SG-1* (1997–2007), *Eureka* (2006–), *Stargate Atlantis* (2004–9) and *Mystery Science Theater 3000* (1988–99). It is also famed for its miniseries: *Steven Spielberg Presents: Taken* (2003), *Frank Herbert's Dune* (2000), *Children of Dune* (2003) and *Five Days to Midnight* (2004). The network extended its distinctive brand to its web site SCIFI.com, a highly successful site known for its impressive coverage of science-fiction subjects as well as deep background on the programme topics, creating rich transmedia narratives. Launched in 1995, it publishes not only material devoted to the network but has won awards for its original science-fiction and weekly newswire devoted to the science-fiction world – a solid example of building its brand.

However, the FX Network (Fox eXtended Network) has achieved the greatest reputation for original programming in American basic cable. Owned by Fox, FX stands as its flagship general-entertainment cable network, but its content has escaped the conservative agenda of its parent company. Founded in 1994, its originators conceived of the network as existing somewhere in the middle, between the broadcast networks (with their dependence on original programming) and HBO (with its originality and lack of censorship). It successfully branded itself as a network that produces gritty drama known for violent and sexual explicitness. Three programmes have particularly defined its style and content: *The Shield*, *Nip/Tuck* and *Rescue Me* (2004–). *The Shield* was a police drama but one where the police were modelled on the corrupt LA unit, Ramparts. It won critical praise for its edgy depiction of gang life in LA despite being controversial for its extreme violence, sexual explicitness and depiction of police corruption. This low-budget series used handheld cameras, on-location shooting on the streets of LA's South Central, unknown actors and kinetic editing, lending it a highly distinctive look. It remains one of the best examples of how cable, because of its narrowed interests, is more willing to take on innovative and complex programmes. The series won cable's first Emmy for series and actor, along with a Peabody Award.

Beginning in 1993, *Nip/Tuck* follows in the medical-drama tradition but focuses on plastic surgery and its attendant subjects of the body and sex. Its explicitness has led the Parental Television Council to call for a boycott, even though the programme is shown at a late hour. *Rescue Me* chronicles the lives of New York City firefighters post-9/11. The characters roil in a sea of alcoholism, depression and sexual dysfunction; one storyline graphically portrayed the lead character raping his ex-wife. FX has other noteworthy original work: *It's Always Sunny in Philadelphia* (2005–), *Dirt* (2007–8), *The Riches* (2007–8) and *Damages* (2007–). Yet for all its successful 'gritty realist original programming', the majority of FX's schedule is devoted to second-run showings of programmes originally aired on Fox – the basis of basic cable's fictional programming.

THE DISNEY CHANNEL AND *HIGH SCHOOL MUSICAL*

By the mid-2000s the Disney Channel stood as the matchless cross-promotion vehicle for Disney – the largest media corporation in the world as of 2009. Launched in 1983, the network was initially a premium channel devoted to children's fare. It showed primarily Disney programmes – *The Mickey Mouse Club* (1955–96), *Welcome to Pooh Corner* (1983–6), *Donald Duck Presents* (1983) and numerous original teen evening programmes such as *Kids Incorporated* (1984–93). The schedule was supplemented by other foreign and non-Disney-made programmes. By 1989 the phenomenal popularity of its relaunched *The All-New Mickey Mouse Club* (1989–93) cemented the channel's return to music and variety as a focus. By the mid-1990s 'Disney' (its re-branded name) could be found in over 8 million homes. By 2000 the channel was in search of a hipper image trying to throw off its conservative reputation. In 2004 Ann Sweeny was hired as the head of the Disney-ABC Group and began her strategy of nurturing teen stars, which Disney massively cross-promoted to the pre-teen audience with hopes of capturing their allegiance into their teens.

High School Musical, a January 2006 Disney Channel film, best exemplifies the synergy of the Disney multiplatform strategy. It chronicled the difficulties of a budding romance between a basketball player and a math student who want to be in a high school musical together. The film intercuts highly choreographed musical numbers of tryouts, basketball and family life, climaxing in the musical where all the school's factions unite. The channel has always produced original movies but HSM (as it is affectionately known) achieved the all-time highest viewer figures with 7.7 million viewers. Not only did the channel advertise the film and its repeats, it also promoted the album – the biggest-selling LP of 2006.

The song-and-dance sequences in *High School Musical* were repackaged for CDs, music videos, DVDs and retail clothing

Disney released a two-disc DVD set six months after the cablecast – the fastest-selling made-for-TV movie in history. By November the cast and new members had begun a concert tour. The musical spun off as various summer camps and dinner theatres vied to be the first to produce a stage production. In 2007 *High School Musical: The Ice Tour* slid into being, while various video games featured song-and-dance competitions. Not only was a 2006 novel published, Disney Channel produced a less than successful reality TV series – *High School Musical: Get in the Picture* – in 2008. The film sequel *High School Musical 2* premiered in August 2007 and *High School Musical 3: Senior Year* rolled out in October 2008 making $80,000,000 in one weekend – the most profitable musical in history. By 2008 the Disney Channel stood as the highest-grossing revenue stream of the Walt Disney Corporation.

HOME BOX OFFICE

In 2004 *BBC News Online* proclaimed that HBO was 'The Channel That Transformed TV'. The author argued that the network had become 'a benchmark for quality television internationally'.[17] In fact, the network had solidified the newest TV dramatic format: 'quality TV' – a genre historically associated with an audience interested in 'high' cultural pursuits and their accompanying urban, coastal, major-market, 'niche' viewer-consumers'.[18] Because of its high-end audience and subscription income, HBO became the major outlet for original TV on cable. With its subscriber payments and Time Warner financial muscle, it could support the higher cost of fictional programming and the production values of broadcast networks. The subscription basis gave HBO licence to break from the stranglehold of mass tastes that keep much of network and even basic cable from producing original or possibly questionable content. In short, HBO produces high-budget independent films as TV series.

Oddly enough, America's leading premium channel grew out of a small company that won the right to lay the first underground cable in lower Manhattan in 1965. By 1972, the company primarily aired sporting events. A year later, it convinced Time-Life to back it and was absorbed by Time Inc. as a subsidiary. With Time's financial backing, the cable service became a subscription service, continuing its presentation of sports events but also expanding its programming to screening recent movies. By 1986, the channel ran twenty-four hours a day, offering theatrically released movies and sports. Time merged with Warner Bros. in 1989 to become HBO's parent company. The parent company provided an infusion of money to the TV network in the 1990s, and by 2002 HBO represented less than 7 per cent of AOL Time Warner's revenues, but the network was one of its top brands and success stories with its audience of one-third of American households.

In addition to its new financial clout, the growing competition in the cable industry forced HBO into original productions. The success of other premium television networks which showed recently released movies – Showtime (1976), the Movie Channel (1979), Cinemax (HBO's sister network, 1980) and Encore (1991) – burgeoned in the 1980s. These various networks often negotiated exclusive deals with motion-picture companies (e.g., the Movie Channel and Paramount) for the television premiere of their films. HBO countered by forming its own motion-picture production company, TriStar (with Columbia Pictures and CBS). The cable company was strengthened when it received exclusive television rights to Columbia's, 20th Century-Fox's and Silver Screen's movies. In 1983, HBO Pictures began with the first made-for-pay-tv movie, *The Terry Fox Story*. Then HBO Showcase began as HBO's movie studio and was folded into HBO Film. In 1999 HBO Pictures and NYC Productions consolidated as HBO Pictures, which started to distribute HBO films in theatres. Since 2003, HBO Films has received three Oscar nominations: Catalina Sandino Moreno in the Best Actress category for *Maria Full of Grace* (Joshua Marston, 2004, US), *Yesterday* (Darrell Roodt, 2004, US) in the Best Foreign Language Film category and *American Splendor* (Shari Springer Berman/Robert Pulcini, 2003, US) for Best Adapted Screenplay. By 2004, industry newspaper *Screen International* had declared that HBO Films was 'the beating heart of US independent cinema'.[19]

HBO: 'ORIGINAL PROGRAMMING' AS QUALITY BRANDING

In 1983 the *New York Times* described a 'quiet revolution within the television entertainment industry' as the cable networks had begun to earn enough profit to enable them to produce original programming whose quality rivalled if not topped the quality of the best network television.[20] HBO's original programming had begun as early as 1975 with *On Location* (stand-up comedians in concert). Its frank content broke from the constraints of broadcast television and presented a substantive shift in the style and content of American TV. As a cable network, HBO has never been held to the strictures concerning nudity, profanity and violence that affect broadcast media. The subscription nature gave the network licence to show explicit material, up to and including soft pornography such as *Taxicab Confessions* (1995–). More importantly, without advertisers it did not have to attract the broad audience that commercial broadcast TV predicates. It had a potential for creative latitude not seen in any other TV network. Nevertheless, HBO had to attract subscribers. It needed to differentiate its product so that subscribers would be willing to pay the premium cost of $10–12 a month. HBO furnishes a casebook example of how 'quality' can be branded as a product. Original programming became a central part of HBO's branding strategy.

HBO executives pinpoint 1983 as the year that HBO got serious about original programming. The arrival of the VCR and video-rental market caused interest in viewing movies on TV to plummet. Network-made series allowed a measure of financial independence from movie distributors who were exacting high prices for screening films on TV. But it also permitted an increase in the variety of programme types that most viewers associated with TV so HBO was able to present a breadth of offerings.[21] *Not Necessarily the News* (1983–90), a mixture of news and sketch comedy premiered on HBO as its first foray into fiction. Then *1st & Ten* (1984–91) introduced its subscribers to the vagaries of a fictional football team. *Fraggle Rock* (1983–7), a children's programme featuring Muppets was co-produced with the Canadian Broadcast Corporation. Two anthology series also aired: *The Hitchhiker* (1983–7) and *Tales from the Crypt* (1989–96). *The Larry Sanders Show*, a sitcom about a neurotic talk-show host, was the first original show to attract new subscribers due to its critical success. It stood as HBO's flagship programme throughout the 1990s without any other HBO series coming close in popularity.

For all its desire to produce original programming, HBO provided only small production budgets when it commissioned series in the early 1990s. For example, a 1991 HBO series, *Women and Me*, consisted of three thirty-minute shows that adapted short stories. It had a budget of around $3 million. The stars, Melanie Griffith, James Woods and Elizabeth McGovern, got $50,000. The producer David Brown, who gave up his salary to make the series, claims: 'This was an opportunity to do something perfect and small, to flex our muscles, and do it quickly and exquisitely'.[22] The business logic of producing low-budget, somewhat off-beat programming lay in the hope that HBO would attract critical praise and would be seen as the 'quality' network. One network vice-president argued:

> When we green-light a programme, we may say it's not going to get great ratings, but it will get unbelievable reviews and get awards … . We are very strategic about each show. One might be for ratings; one for the press. That's part of HBO's mission.[23]

HBO strategy was to draw elite or quality audiences willing to pay a fee for a premium service. As its subscription base grew across the 1990s, so did HBO's interest in more expensive and provocative programming. In 1999 the network commissioned two well-known directors, Barry Levinson and Tom Fontana, to develop and produce a series. The result, *Oz*, was the network's first hour-long dramatic series. More importantly, it was highly controversial in that it depicted prison life with all its graphic brutality. The producers took advantage of the freedom allowed on cable to create a new kind of TV realism: violence, drugs, homosexuality, nudity, rape and racial conflict. The six-year-long series gave HBO a product that featured a qualitative difference: original programming with an explicitness not found on broadcast TV.

The network's 'golden years' were from 1998 through 2007 as it consolidated its 'quality' brand. By 2001, HBO was spending $1 billion on original programming per year. It generated an array of original programme types: sports, original movies, documentaries, original series and specials. But it was its original scripted programming – specifically, two solid hits – that drove its reputation and ultimately its success. *Sex and the City* was a sitcom devoted to the complex lives of single women in New York in the 1990s. Its final episode in 2004 played to 10.6 million viewers. *The Sopranos* premiered in 1999 and lasted until 2007 (see below). The network's other solid successes in that period were: *Six Feet Under*, the saga of a family which runs a funeral home; *Deadwood* (2004–6), a violent Western set in South Dakota in the 1870s; and *Curb Your Enthusiasm* (2000–), Larry David's socially 'uncomfortable' sitcom about life after producing *Seinfeld*.

Entourage (2004–) – a comedy about a Hollywood star and his high school friends in Hollywood – drew only 1.5 million viewers per episode (about half the audience of *Curb Your Enthusiasm*). But in the world of premium TV, 'who watches' is more important than the size of the audience. The series appeals to the young city dwellers who are perceived to drive the pop-cultural chatter. 'It's absolutely doing what it should be doing', says HBO's Carolyn Strauss. 'The numbers don't play into our thinking as much as the buzz.'[24] Although sub-scriptions are the bedrock of premium TV, a newer driving force in HBO's original programming is the through DVD sales by 2004. Both *The Sopranos* and *Sex and the City* were able to recoup production costs in sales of the early sea-sons. Between DVDs, syndication and theatrical movies, 20 per cent of HBO's revenue came from non-subscription sources.

When *The Sopranos* ended in spring 2007, HBO had no comparable hit to keep up its reputation and therefore viewership. *Curb Your Enthusiasm*'s popu-larity soared in its third season, only for it to suffer a 50 per cent decline in its viewership in 2005. That year critics began to question the network's ability to maintain its level of success as many of its series declined in popularity. Although HBO had 28 million subscribers, other premium networks were beginning to mount a challenge. In particular, Showtime, with only 13 million subscribers, began to diversify its programming from being a niche network friendly to gay programming (*Queer as Folk*, *The L Word* and *Queer Duck*, 2002–4) to a more diverse and highly touted premium network in 2006–7 with *Weeds* (about a pot-selling suburban soccer mom, 2005–), *Dexter* (about a sympathetic serial killer, 2006–), *The Tudors* (a BBC period drama series, 2007–), *Sleeper Cell* (about an American terrorist group, 2005–6) and *Californication* (about a dissolute novel-ist, 2007–) – all series which offered the edgy, socially relevant content for which HBO was known. Additionally, FX began to make HBO-style original pro-grammes that explored the grey areas and shadiness of American life with *The Shield*, *Nip/Tuck*, *Rescue Me*, and *30 Days* (2005–8). HBO subscriptions began to flatten out by 2001 as the network lost its reputation as the only source of novel TV. By 2000, compression and the resulting increase in bandwidth allowed for an increase in the number of premium channels on cable. HBO packaged the original network with six other HBO channels: HBO2, HBO Latino, HBO Signature, HBO Family, HBO Comedy and HBO Zone. Epstein, Reeves and Rogers maintain that this bundling of seven networks under the HBO banner most probably diluted its audience and therefore its brand.[25]

CASE STUDY: *THE SOPRANOS*

When **The Sopranos** – the story of the trials and tribulations of a modern Amer-ican mob boss – premiered in 1999, it was immediately apparent that this was no ordinary gangster TV series. Slowly, a complex vision of the failure of the American Dream unreeled as it took on old and new money, class mobility, the psychology of violence and the fine line between capitalism and criminality in America. Its qualitative difference was ensured by its film production methods. Filmed on location in the butcher shops and strip joints of New Jersey and on the lot at Silvercup Studios in Long Island City, Queens, the series drew its directors from television and the New York independent film scene. It was filmed primarily by the Russian-born cinematographer Alik Sakharov, who broke scenes down into single shots before shooting to give it a feature quality. The programme began with an audience of 13.4 million viewers but by its fourth season that number had increased to 24 million – making it the most-watched show in the history of HBO and a defining cultural event. According to Epstein, Reeves and Rogers, HBO valued the series not only for its critical praise but also because it created 'buzz' – industry slang for word-of-mouth marketing. It made viewers want to pay a premium rate to subscribe to HBO and to be in the 'know' about a cultural event. Many industrial analysts credit *The Sopranos* for driving HBO subscription up to 28 million by 2005. When the show ended in 2007, HBO had more than 40 million subscribers.

HBO's 'quality' marketing campaign, which focused on the making of *The Sopranos* (the aesthetic process), was so successful that it has entered American lore as the Internet, newspapers and magazines created a media frenzy around the series. The pilot 'Made in Jersey', with the basic conceit – a mobster sees a psychiatrist – was commissioned by Fox but the network then turned it down. HBO then picked the series up as a result of its growing commitment to producing original programming. In total, the series encompasses eighty-six episodes that aired over six seasons. Without the pressure of commercials, advertisers or a network schedule, the series had more latitude to create its drama with varying season and episode length. Typically, a season ran thirteen episodes. But the last or sixth season was split into two parts and ran for twenty-one episodes with some commentators arguing that it really constituted two separate seasons. Episode length varied from just under sixty minutes for its pilot to forty-five minutes for a number of episodes. Additionally, there were major delays between seasons, unlike broadcast's predictable three–four-month summer break. The final season appeared after an eighteen-month hiatus. Such flexibility allowed the series to develop a richer, four-act storytelling structure than network drama, which typically depends on three acts. As a serialised work, the programme typically closed one or two plotlines in an episode. When it began, the series interwove four or five ongoing plotlines across a series of episodes. As it gained stability as a series, the producers simplified its drama by reducing the number of continuing plotlines.

Without the strictures of broadcast television, *The Sopranos* broke a number of American TV drama taboos. The subscription basis of HBO allowed *The Sopranos* to engage in the filmic conventions of the genre with the requisites of extreme violence and sex affording a scandalous (and much publicised) alternative to sanitised network drama. However, the series was infused with irony. It often portrayed its violent moments right up against classically sentimental family scenes,

The 'Pine Barrens' episode of season 3 of *The Sopranos* exemplifies how the series combined the gangster genre with the lack of clear closure common in the art cinema

producing a rich play of mockery with the Soprano clan's pretension to normalcy. The series continued to undercut its construction of the American Dream through its play of camerawork as it refocused on a telling detail or a single song at the end of an episode which commented on the overt plot.

Nevertheless, it was the psychological depth of the series that generated the greatest critical praise. By interweaving aspects of Tony Soprano's violent life as a New Jersey mob boss with his visits to his psychologist, the producers created a work that entered the worlds of high and low cultures. The crime story is an easily recognisable example of a popular-culture tradition based on the arc of the rise and fall of a gangster and his family. However, the generic shift into the realm of art comes with its parallel plot: the therapy sessions. David Bordwell has outlined the five main traits of the art cinema and art television: violations of classical space and time, a loosening of causality, a greater emphasis on psychological or anecdotal realism, authorial commentary and ambiguity. Thompson cites *The Singing Detective* (BBC, 1986) and *Twin Peaks* (ABC, 1990–1) as examples of art television.[26] Both moved between a number of very loosely connected plots, creating an ambiguity that could only be resolved by understanding that there is an author/director commenting on the irony of the content through breaks in traditional causality. *The Sopranos* does not rival these two well-known art television works, which tested the popular audience's ability to enjoy modernist storytelling. Rather, the HBO series offered the parallel world of psychological explanation – Melfi's Freudian rewritings of Tony's stories of macho bravado – to the traditional cause-and-effect storytelling of television. Further, it nods to the notion of psychological realism that pervaded the European art-cinema films of Ingmar Bergman and Federico Fellini. The irony of camerawork and music can further be understood as an art-cinema technique where writer/executive producer David Chase ('the author') is commenting – another double text. Finally, the much-disputed close of the series – the abrupt cut to black from a tension-filled scene of the Soprano family in a diner – can be understood as an ode to art-cinema realism: the refusal of a neat explanation.

CONCLUSION

It's no surprise: TV programming is narrowing its scope to much more specific content than the family-appeal shows of the broadcasting era. More fascinating are the diverse paths that unscripted and scripted programming have gone down. Information has gone the way of popularising narrow educational TV genres – nature, do-it-yourself and documentaries. Cable networks have taken unexciting and intellectual material and made it accessible by putting humans at the centre of every filmable situation and then 'narrativising' it by imposing a conflict, a climax and a resolution. These effective tools increase audience identification and breadth whether this involves interactions with animals, natural disaster or economic news. With stories of battles and triumphs, the producers broaden the appeal of what were once dry and uninteresting subjects. So effective is this strategy that when Queen Flower, the lead matron meerkat, died on Animal Planet's *Meerkat Manor*, it was a top news item.

Original scripted TV programmes produced for cable such as HBO's *The Sopranos* or FX's *The Shield* have done the opposite. Narrowcasting for cable drama has meant tightening the focus to reach a more rarefied 'quality audience' with complex stories, more socially relevant topics and potentially objectionable content. Consider the 'Pine Barrens' episode of *The Sopranos* where small-time criminals Paulie and Christopher wander without aim, freezing in a woods, for an entire episode only to find their way without fanfare – much like the art-cinema classic Antonioni's *L'avventura* (Michelangelo Antonioni, 1960, Italy). Both art film and TV show make a statement about the arbitrariness and meaninglessness of life – a far cry from the easy resolutions of network dramas. Consider the character of Vic Mackey of *The Shield* as a corrupt police detective who, to the very end of the series, remained a violent and morally ambiguous figure that could rival any of the complex characterisations in *The Godfather* films (Francis Ford Coppola, 1972, 1974, 1990, US). The narrowcasting or 'niching' of American TV cannot be categorised as a simple broadening of tastes or a more rarefied experience. Rather, it is more about dividing the audience into subgroups based only in part on tastes. It is a much more complex system of marketing based on social economic class, education, race and gender. Those possible combinations have made the narrowing of television a less predictable and perhaps more rewarding experience than any other moment on network TV.

NOTES

1. Christopher Anderson, 'The Long Tail', *Wired* vol. 12, no. 10 (October 2004) <http://www.wired.com/wired/archive/12.10/tail.html>.

2. Owen Gibson, 'The Story of the Long Tail', *The Guardian* 10 July 2006: 5.

3. Christopher Anderson, *The Long Tail: Why the Future of Business Is Selling Less of More*. New York: Hyperion, 2006: 166.

4. Sylvia Chan-Olmsted and Yungwook Kim, 'The PBS Brand versus Cable Brands: Assessing the Brand Image of Public Television in a Multi-channel Environment', *Journal of Broadcasting and Electronic Media* vol. 46 (2002): 305.

5. Amanda Lotz, *The Television Will Be Revolutionized*. New York: New York University Press, 2007: 14.

6. Julie Salamon, 'History That Calls for a Bit of the Ham', *New York Times* 3 November 2002: 2.1.

7. Ibid: 2.

8. Gary R. Edgerton and Kyle Nicholas, 'I Want My Niche TV', in *Thinking outside the Box: A Contemporary Television Genre Reader*, eds. Gary R. Edgerton and Brian G. Rose. Lexington: University Press of Kentucky, 2005: 256.

9. Kate Coe, 'On the Prowl for Telegenic Experts', *Chronicle of Higher Education* vol. 49 (1 August 2003): C3.

10. Kevin Mattson, 'Channeling History', *Dissent* vol. 52, no. 4 (Fall 2005): 74.

11. Ronald J. Grele, 'An Interview with Charles Maday Jr. of the History Channel', *OAH Newsletter* vol. 28, no. 4 (2000) <http://www.oah.org/pubs/nl/2000nov/maday.html>.

12. Mattson, 'Channeling History': 76.

13. See <http://www.wellergrossman.com/.>

14. Steve Schneider, 'Cable TV Notes: A Channel with a Difference', *New York Times* 16 June 1985: 28.

15. See <http://corporate.discovery.com/our-company/company-timeline/>.

16. 'A World of Discovery: Facts & Figures', *Globe: A Quarterly Newsletter from Discovery Communications* September 2008: 11.

17. Neil Smith, 'The Channel That Transformed TV', *BBC News Online* 25 February 2004 <http://news.bbc.co.uk/1/hi/entertainment/tv_and_radio/3485916.stm>.

18. Catherine Johnson, 'Tele-branding in TVIII: The Network as Brand and the Programme as Brand', *New Review of Film and Television Studies* vol. 5, no. 1 (2007): 5–24.

19. Smith, 'The Channel That Transformed TV'.

20. Sally Bedell, 'Pay TV Challenges the Networks', *New York Times* 3 April 1983: 2.1.

21. Deborah L. Jarmillo, 'The Family Racket: AOL Time Warner, HBO, *The Sopranos*, and the Construction of a Quality Brand', *Journal of Communication Inquiry* vol. 26, no. 1 (January 2002): 59–75.

22. Ann Hornaday, 'Television; Programming for Reputation. And Profit', *New York Times* 7 November 1993: 2.37.

23. Devin Gordon, 'Part of the "Entourage"? *Newsweek* 22 August 2005 <http://www.newsweek.com/id/56509>.

24. Ibid.

25. Michael M. Epstein, Jimmie L. Reeves and Mark C. Rogers, 'Surviving "The Hit": Will *The Sopranos* Still Sing for HBO?', in *Reading The Sopranos: Hit TV from HBO*, ed. David Lavery. New York: I. B. Tauris, 2006: 19.

26. Kristin Thompson, *Storytelling in Film and Television*. Cambridge, MA: Harvard UP, 2003: 110–35.

6

The New Economies of TV Information

Post-network TV is marked by the growing dominance of unscripted television in all its variety. TV is shifting from a medium known primarily for fictional programming to a vehicle for information. It is important that we shift our thinking away from the term 'reality TV' and look at all its complex manifestations within six major subgenres as television takes on special or narrowed interests. This development involves tracing the industrial and cultural origins of each subgenre, as they have moved away from mimicking the US networks to raid the TV formats of other countries (Britain and Japan) as well as magazines and newspapers in the search for network brands or programme concepts. All news cable networks (CNN, MSNBC and FOX News) should now be understood as a form of the branding of political difference as they set brands based on liberal, middle-of-the-road and conservative values. The daytime issue-oriented topics of *The Oprah Winfrey Show* and *The Phil Donahue Show* (1967–96) have evolved into new reality subgenres (blind dates, contests and confessions) that feature 'real' events and people. Network game shows have evolved into the contest and contrast-and-compare formats and their various derivations: *American Idol*, *Wife Swap* (2003–) and *The Apprentice*.

This chapter looks at how American TV has transmuted, from the serious public-service orientation of the networks and PBS when delivering information, to the growing cable phenomenon of infotainment – nonfiction and entertainment in the quest for greater audiences and profits. Consider how the history of the cinéma vérité documentaries from public television has been incarnated commercially, beginning with *COPS*, then MTV's *The Real World* and later *The Osbournes* (2002–5) and *The Simple Life* (2003–7). The rise of makeover programmes (whether the subject is the body or home) serves to demonstrate our fascination with watching the transformation of average people's circumstances – *Queer Eye for the Straight Guy* (2003–7), *Extreme Makeover*, *Trading Spaces* or *Black.White* (2006). Even the 'do-it-yourself' format brings together the makeover element and the direct-sell format of QVC to advertise with product tie-ins. But ultimately what holds all these together is infotainment – the popularisation of information.

NETWORKS AND INFORMATION

Serious informational programming was never lucrative for the broadcast networks. NBC, ABC and CBS were primarily concerned with entertainment rather than education. There were two main reasons behind the rise of news networks and related programmes. First, the networks wanted to prove their seriousness and social responsibility in the face of criticism of their crass commercialism. Second, such programmes were motivated by the requirement to provide public-service programming in exchange for lucrative station contracts. During their first thirty years, the networks conveyed their civic engagement primarily through three genres: news, news magazines and talk shows. In 1948/9, all three networks had ten- to-fifteen-minute nightly news broadcasts. By the 1960s the networks felt even greater pressure to prove their worth after Newton Minow's famed speech that declared television to be a 'vast wasteland'. The networks turned to their news divisions to reclaim their reputations. They increased the news to its present half-hour format in 1963. Nightly news then became a staple of the networks – the flagship programme.

During the network radio period, news had always been seen as a prestige format (albeit a less than profitable one). In the 1930s, NBC had cornered the market on entertainment and star-driven programming. CBS under William Paley calculated that the listeners might want more information. In 1931, Paley hired Edward Klauber from the *New York Times* and Paul White from United Press and began putting together a rock-solid news division. CBS radio news laid the foundation of a reputation that carried into television. In 1937, Edward R. Murrow started reporting from London; his first-person reportage of events like the Anschluß, the Blitz and later the Nazi death-camp liberation became a standard of detailed hard-hitting news. His programme and staff evolved into CBS's news division of the 1950s. Throughout the 1960s network news was defined by a half-hour evening programme hosted by signature anchormen, which led into the primetime programming. From 1962 to 1981 Walter Cronkite anchored CBS News – the top-rated news show for nineteen years. NBC's *Huntley-Brinkley Report* began in 1956 with an anchoring duo that lasted twenty-six years. Peter Jennings anchored *ABC World News Tonight* (1983–2005) for over twenty years. At the time news was understood to be in the public interest and was therefore limited to national and international events that affected the social, economic and political lives of Americans. But by the 1990s the creeping pressures of ratings overwhelmed the genre. National evening news had become more upbeat and driven by visuals and entertainment.

Long-form documentaries were the offspring of the news-focused 1950s and 1960s. Both CBS and NBC began with compilation documentaries of previously shot footage, forerunners of the programmes broadcast by the History and Military Channels. NBC's *Victory at Sea* (1952–3) aired patriotic programmes showing World War II sea battles (see previous chapter). CBS's *Twentieth Century* (1957–66) used newsreel footage to tell the history of the first half of the century. Fearing government regulation and trying to maintain their reputations against the 'wasteland', the networks began to produce more full-length non-fiction works. The accessibility of 16 mm technology helped create a generation of independent makers.

As America liberalised, the early 1960s marked the glory days of the independent TV documentaries. Drew Associates screened *Primary* (Robert Drew, 1960, US), *Yanki, No!* (Robert Drew, 1960, US) and *In Crisis: Behind a Presidential Commitment* (Robert Drew, 1963, US) on TV at the start of the 1960s. In fact, many critics describe 1961/2 as the high watermark for TV documentaries, with over 250 hours airing and each network featuring a weekly show dedicated to the form – NBC's *White Paper* (1960), CBS's *CBS Reports* (1959–95) and ABC's *Bell and Howell Close Up!* (1960). As America began to polarise over the Vietnam War, it had a cooling effect on the networks' desire to be political. President Richard Nixon actively attacked the networks as bastions of liberalism. The last hurrah of advocacy documentaries on the networks came in 1971 when CBS ran *The Selling of the Pentagon*, which provoked a Congressional investigation into the questionable manipulation of public opinion by the military. By the Reagan years in the 1980s, the long-form documentary had disappeared from the networks.

Beyond news programmes, news magazines have been the second most common way to convey information on networks. In 1951, Edward R. Murrow and Fred Friendly invented the American news magazine. Their series, *See It Now* (1951–9), stood as the model for television documentaries for years. Instead of a one- or two-hour length, this programme distilled issues to several short documentaries in an hour. The *See It Now* producers did not shy away from controversy: they simulated a nuclear attack on New York; they chronicled the plight of migrant farmers; and they famously probed McCarthyism. They generally began their investigative reports from scratch, without recourse to prior material. They created powerful news stories, filming their own material without a script. It resulted in enlightening and spontaneous interviews such as the one with Joseph McCarthy. The programme acquired a reputation for fierce independence. In 1955, its sponsor, Alcoa, refused to publicise some programmes and finally withdrew its sponsorship. By 1958 the series was reduced to occasional broadcasts. Not only did Murrow and Friendly invent the news-magazine format for TV documentaries but they also tested editorial advocacy for documentaries on a commercial medium.

News magazines have been a more profitable but small portion of the schedule over the years. CBS's *60 Minutes* remains the longest-running and most influential. Started by *See It Now* alumni, the programme is structured around three long-form news stories with the expressed logic of lending greater investigative depth to news stories. The programme can be equated with *the fifth estate* (1975–) in Canada and *Panorama* (1953–) in Britain. Although the series has involved serious investigative journalism (tobacco companies, the US Army and chemical companies), *60 Minutes* structures its confrontational news stories as dramas revolving around clear protagonists and antagonists. The programme has built up its correspondents to be well-known personalities. It eschewed the detail and moral complexity of hard news as it grew to be more entertaining and broadly acceptable. Often it mixes in entertainment news and interviews with entertainers. Relatively cheap to produce in comparison to TV drama, the format has succeeded commercially; *60 Minutes* has been one of CBS's most highly rated programmes. By 1993 it competed with six other news magazines in primetime e.g., NBC's *Dateline* (1992–) and ABC's *Primetime Live* (1989–).

Infotainment, or the presenting of information in entertaining ways, seemed to have triumphed in the 1990s. From the evening news to the news magazine, the traditional division between the public and private sphere became more ambiguous under the growing pressure for larger profits as the networks shifted ownership. Programmes shifted from covering politics and world events to concentrate more on human-interest and celebrity-culture stories. However, this mixing of light entertainment with the news began in 1952 with NBC's *The Today Show*, the third-longest continuously running network programme. Known elsewhere as 'breakfast television', this morning format mixes news and talk show. *Today* has remained the most popular breakfast magazine despite attempts by the other networks to create comparable programmes (ABC's *Good Morning America*, 1975– and CBS's *The Early Show*, formerly *The Morning Show*, 1989–). As weekday-morning programmes, they slowly shift their focus across the two- to four-hour length: first comes the breaking news needs of the commuter (hard news and weather) then a slow move to the domestic issues of the stay-at-home viewer (cooking, how-to-dos and entertainment chat). Anchored by female/male duos and a set of secondary personalities (weatherperson and interviewer), the programme signifies the persona of the networks as a morning parallel to the nightly news. Highly popular (*The Today Show* with its 5–6 million viewers in 2005/6), these news/entertainment hybrid shows have served as staging grounds for network news personalities and future evening anchors. However, the networks have traditionally divided the day into daytime for light entertainment or female-oriented programmes and reserved evenings for serious or male-oriented programming. For example, Katie Couric departed from her successful morning news position on NBC's *Today* in 2006 to become the first solo female anchor for CBS's evening news. This was a highly controversial move given not only her gender but her association with light entertainment.

Infotainment genres have always been associated with such liminal periods of the network schedule. Entertainment news magazines such as the tabloid-oriented *Entertainment Tonight* (1981–) and *Inside Edition* (1989–) act as a segue between the evening news and primetime fictional programming. The network celebrity talk shows such as NBC's *The Tonight Show*, CBS's *Late Night with David Letterman* (1982–93), and NBC's *Late Night with Conan O'Brien* (1993–), where hosts conduct interviews with celebrities and newsmakers between performances have been relegated to 'late night' (10:30 pm to 2:00 am). Nevertheless, these shows have been central to the networks' revenue. *The Tonight Show*, running continuously since 1954, has been the biggest money-maker in the history of the networks. A very different kind of talk show – the confessional – can be found mainly during the daytime as an outgrowth of public-affairs- and women-oriented programming. Programmes such as *The Phil Donahue Show* and *The Oprah Winfrey Show* began with an issue-oriented format where average people discuss a personal or personalised political issue (obsessive compulsive disorder, teenage pregnancy or racism) with the host, an expert and the audience. They also revealed a lighter side when they veered off into self-improvement episodes (personal makeovers, home improvement and 'meeting the right man'). But as the networks were bought by conglomerates in the 1990s, these talk shows – produced cheaply by non-network companies – proliferated both in number and in the degree of sensationalism, becoming exercises in quick profit. Increasing revenue drove them to greater tabloid extremes as guests screamed and fought over infidelity, incest and homosexuality. *The Jerry Springer Show* remains the most infamous example of this tendency, with highly visible bodyguards to maintain the show's equilibrium.

PBS AND INFORMATION AS PUBLIC SERVICE

In many ways the informational cable networks have evolved into a popularised form of what the Public Broadcasting Service network has been doing from its inception. When the Carnegie Commission on Educational Television defined public television in 1965, the panel proclaimed that the network should be the broadcast equivalent of Lyndon Johnson's Great Society and needed to show America 'in all its diversity'.[1] Unfortunately, the powerful commercial networks feared the competition of this fourth network and many politicians worried about the liberal nature of the network's founding. They lobbied intensely against public TV. So PBS's mission began ambiguously: producing 'non-commercial' works not seen on the commercial networks. Beyond this nebulous aim, its quality of output was hampered from the start by underfunding.

A 1967 law created the Corporation for Public Broadcasting (CPB). This private corporation distributes public tax dollars as grant money to the various stations that make up the loose decentralised consortium that constitutes PBS. The 360 stations operate most often through public institutions such as universities. With the federal government providing less than 20 per cent of the financing, public television has had to rely on these state institutions, commercial sponsors and private donations to maintain its existence. The stations preserve their independence producing an array of local and regional programming (e.g., *Outdoor Wisconsin*, 1993–2009 and *Texas Monthly Talks*, 2003–9).

But what most Americans know as 'PBS' is the shared or national programming primarily produced by three stations on the East Coast: WGBH in Boston (educational), WETA in Washington, DC (news) and WNET in New York (news and educational). The individual stations pay considerable fees to PBS for the right to show individual programmes. The network requires the stations to show the programmes as part of a national schedule so that they may be marketed nationally. The offerings fall loosely into five categories: fine arts, science, history, public affairs and independent films. WGBH is the single most prolific PBS production house, producing one-third of its primetime schedule and a large portion of its daytime children's TV in a large studio facility on the outskirts of Boston.

Over the forty years of its existence the station has translated a large part of its 'non-commercial' TV into adult and child education. Because PBS cannot compete with the production values of commercial TV, it rarely produces dramatic series. Even though *American Playhouse* (1982–93) played off and on for a decade, drama on PBS is defined as British. For fictional programming, PBS has relied on imports. WGBH groups them together as *Masterpiece Theater* (1971–) for historical dramas and *Mystery!* (1980–) for detective works. They come primarily from the BBC and other British broadcasters such as Channel 4 and ITV. As a result PBS is often jokingly referred to as 'Primarily British Series'.

PBS's strongest suit is public affairs. WNET (along with Liberty Media) produces *Newshour with Jim Lehrer* (1975–) as PBS's weekday evening news. This hour-length episode allows greater depth for reports and interviews than the half-hour broadcast news. When documentaries had all but disappeared on broadcast TV in the 1980s, they thrived on PBS. WGBH became the leading production house for documentaries in the US. Begun in 1982, its *Frontline* exists as the only hour-long investigative documentary series on American TV. The station also produces *The American Experience* (1988–), which made the multi-episode summative and politically important documentaries about American history such as *Vietnam: A Television History* in 1983 and *Eyes on the Prize* (the history of the American civil rights movement) in 1987.

To compensate for the lack of science programming on broadcast TV, PBS has created two long-lived programmes. Modelled on the BBC2 series *Horizon* (1964–), WGBH's *Nova* (1974–) has won many awards for its willingness to tackle complex subjects such as Fermat's last theorem, string theory and acid rain. In classic PBS fashion it is funded by a corporation e.g., Dow Chemical Company. WNET's *Nature* (1982–) presents documentaries on wildlife, becoming the longest-running nature programme in the US. PBS also provides a haven for independent American film-makers. *POV* (1988–) is made by American Documentary which sells its twelve to fourteen nonfiction films as a package to PBS. The films are eclectic in style and content. More importantly, they each advance a different political point of view. The series has attracted such talent as Errol Morris, Jonathan Demme and Michael Moore as well as unknown film-makers. Importantly, its emphasis on single political points of view has politically tested the Fairness Doctrine, which had previously been interpreted to mean that different points of view had to be expressed within a programme.

Over the years PBS has proffered two kinds of documentary form. It pioneered cinéma vérité documentaries for television, funding most of Frederick Wiseman's direct-cinema works such as *Titicut Follies* (1967), *High School* (1968) and *Welfare* (1975). In a similar vein it pioneered a vérité reality form with *An American Family* in 1973. The twelve-episode series followed and chronicled the experiences of the Louds, a real, 'average' American family. During the documentary Pat Loud asked her husband for a divorce and their son Lance came out of the closet while one of PBS's largest audiences (10 million) looked on. By the 1990s PBS had become a political battleground as conservatives attacked what they perceived as a liberal bias. The most prevalent style then became the compilation work with found footage, interviews and a strong voiceover narrator. Given its federal funding, the network increasingly tended to produce non-controversial summative histories of America. Through WNET Ken Burns was commissioned to make a much-watched series of multi-episode works: *The Civil War* (1990), *Baseball* (1994), *Jazz* (2001) and *The War* (2007).

Children's programming became an important part of PBS's educational mission. *Sesame Street*, the preschooler-oriented programme that combines Muppet entertainment with education, has run non-stop since 1970. Produced by the non-profit Sesame Workshop (formerly Children's Television Workshop), a dubbed version is seen in 130 countries; thirty other countries turn out their own cultural versions such as China's *Zhima Jie* (1998–2001), Egypt's *Alam Simsim* (1997–), and Mexico's *Plaza Sésamo* (1972–). Big Bird, Elmo and a crew of other puppets help children through rudimentary spelling, mathematics and story-telling. *The Electric Company* (1971–7) helped elementary schoolchildren to read through sketch comedy. With its slogan 'Turn off the TV and do it!' *ZOOM* (1972–8 and 1999–2005) was an unscripted show created by an on-camera group of children and the viewing audience. With an emphasis on diversity of race and cultures, children generated and sent in ideas for sketches, games, science projects and jokes and then performed them.

Over time, PBS has slowly moved away from its educational aim and begun to make entertaining series that emphasise a 'prosocial' logic, socialising children in a complex and multicultural world. *Arthur* (1996–) made by WGBH and a Canadian firm, tells socially relevant cartoon tales through the experiences of a young aardvark. *Dragon Tales* (1999–) engages a cartoon format of imaginary dragons and magic to teach its life lessons. *Barney & Friends* (1992–) presents an actor in a purple dinosaur costume who sings and dances with preschoolers to produce an upbeat view of the world. *Mister Roger's Neighborhood* (1968–2001) was created by its host Fred Rogers (a former Presbyterian minister) and WQED Pittsburgh. The series constituted one of the gentlest moments on American television, with a cardigan-wearing Rogers interacting with puppets, music and a make-believe neighbourhood (a wooden model of a miniature town). He discussed anger, divorce, death and war in soft, comforting tones. For many critics the predominance of the prosocial sensibility was at the cost of PBS's charge to educate children.

However, education found its home in 'how-to-do' programmes. The infamous *The French Chef* (1963–73) began this applied schooling. Through the broadcast and reruns until 1987, Julia Child taught the art of French cooking, ending each episode with a glass of wine and oddly accented '*Bon Appetit!*' Another WGBH-created series, *This Old House* (1979–), has energised the do-it-yourself renovation movement in the US, showing the restoration of old New England homes. The programme has never used PBS money as it is entirely supported by sponsors: Ace Hardware, Kryton Paints and State Farm Insurance. *Victory Garden* (1971–) was the only gardening programme until the advent of cable. *Antiques Roadshow* (1997–) copied the BBC's programme of the same name and started appraising American antiques.

PBS has augmented its programming in two central ways. First, it has become a premium merchandiser. In 1999 *Strategy+Business* described WGBH as the 'Procter and Gamble' of non-profits in that it marketed its name, which had become synonymous with 'quality' in broadcast TV. As money from the federal government diminished, the station exploited its branding as the most highly respected PBS station and began merchandising. It put its name to Learning-smith, a chain of educational toy stores; it published a *This Old House* magazine with Time Inc.; and it sells tools with the show's logo on them. *Signals* is its online catalogue, selling PBS tapes, DVDs and books but also clothing, jewellery and wall decor. The station instigated aggressive marketing to schools with over 90,000 teachers adopting *Nova* programmes in the classroom. Further, children's programming has grown into a financial asset. For the series *Arthur*, WGBH takes home a percentage of the book, video and DVD sales as well as a percentage of profits from the popular toys, games and electronics.

Initiated in 1995, the network's web site, PBS.org, promotes the network's schedule and enhances the informational depth of programming. With its large size (over 200,000 pages), it has kept its programmes alive after their airing through streaming video. It will show a *Frontline* and *Nova* programme for a discrete amount of time before it goes to DVD sale. It provides transcripts of programmes. Each programme has its own web site with the PBS.org site; *Frontline*'s web site, for example, carries an array of information and interviews that extend its investigative information. And its popular PBSkids.org allows children to spin a wheel of programme information and to find related coloring opportunities, music and games. Parents and teachers can link to educational material but are warned about the 'cookies' that will record their tastes and link them to advertisers. In fact, PBS.org is adding advertising, sponsored links and premium games for which children would have to pay. These commercial moves have caused viewers and producers to question whether PBS is losing sight of its commitment to 'public service'.

CABLE AND INFORMATION: RECYCLING INFORMATION GENRES AS CABLE NETWORKS

Cable networks are primarily founded on the informational genres of broadcast TV. The economical way to create a branded cable network is to remake what has already succeeded on the established networks. Cable has taken the established genres of television (news, movies and sports) and created networks with a narrower scope (CNN/News, TNT/Movies and ESPN/Sports). Generally, the broadcast network and premium channels are still in the main responsible for TV's fictional programming, because of its high cost. But basic cable has limited its purview primarily to formats that do not have high costs: information genres. Although PBS has founded its own cable network (Kids Sprout, a preschooler network), its greatest nemesis is cable TV. With its record of successful public affairs, arts and documentary programming, PBS remains the central source of models for cable networks. Public TV was the first to succeed with do-it-yourself programming. Now we have the Home and Garden Television (HGTV), the Food Network and the Do-It-Yourself Network (DIY) whipping up projects twenty-four/seven. When the broadcast networks jettisoned documentaries as too unpopular and controversial in the 1980s, PBS weathered the political problems and low viewer numbers. Now, cable makes available the Discovery Channel, Military Channel, History Channel, National Geographic and Biography, pumping out seemingly endless wildlife, military, life-story and paranormal nonfiction programmes. PBS's *Austin City Limits* (1976–), TV's longest-running music series, is now mimicked by Great American Country Network and Music Television Network (MTV). Arts and Entertainment Network (A&E) aspires to be an entertaining PBS. The 'Primarily British Series' network is not surprisingly now BBC America – a cable network owned by BBC Worldwide Americas that shows programmes primarily from the BBC. And Fox Reality Network relies on formats once alive and well when WGBH produced the documentaries of Frederick Wiseman in the 1960s. Instead of being chained to the PBS programme schedule, a viewer now enjoys access to similar programming at a moment's request with cable. This cannibalising of public television forms has led to questions about the relevance of the PBS network in the age of cable.

Cable's borrowing also extends to commercial television during primarily the secondary time periods before and after primetime: daytime, weekend afternoon, and early evening. With the ubiquity of daytime talk shows in the 1990s, cable networks have sprung from the subgenres of these talk shows. *The Oprah Winfrey Show* with its self-help format evolved into OWN (Oprah Winfrey Network), a conflation of her former Oxygen Network and Discovery's Health Network. The personal makeovers that were the daytime staples of the 1990s now constitute the fodder of many cable shows devoted to plastic surgery and redecorating. The entertainment news magazines that typically filled the dinner hour have expanded into a whole network (E! Entertainment Network) devoted to celebrity gossip. Perhaps more strikingly, the less popular sports – golf, tennis, bicycling – that tended to be relegated to the margins of the network sports schedule on Saturday and Sunday afternoon have their own respective networks (Golf Channel, Tennis Channel and Versus).

Nevertheless, the cable networks have changed the original premises of the genres in important ways to be either more entertaining or to stretch the programme format out to cover a day's schedule. With more focus on personalities, less details and conflict-driven drama, cable has popularised information. In many ways cable represents the triumph of infotainment.

CABLE NEWS NETWORK (CNN)

On 1 June 1980, CNN went on the air and changed the landscape of journalism. Founder Ted Turner said: 'We will stay on the air till the end of the world and then we will cover the story and sign off playing "Nearer My God to Thee". '[2]

With this American sense of hubris, CNN began as a twenty-four-hour live cable news network headquartered in Atlanta – a sign of its break from the broadcast news establishment. Initially, the network set up bureaux in New York and Washington and later in London and Rome. Losing $2 million a month, the network stayed afloat with money from Turner's highly profitable superstation WTBS. It faced tough competition from Satellite News Channel (SNC, an ABC and Group W Westinghouse co-endeavour), created in 1982. Nevertheless, Turner expanded to a second network, CNN Headline News. With the expanding presence of CNN, SNC gave up after little over a year and ABC/Westinghouse sold it to CNN for $25 million. By 1985, CNN began to make a profit with over 30 million viewers.

CNN is a prime example of the first generation of cable networks (which included ESPN for sports and MTV for youth culture) that based their services on a broad need – what is called a 'utility brand'. Its success lay in its stripped-down, low-overhead, twenty-four-hour service when no other network filled the role. It employed non-union personnel who were paid less than their broadcast network equals. It was bought by Time Warner in 1996, becoming part of its large media constellation of subsidiaries that presently includes AOL, Home Box Office, New Line Cinema, Time Inc., Time Warner Cable, Turner Broadcasting System, CW, Warner Bros. Entertainment and the Cartoon Network. Under Time Warner's direction, the network laid off many reporters connected with its Atlanta headquarters, and it began to rely more heavily on network affiliates for newsgathering. This cost-saving shift was branded as part of the distinctive CNN news style: more reporters and more news outlets.

What distinguished CNN in the 1980s was the breadth of the reach of its newsgathering – it is the only truly international cable news network in America. While the broadcast news divisions were closing down foreign bureaux, CNN opened up offices in Bonn, Moscow, Tel Aviv and Cairo. By 2007 it had forty-two bureaux, 400 affiliated local stations and a number of foreign-language networks around the world. In 1985, CNN launched CNN Europe (which evolved into CNN International) as a service for foreign hotels. The power of CNN's live twenty-four-hour news service was attested to in the early 1990s when the Pentagon coined the term 'the CNN effect' to describe how the twenty-four-hour or 'real-time' news was affecting the decisions of the American government.

CNN's coverage of the First Gulf War in 1991 turned the relatively unknown network into an international household name. The cable network was the only news organisation able to sustain a live news feed out of Baghdad during the American bombing operation. By the early 1990s, CNN's international news division (CNNI) had grown considerably. As opposed to the BBC and many of the

American broadcast news operations, whose reporters are from their respective countries, CNN enlists affiliated local reporters. These individuals live in the area where the news story has arisen and are often invested in the issue concerned. This system costs a lot less than a bureau. By the mid-1990s, CNN ranked second only to the BBC, reaching only half the audience that the British channel does.

One critic argues that CNN's coverage of the 2003 invasion should also be remembered as the 'digicam war'. These are:

> tools that have created the so-called Sojos: solo journalists who report, act as their own producers, shoot their own film, edit on laptops and beam the results back to the network by satellite phone – all in a matter of an afternoon, in time for the evening broadcast.[3]

In a 4 February 2004 press release, CNN launched a new 'video correspondent' formula, by which the network compressed the normal fifty pounds of gear a crew travels with into a single laptop so stories could be reported, edited and transported more easily.[4]

CNN's willingness to experiment with technology has led to the early creation of CNN.com – the leading online source for news in America. Launched in August 1995, the web site relies on the established news outlets of CNN and CNN International. Initially called CNN Interactive, it pioneered live streaming of video and audio as well as a search news archive. The web site has been distinguished by its attention to interaction with its users, featuring blogging, social media and user-generated content. By 2000, CNN.com was getting 400 million hits per month with 30 per cent coming from foreign users.

By 2007, three editions of the web sites had been established: CNN.com (for domestic news), CNN.com International and CNN.com Arabic. Following the television network's method, CNN.com has gone into foreign markets with local partners and created a number of foreign-language web sites starting with Sweden in 1997 and Japan in 2000. Nevertheless, CNN.com is often criticised, much like the CNN TV network, for the American bias of its coverage.

FOX NEWS CHANNEL

The problem for CNN is that as a successful utility brand – cable news – its content is generic and therefore easy to duplicate. It was inevitable that another news network would evolve: FOX News Channel (FNC). Launched in 1996, it is distinguished by its focus on American news and perspectives as opposed to CNN's 'international' sensibility. Like CNN, FOX News is a twenty-four-hour cable and satellite news network. It is owned by Fox Entertainment Group, a subsidiary of Rupert Murdoch's media conglomerate News Corp. Murdoch said he was filling a void for 'fair and balanced news'.[5] FOX News has successfully branded itself (although it would deny it) as the 'fair news' outlet because it airs conservative positions that appealed to an untapped target audience in the 1990s. In other words, FNC's success lay in its ability to move beyond the utility branding of a news network and move into a new phase of TV branding based on identity. Such branding creates an emotional connection between a product and its consumers. By placing FNC in opposition to the 'liberal bias' of all other news, Murdoch and his executives (he picked Roger Ailes, a former political consultant for the Republican Party, as the founding CEO) created a powerful bond with conservative consumers. With their conservative brand, they also spurred the labelling of CNN as the 'liberal' network. Interestingly, MSNBC (see following profile), a third news network, has a similar broadcast model to CNN (appealing to the widest possible audience) but escaped the liberal label until the Obama campaign in 2008. FNC has found its niche by narrowcasting to viewers who wanted news from a particular perspective, according to the *American Journalism Review*.[6] FOX's conservative content represents the growing multichannel sensibility where news is tailored to serve a specific audience (e.g., the news on Univision repurposing national and international news from Mexico City).

Beyond its shrewd product differentiation, FOX News also succeeded in part due to News Corp.'s unusual strategy of paying cable companies $11 per viewer to distribute its network. When the network was launched, it was available to only 10 million viewers and had no outlets in New York and Los Angeles. Time Warner Cable (sister company to CNN) chose not to carry FOX News Channel, instead selecting MSNBC as its second news service. This led to a series of acrimonious antitrust lawsuits (where Ted Turner famously compared Rupert Murdoch to Hitler and Murdoch's *New York Post* ran an editorial questioning Turner's sanity). The suits resulted in a settlement; Time Warner began to carry FNC in New York in 1997 and as part of all of Time Warner Cable by 2001. Nevertheless, this highly publicised battle served to underline the brand opposition between two news networks in the eyes of the public.

FOX's branding was phenomenally successful. By its fifth year of existence it had become the most popular cable news outlet based on its regular viewership while CNN exceeded FOX News in terms of its number of unique viewers. By 2007 FOX News Channel pulled in an average of 840,000 viewers daily (6:00 am to 11:00 pm) compared with CNN's 448,000 and MSNBC's 270,000. FOX News has sought to broaden the appeal of its news with gaudy graphics, a feeling of intense speed created by quick editing and the emotional delivery of its hidebound hosts. It created the 'FOXNews Alert' which breaks into regular programming with a flashy logo bearing breaking news. Whereas CNN depends on its reporters for narrating the news, FOX relies more heavily on its anchors and hosts. As a result, FCN is personality-driven. The daily *The O'Reilly Factor* (1996–) with Bill O'Reilly, an inflammatory political commentator, scored regularly as the highest-rated programme on any cable news network.

FOX News is also available internationally but its content is the same as FOX News in America. The network is carried in Britain on its sister network: British Sky Broadcasting (BSkyB) – a News Corp. subsidiary. In Australia, the news network is available with local advertising on Austar, Optus TV and Foxtel (a News Corp. subsidiary). In Brazil it is carried by Sky, a satellite network run by News Corp. and Globosat. The network inserts local advertisements and weather reports to regionalise its appeal. In 2000, FOX News was granted the right to begin a domestic or Canadian FOX News network. However, it did not air until 2004 because the Canadian government refused FOX a licence on the grounds that it was a foreign company. Further, FNC's lack of international presence is attested to by its web site. Launched in 1995, it is consistently ranked low in popularity among news sites, reporting just fewer than 9 million unique viewers per month. FOX News has a limited audience because of its focus on America and 'objective' newsgathering. Nevertheless, the fact that cable serves up two clearly differentiated brands of news speaks to the distance that TV has travelled since the network news programmes all spoke with a similar voice.

MSNBC

During the Presidential election in 2008 MSNBC emerged from its weak third position among cable news networks by unofficially branding itself the liberal alternative to FOX News. Founded in 1996 by Microsoft and General Electric's NBC division, the venture was intended to combine a twenty-four-hour news cable network and an equivalent online site. Microsoft agreed to pay $200 million for half of America's Talking, an all-talk NBC cable network to be renamed MSNBC. Both companies agreed to put another $200 million into MSNBC over the next five years. The new network was publicised as a great synergy with its TV news augmented by the deeper background understanding available on MSNBC.com, whose news headquarters was in Redmond, Washington. TV news would become 'more interesting' according to Bill Gates. The combination was to attract the Internet-savvy by connecting its TV programming via Microsoft to create MSNBC.com as the leading online news source.

Initially MSNBC was kept separated from NBC with its production house in Fort Lee, New Jersey. Nevertheless, NBC shifted some of its established correspondents over to the new network. Positioning the NBC White House reporter, Brian Williams, as anchor of the primetime news show – *The News with Brian Williams* (1996–2002) – intimated that the broadcast network wanted the cable network to be competitive. The show gained a solid following because it premiered a few days before MSNBC's non-stop reportage of the TWA Flight 800 explosion. *Internight* (1996), which showcased a number of NBC news personalities, boosted the ratings as a lead into the news. After the news ran *The*

Site (1996–7), a show about the Internet and computer technology. Many NBC affiliates were unhappy with NBC's cross-promotion, fearing that it would cut into its audience.

Although there was interest in a niche market of a new generation of computer users, the main criticism was initially directed not at the programmes but at the online component. The Internet site was considered too slow. Also it did not vouchsafe much depth, especially around the Flight 800 disaster – the first test of its producing ability. But by the 1997 Presidential election the online news had improved and was able to declare Clinton the winner quickly. Nevertheless, the Internet part remained a weak link and that year NBC laid off 20 per cent of its news team. It cancelled *The Site* and moved away from its stated connection to the new media. Its ratings increased during the Clinton impeachment proceedings due to MSNBC's new tactic of saturation coverage of the 'big story' of the day. It still lagged a weak third in terms of cable-news audience share with the younger FOX News boasting 30,000 to its 24,000 households (CNN outstripping them with 578,000).

Following FOX's lead, the cable network began filling its schedule with opinion talk shows. Although MSNBC's daytime schedule is filled with breaking news, the evening became a haven for political discussions. It hired a quirky Keith Obermann to host *The Big Story* in 1997, which evolved into *Countdown with Keith Obermann* (2003–). The popular programme involves a countdown of the five top stories of the day, interviews and the host's commentary. Obermann created *Bloggermann* (later called *The News Hole*), an online forum for him to expand on his show's content and his own thoughts. Moving from CNBC in 1999 *Hardball with Chris Matthews* too belonged to the opinion-talk genre but with the addition of a group of pundits. Throughout the 2000s, the network moved away from straight news stories to more opinion shows. In 2002 *The News with Brian Williams* was moved to CNBC becoming the central source for election news on MSNBC. In 2007 MSNBC moved from New Jersey to NBC's headquarters in New York City, branding itself as the 'politics network' for NBC. MSNBC began to gain in the ratings. And in September 2008 during the heat of the election, the network added *The Rachel Maddow Show*. Maddow made a name for herself as a substitute on various network programmes. By November of 2007 the press began to argue that MSNBC was politically biased to the left and was openly casting itself as the liberal alternative to FOX News. Both Matthews and Obermann were famed for taking on conservatives. As early as the 2004 election Matthews began to challenge the veracity of the statements of conservative commentators on his show. But Obermann cemented MSNBC's liberal reputation by taking on FOX's *The O'Reilly Factor*, which aired in the same time slot. Nominating O'Reilly as 'the worst person in the world', 'Bill-O

the Clown', and 'the Big Giant Head' (to name a few), the MSNBC host introduced a segment called 'Factor Fiction', which involved fact-checking of
O'Reilly's statements. O'Reilly fired back by petitioning NBC Universal to fire
Obermann for his 'cheap pot shots'. In fact, on his radio show he told a caller
who 'liked' Obermann's show that he had his address and he would send FOX's
security to his home to hold the caller 'accountable'. Beyond this ongoing skir-
mish, MSNBC's general bias came to a head in 2008 when Obermann,
Matthews and Maddow openly voiced their support for Barack Obama's Presidential campaign during their programmes. Recognising an opening, CNN
pursued a branding strategy of representing the 'middle ground'.

In December 2005, MSNBC dissolved its joint venture with Microsoft leaving the computer company with only an 18 per cent interest. From the beginning
the two companies had had a rocky relationship. The computer company had
initially wanted to partner with a news outlet, recognising that news ranks second only to email in online pursuits. However, NBC negotiated a stronger part
in the initial partnership with Microsoft having to pay $30 million a year for
licensing fees for NBC News even when MSNBC was losing money. The shift
allowed NBC News to consolidate its control of the MSNBC network. NBC
still remains the news provider for Microsoft Network (MSN), the company's
portal. In November 2008 MSNBC.com ranked number one as a news site with
nearly 42 million unique users. CNN.com and Yahoo News ranked second and
third respectively.

FROM NEWS MAGAZINES TO E! ENTERTAINMENT CHANNEL

E! is a celebrity-news cable network (originally called Movietime 1987)
launched in 1990. It exemplifies how the news has come to consist of infotainment or celebrity culture. As the first network entirely devoted to tabloid-style
news, it plays out America's love/hate relationship with celebrity culture. The
cable network takes its inspiration from the syndicated evening magazine programmes seen on broadcast TV throughout the 1990s. It involves similar content
– coverage of celebrity lives and scandals – to that furnished by *Entertainment
Tonight* (1981–) and *Hard Copy* (1989–99). But now it is twenty-four hours a
day. With its programmes hosted by well-known personalities, there is an odd
narcissism to the network: publicity about publicity.

Historically, broadcast TV became more celebrity-oriented in the 1990s as the
new mergers demanded higher profits. Further, the networks aired increasingly
volatile daily talk shows that combined human interest and confessions. The
once hard-news magazine programmes grew to be driven by entertainment.
CBS's investigative news magazine *48 Hours* (1988–) was revamped in 2004 and
entitled *48 Hours Mystery* to feature hour-long investigations into a mystery or

true crime, a format which found success on a cable network (A&E). By the spring of 2005, ABC's news magazine *Primetime Live* (1989–) allotted an entire programme to a brewing sex scandal on *American Idol*. Similar reports fill the Entertainment Network.

With E!, the '!' astutely exclaims its excessiveness. Its signature programme is *E! News* (1998–) which features a nightly and timely wrap-up of the day's celebrity goings-on and gossip. It mimics the nightly news with an evening and nighttime scheduling. The host is the celebrity Ryan Seacrest, the emcee for *American Idol*. A female host plays a secondary role. A typical news 2008 programme begins with a leading report on the highly speculative details and questions around the death of a young actor. It moves to a pregnancy theme section called 'Baby Talk', with cuddly interviews with pregnant actresses (replete with gushy statements from the reporter and presenters from *E! News*). The next segment has viewers describe what TV programmes they miss during a Writers Guild of America (WGA) strike. The programme chips away at the practice of political reporting and objective distance in hard news. It trades on lurid speculation, syrupy interaction and the details of the entertainment industry, specifically the private lives of celebrities. Similarly, *The Girls Next Door* (2005–), an E! reality series about the goings-on at the Playboy mansion, highlights the tabloid character of E! as it focuses on Hugh Hefner's live-in girlfriends, who have been featured in a *Playboy* centrefold. *Snoop Dogg's Father Hood*, a 2007 reality show, chronicles the life of the famed rapper, especially the vagaries of marriage and fatherhood as it unrolls in his LA mansion. It plays on the celebrity culture conceit that stars, even rappers, are just like all of us. The *New York Times* nicknamed this genre 'celebreality'.[7] And finally, the pleasure of dressing down celebrities is highlighted in *Fashion Police* (2002) where Joan Rivers (a celebrity in her own right) and her daughter criticise the clothing of stars with warm campy cajoling. But again, the show, like the network, revels in the averageness of celebrities.

FROM DIRECT-CINEMA DOCUMENTARIES TO MTV'S *THE REAL WORLD* AND *THE OSBOURNES*

One of the earliest commercial reality forms is the documentary. If reality TV is defined as the use of non-actors in relatively unscripted situations, *Candid Camera* does not fit; it manipulated people the producers found on the street into being the butt of the joke. However, *COPS* became one of the first reality documentary programmes; it is a rather gritty observational study of crime and police work in US cities. Then came MTV's *The Real World* in 1992, the first documentary soap opera created for commercial television. The formula was simple: put a group of similar young adults in a confined situation and watch how they behave.

As previously stated, PBS pioneered the observational cinema work on TV in its attempt to document everyday life with a camera watching like a fly on the wall. In *An American Family*, the Loud family (parents Pat and Bill and their five children Lance, Grant, Kevin, Michelle and Delilah) allowed a PBS film crew to chronicle their lives with handheld cameras for seven months. The series let the footage speak for itself – no narrator or interviews were involved. The seemingly straightforward nature of this form belies the degree to which the editing of footage geared the structure and meaning of the series of twelve hour-long episodes. Although viewers remember the series as observational, it is much more self-conscious and directed as a critique of the American family. The son Lance constantly acknowledged the camera and crew, and the film-makers engaged Hollywood editing techniques to create narrative. Nevertheless, the series is remembered for its open-endedness—a characteristic of direct cinema. It finished without a clear sense of closure as the mother Pat is considering a divorce. Its final shot was a freeze-frame of her wry but ambiguous smile. This refusal to offer a clear ending represented a rare moment in American television.

For many critics, direct cinema is indistinguishable from cinéma vérité. Both are concerned with social and ethical issues. The movements wanted to convey 'real life'. They both employed handheld cameras and available light. Their art was in the editing – taking a vast amount of footage and editing this down to an hour and forty-five minutes for standard TV and film documentary length. Often the ratio of what was shot and what was seen is 40 to 1. Cinéma vérité was produced by French film-makers such as Jean Rouch, who used their presence to provoke a reaction in their subject – refusing the concept of objectivity. Contrastingly, direct cinema emanated from the US and was more observational. There was an awareness of the presence of the camera but that awareness was not thought to affect the event. Erik Barnouw describes the makers' presence as similar to an 'uninvolved bystander' —a near impossibility given that a camera is filming events.[8]

Many historians argue that Robert Drew started the direct-cinema movement in the United States as he applied his photojournalism training to film. He formed Drew Associates (Richard Leacock, D. A. Pennebaker and Albert and David Maysles) and made *Yanki, No!*, *Eddie* (1960) and *Primary* (1960) – all observational but still socially critical programmes for Time-Life broadcasting stations in 1960. Drew never found a home on network television. Rather, Frederick Wiseman has perhaps become the leading maker of observational TV documentaries. He received two successive five-year contracts with PBS's WNET, making one film a year from 1971 to 1981. WNET paid for the film-to-tape transfer for these ten films and gave him a national platform by broadcasting his documentaries. But the funding for the programmes came from private sources. With no voiceover, music or interviews, Wiseman called his works 'reality-fictions'.[9] The films' focus was on no central individual but rather concentrated on institutions such as a mental hospital, a high school or a welfare agency.

Before his PBS work, his 1967 documentary *Titicut Follies*, a horrific study of a state mental institution in Massachusetts, had its public screenings banned by the state Supreme Court because of its filming of unwitting mental patients. Wiseman maintained that he had obtained permission from the individuals or their guardians and that the real reason for the court order was that he had embarrassed the state. With this muckraker reputation, he began his work for PBS. The titles of his best-known works describe the content: *Basic Training* (1971), *Primate* (1974) and *Meat* (1976). Although an observational style typically demands chronological order, he edited based on a 'mosaic style', structured on comparisons, contrasts and ironies to express his moral outrage at the institution in question.

In many ways MTV's *The Real World* owes its logic to Frederick Wiseman. Nick Poppy quips in *Salon.com*: 'Think of the vérité filmmakers as the very disappointed stepfathers of *The Real World* and *Cops*.'[10] Labelled as a docusoap, this particular subgenre of reality TV continues the fly-on-the-wall camera technique of the observational documentary. However, the series producers do not film an established situation such as the goings-on of a hospital, welfare agency or an election, rather they create the event and pick the participants – normally a house and a group of strangers. In other word, in its attempt to popularise vérité, commercial TV produces drama (people living in close confines) with characters that happen to be non-actors.

The stories that evolve on *The Real World* tend to follow classic melodrama or soap-opera scenarios: betrayal, love, flirtation, rejection and estrangement.

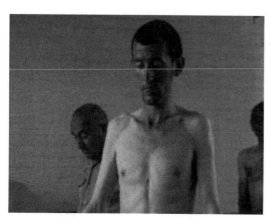

A court order meant that Frederick Wiseman's 1967 *Titicut Follies* could not be shown on PBS until 1992 because it showed real inmates in a mental hospital and allegedly violated their right to privacy

The Real World: Brooklyn Episode 2 (Season 21, 2008) exemplifies how the series highlights participants' first sexual experiences. Here Brian washes out his mouth after kissing a drag queen

Bunim/Murray Productions picks young, inexperienced adults, often living away from home for the first time. The subjects tend to be diverse: regionally, sexually and racially. Each season the company singles out a new setting, moving from big cities such as New York and Boston, where individuals considered careers, to more exotic playgrounds such as Key West and Las Vegas as the series evolved into what critics call its 'party' sensibility. Much of each episode involves mundane everyday activities such as sleeping, cooking and sunbathing. But the structure also creates a pressure-cooker environment. The participants seemingly mirror soap-opera behaviour due to an awareness of the producers' vision. They frequently explore their first sexual relationships. The people in the house often have to confront racial and sexual differences for the first time.

Some critics have lauded the programme for its frank portrayal of racism and exploration of sexual differences. Others argue that the casting method tends towards stereotypes such as city liberals and racist southern and midwestern hicks, which have underlined popular portrayals for years. Further, its ethos was that racial and sexual prejudice results from individuals rather than larger social formations.[11] As a cable series, *The Real World* did not have the impact on the creation of reality shows that CBS's *Survivor* had in 2000, but the producers spun off *Road Rules* (1995–2004 and 2007–), MTV's second reality series, where five strangers travel from location to location in an RV without money with a goal to complete a mission at each stop based on a set of clues. It took nearly a decade before similar scenarios appeared with MTV's *Laguna Beach: The Real Orange County* (2004–6), a highly scripted story of real California teens.

The Real World invented this logic but *Big Brother* extended it in 1997 when Dutch TV executives turned it into a game show by offering cash rewards for winning the show by not being nominated for eviction or voted off by the viewing audience. This programme increased the dramatic tension by cutting the house of up to fifteen people off from the rest of the world, making it into an emotional pressure cooker. This isolation extended to the absence of Internet, radio or TV as interpersonal conflict became the entertainment. The participants did interact with the *Big Brother* voice, as it instructs them what to do, enhancing the sense of control and lack of volition. *Big Brother* has been adapted in various areas such as the Middle East, the Balkans and Latin America. The US version (2000–) the CBS programme premiered a few weeks after *Survivor*.

Although docusoaps featuring 'average' real Americans had diminished in popularity by the 2000s, reality shows portraying the lives of celebrities in a candid manner flourished. This 'celebreality' phenomenon results from the greater profits garnered when producers focus on 'known' or, even better, infamous, figures. Ozzy Osbourne, former lead singer for the band Black Sabbath, was one of the first celebrities to allow producers to come into his home and chronicle the everyday doings of his family in MTV's *The Osbournes*. The success of the programme stemmed from the series' ability to make the Osbournes seem average. They experience the trials that affect everyday families from new vacuums, pet allergies, accidents and even cancer. But the Osbournes yell at each other at top volume, and have to have their language censored continuously as they walk around setting up concerts in post-heavy metal regalia and enjoy an opulent Malibu lifestyle. Similarly, socialites Paris Hilton and Nicole Richie moved in with an Arkansas family and worked on a 'real' farm like average Americans in *The Simple Life*. Produced by *The Real World*'s production house, the programme started at Fox but, as the celebrities began to fight and prove unpredictable, it shifted to E! Network. But it never made it to its fifth season because of the stars' extraordinary behaviour, which included arrests and hospitalisations. This reality type extends tabloid culture; it often chronicles the more marginal actors or entertainers (Jessica Simpson and Nick Lachey, wrestler Hulk Hogan's family and rap artist Flavor Flav) who are willing to expose their private lives to extend their careers and notoriety via such publicity.

FROM PUBLIC AFFAIRS TO DAYTIME TALK SHOWS: MAKEOVER SHOWS

Appropriately, the transformative power of American television can be found in makeover TV. The success of such shows seemingly speaks to a very American sensibility: reinventing oneself. Unfettered by the traditional class prohibitions, it demonstrates that we now inhabit a 'can-do' culture. It popularises the lifestyles associated with the wealthier classes of the celebrity and professional worlds. The TV version of this ethos subdivides into two forms: self-improvement and home improvement. Personal makeovers have remained an important facet of women's fashion magazines, with subjects paraded in 'before-and-after' images, for over a century. The first television form to take an interest in makeovers was the daytime talk show. In the 1980s, *The Oprah Winfrey Show* devoted episodes to shopping sprees, makeup or designer clothes, allowing ordinary women to live a fantasy that wiped away the class, race and gender problems discussed on other episodes. Political empowerment became personal. For example, an episode entitled 'Home Hair Care' featured women who used affordable, across-the-counter hair products being critiqued by experts. The programme then gave them a $500 designer haircut to demonstrate the mis-guidedness of their choices. Oprah Winfrey became a poster child for makeovers when she carted out a wagon of sixty-seven pounds of fat to represent the weight she had lost in 1988. Much of her female-empowerment philosophy is based on an individual's power to change him- or herself – a self-help sensibility common in American popular culture.

Queer Eye for the Straight Guy marked the advent of primetime interest in per-sonal makeovers, as five gay men ('the Fab Five') transformed the appearance, the living quarters and the taste of schlumpy straight men. As opposed to PBS's *An American Family*, the series was accused of stereotyping gays as servants to, and tastemakers for, heterosexuals. Nevertheless, the show succeeded with a broad audience. It jumped to become the cable network Bravo's number-one programme with over 3 million viewers. The five men became taste icons in the US. Nevertheless, the foreign versions did not succeed. For example the origi-nal US version did well in the UK but the Australian version was cancelled after three episodes. An American spin-off, *Queer Eye for the Straight Girl* (2005), lasted a single season.

NBC's *The Biggest Loser* (2004–) makes a game out of transformation. It fea-tures obese individuals fighting it out to see who can lose the most amount of weight through diet and exercise in order to win $250,000. With the beginning contestants ranging in number from twelve to fifty, the programme centres on teams and puts them through a number of tests or temptations. Slowly the num-bers diminish as contestants weaken and fail to lose as much weight. In the first season, the winner lost 122 pounds or 37 per cent of his weight.

With the combined success of FX's fictional plastic-surgery series (*Nip/Tuck*) and the rise of reality's popularity, makeovers became 'extreme' – plastic-surgery programmes evolved as the newest permutation. In series such as *I Want a Famous Face* (2004–), *Extreme Makeover, Dr. 90210* (2004–) and *The Swan* (2004), average people elected to radically change their body for cable-network profit as a transfixed audience looked on. The best known is ABC's *Extreme Makeover*, which involves plastic surgery, weight loss and clothing and hair change. Each episode ends with the family of the participant critiquing the changes. Fox's *The Swan* gave average women extreme makeovers over a three-month period. Those who succeed in their swanlike transformation compete in a 'swan pageant' at the end of the season. MTV's *I Want a Famous Face* features twelve individuals who covet celebrity faces such as those of Janet Jackson and

Pamela Anderson (celebrities famed for their own facial plastic surgery). Interestingly, much of makeover TV is guided by current tastes and looks where the metamorphosis from ordinary to extraordinary is understood as the achievement of a manufactured look that anyone can construct through the magic of TV. Deeply embedded in this ethos is American egalitarianism – the removal not of social inequalities but physical ones.

DOCUMENTARY MEETS GAME SHOW: REALITY TV

As already discussed, the success of *Survivor* and *Who Wants to Be a Millionaire* signalled a major shift in television programming. Hungry for cheap programming Fox and cable networks became the leading purveyors of this form of reality TV. What is less expensive to stage than a game or a competition between average citizens? It has no writing or acting costs. It entails classic narrative principles: humans in conflict reaching a climax and eventual closure (winning or losing). Game shows have been central to television since its genesis in the 1940s. In fact, they were once a prominent format of primetime as Americans tuned in to *What's My Line?* (1950–67) and *The $64,000 Question* to watch average people matched against not-so-average experts or celebrities in a battle of minds. The game show fell out of favour in the 1980s and became primarily a daytime format (e.g., *The Price Is Right*, 1956–65). However, since the turn of the twenty-first century the game format has returned to the centre of primetime. It has subdivided into two forms based on European imports: *Survivor* propagated a specific subgenre as in the game documentary and the triumph of *American Idol* pointed to the growing interest in the second subgenre: the talent competition.

Although game documentaries (gamedocs) are based on a competition, they have their own specific characteristics: non-actors in a narrative-based competition. Individuals or teams have always competed against each other, but how this new form innovated was to have the producers set out the broad premise (date, resort stay, sport or wilderness experience), the rules and challenges and then allowed participants to go their own way. What was once a half-hour affair got lengthened to an hour and then extended through multiple episodes as endless hurdles were put in place. Rather than being limited to a week or a single episode, competition often stretches out over an entire season.

This reality format is often more expensive to produce and had been the province of the broadcast networks – especially the newer networks, which were more willing to play fast and loose with the premises. Fox fuelled the interest in the competitive documentaries with a controversial succession of them: *Boot Camp* (2000–1) with its military-style boot camp created by Mark Burnett in the style of *Survivor*; *Temptation Island* (2001–3) turned up the temperature as couples tested their relationships with other couples at exotic resorts; *Joe Millionaire* featured women competing to marry a millionaire. Unfortunately, he turned out not to be a millionaire. And *The Rebel Billionaire* (2004) showed Richard Branson, founder of Virgin Worldwide, judging which of the contestants would be able to take over his corporation. One of the more staid competitions, the latter failed to gain an audience. The dating programme variation has done particularly well on cable. VH-1's *Flavor of Love* (2006–) focuses on women contestants living in the rapper Public Enemy's mansion and competing to stay with him. And the network's *Rock of Love* (2007) has women competing to date Bret Michaels, the former lead singer of the band Poison. This format is renowned for its sexism with women forced to compete against each other for success defined by a male's desire.

American Idol represents the talent-competition format at its most successful. But it also moves beyond a competition by narrativising the process – a popular textual ploy. It documents the procedure, the participants, their families and hometowns. As it moves across various American cities in search of 'the' American singer, the competition takes on the characteristics of a pop epic. Started in 2002, the singing competition is based on Britain's *Pop Idol* (2001–3), a comparable contest where viewers vote. Contests of this sort are not new; the 'Miss America' pageant has been a yearly televised affair since 1955 with the women competing not only based on appearance but on 'talent'. *Star Search* (1983–95) was a syndicated weekly venue where experts judged singers, dancers, comedians and models. However, talent contests remained a marginal format until the advent of *American Idol*. The programme, which costs Fox $1 million an episode to produce, has turned into the most-watched TV show in America, allowing Fox to reign supreme during Tuesday and Wednesday primetime.

Much of the show's success lies in the fact that it is part of a larger marketing franchise, which involves not only record contracts for the top contestants, but millions of dollars of merchandising under the brand name 'American Idol'. The British executive producer Simon Fuller brought his formula – a series of protracted tryouts leading to a final contest judged by the viewing audience by phone – to America but also to South Africa and Poland. Run by his company 19 Management and another top UK TV producer FremantleMedia, these combined media corporations have successfully combined a talent agency and an international entertainment programme producer. The contestants are treated not as traditional singers with a record contract but rather as a brand. Through binding contracts, each top performer must participate across a series of media platforms. The programme's title also decorates single song downloads, DVDs, concert tours, posters, tattoos, key chains and computer games. Top performers Kelly Clarkson and Justin Guarini starred in a movie about *American Idol*, released not unsurprisingly by 20th Century-Fox. With Coca-Cola (the major sponsor) glasses decorating the judges' table, *American Idol*, the TV programme has almost been regulated to 'a footnote' or a small part in an endless marketing scheme.[12]

Not unexpectedly, 19 Management has spawned a number of *American Idol*-style talent competitions on Fox: *The Next Greatest American Band* (2007), *American Juniors* with children (2003–5), and *American Idol Rewind* (2006–, a programme devoted to previously unseen clips, interviews and auditions related to the central contest). Moreover, the talent-'contest' format has become one of the most popular forms on cable. With the built-in tension of a contest and its belief in the innate talent of average Americans, the talent contest has been applied to decorating (*Trading Spaces*), cooking (*Top Chef*, 2006–), fashion designing (*Project Runway*, 2004–) and amateur film-making (*Project Greenlight*, 2000–3). The Bravo Network, a subsidiary of NBC Universal, has gained a reputation for this reality format, often with openly gay themes, judges or contestants. Not surprisingly, Fox as the leading network for reality, spun off Fox Reality Channel in 2005, which features reality programmes that premiered on Fox and those acquired from other networks when the shows lost their large network audiences.

Cable information programming has made significant inroads into PBS as the number of member stations, corporate sponsors and successful programmes have diminished in the twenty-first century. Although PBS's mandate still requires it produce a diversity of programmes, its educational mission gets in the way of it producing hits. Its forays into commercial TV genres have failed, such as *American Family*, a Latino drama series in 2002–4 which was much criticised for its earnestness. However, PBS, with its over forty years of experience still maintains an audience double the size of any cable competitor such as History, A&E or Discovery, which have only been around for twenty-some years. It remains to be seen whether, as cable networks continue to grow, PBS will be able to strike a balance between its stated mission of education, diversity and non-commercialism and popular programming.

CONCLUSION

The chapter has explored how the information genres pioneered by public television have been made more entertaining by the cable networks. As stated earlier, the success of the cable networks stems from their ability to popularise. This infotainment process involves greater emphasis on the creation of a dramatic narrative structure to make information entertaining. Participants are etched out as characters and episodes depend on producer-constructed conflicts and resolutions. Viscerally appealing visual images become the anchor on which stories are hung. In this process information and history are conveyed with broad brushstrokes on such a large canvas that the results frustrate historians and academics, who argue for the details and moral complexity of history, science and public affairs over spectacle, black-and-white conflicts and easy resolutions. Nevertheless, John Hartley argues:

> Communication – television is still the pre-eminent example – reaches citizens (including women, children, migrants and minorities) who have not been well served by the modernist communication technologies. Far from 'dumbing down' a once-knowledgeable populace, it could be argued that 'democratainment' extends the public sphere to the places where other media cannot reach.[13]

Clearly, commercial cable with its narrow audiences has slowly taken over the concept of PBS's mandate of diversity as Logo, Telemundo and Black Entertainment Television provide platforms for underrepresented groups. Perhaps cable's infotainment channels have achieved that life goal of public television: popular information. However, we need to consider how this 'diversity' of cable channels will always be limited to knowledge that is attractive to profit.

NOTES

1. Patricia Aufderheide, 'Public Television', *Museum of Broadcast Communication On-Line Encyclopedia*:
    <http://www.museum.tv/archives/etv/P/htmlP/publictelevi/publictelevi.htm>, accessed 7 June 2009.
2. Neil Hickey, 'Enter CNN', *Columbia Journalism Review* vol. 40, no. 4 (November/December 2001): 88.
3. Lucinda Fleeson, 'Bureau of Missing Bureaus', *American Journalism Review* October/November 2003:
    <http://www.ajr.org/article_printable.asp?id=3409>, accessed 7 June 2009.
4. 'CNN Deploys Video Correspondents', *CyberJournalist.Net* vol. 7 (9 February 2004) <http://newsattic.com/d/h/cnn_deploys_video_correspondents.html>, accessed 7 June 2009.
5. Marshall Sella, 'The Red-State Network', *New York Times* 24 June 2001: 6.26.
6. Deborah Potter, 'The Secrets of Fox's Success: How Roger Ailes' Game Plan Created Fox's Cable Domination', *American Journalism Review* vol. 28, no. 6, December 2006/January 2007: 78.
7. Virginia Heffernan, 'Hey, Adrift and Famous? Do a Celebreality Show', *New York Times* 5 July 2007: E1.
8. Erik Barnouw, *Documentary: A History of Non-fiction Films*. Oxford: Oxford University Press, 1993: 255.
9. Thomas W. Benson and Carolyn Anderson, *Reality Fictions: The Films of Frederick Wiseman*. Carbondale: Illinois State Press, 2002: 2.

10. Nick Poppy, 'Frederick Wiseman: The Grandfather of Cinéma Vérité Talks about Domestic Violence, "Domestic Violence" and the Reality behind Reality Films', *Salon.com* 5 January 2009:
<http://dir.salon.com/story/people/conv/ 2002/01/30/wiseman/index.html >.

11. Jon Kraszewski, 'Country Hicks and Urban Cliques: Mediating Race, Reality, and Liberalism on MTV's *The Real World*', in *Reality TV: Remaking Television Culture*, eds Susan Murray and Laurie Ouellette. New York: New York University Press, 2004: 193.

12. Gabrielle Dann, '*American Idol*: From the Selling of a Dream to the Selling of a Nation', *Mediations* vol. 1, no. 1 (2004): 19.

13. 'The Infotainment Debate', in *The Television Genre Book*, ed. Glen Creeber. London: BFI: 2001: John Hartley, 120.

Conclusion

Several developments during the 2007–8 season pointed to a historic shift in American television. The season began with an agreement between national networks and advertisers to include DVR audiences in their ratings reports, basing calculations for each show on the number of live viewers plus those that watch within three days via DVR. At the time, close to a quarter of all US households owned a DVR and the major networks had been pressing advertisers to acknowledge some of these viewers since they comprise a substantial share of the audience. In return, the networks accepted advertiser demands for ratings of TV *commercials* as well as programmes. The agreement represented a fundamental change in the ways that audiences are measured and interpreted. It allowed networks to claim larger audiences for their shows, but it also intensified accountability for the commercial minutes they sold to sponsors. Both parties saw it as an important innovation aimed at coping with dramatic changes in media technologies and audience use patterns.

Yet these weren't the only issues troubling the television industry. Executives also expressed concern about growing competition from video games. On 9 March 2008, Nintendo released 'Super Smash Bros. Brawl', updating the enormously popular Super Mario franchise. That evening television ratings among 18–24-year-old males dropped 8 per cent. The following day they dropped 14 per cent (Fritz 2008). Studies furthermore showed that young people spend 25 per cent more time online than viewing television. Just as worrisome, an increasing number of Americans were turning to the Internet for video entertainment and information, a medium that Google and its YouTube subsidiary dominate with 38 per cent of all video streaming. Although television companies remained the leading producers of video content, their historic control of distribution seemed increasingly uncertain.

As these changes unfolded, another daunting challenge emerged as Hollywood writers voted to strike on 5 November in the very heart of the television production season. Late-night talk shows were most immediately affected and in December, drama series were put on hiatus as well, leaving gaping holes in the primetime schedule. Ratings plummeted and by the time a strike settlement was reached in early February, it proved unexpectedly difficult to lure audiences back to network television. Many executives declared the season a washout and nervously shifted their attention to the upcoming fall schedule. Some struck a more contemplative posture, arguing that it was time to reassess the foundational assumptions and practices of the industry. As if to emphasise the point, all four networks announced that they would transform their upfront sales presentations in May, seeking to demonstrate that, despite the apparent slide in ratings, the national networks remain leaders of the overall television economy and that, along with their corporate siblings, they can attract substantial audiences across a range of electronic media, including the Internet.

Interestingly, intermedia rights were the key point of disagreement between the networks and the writers during the strike, with the latter arguing for a share of revenues earned via new delivery systems. During the classical network era when three companies dominated American television, writers were compensated for primetime showings and syndicated reruns, a formula that carried over easily into the cable era. Yet that compact became subject to debate during the 1980s due to the development of VCR technology. At the time, writers tried to convince the studios to share a percentage of video revenues, but executives claimed it was too early in the development of video to establish a revenue-sharing formula and that high royalty rates might smother the nascent industry. After a bitter strike in 1988, the two sides settled on 0.3 per cent royalty on reportable gross sales. As video took off and became a multibillion-dollar industry, the formula was earning writers only pennies from each sale and it therefore became a bitter point of contention, since royalties are often the only source of income for writers during inevitable stretches of unemployment.

In 2007, screenwriters were determined not to let the video rights formula established twenty years earlier become the basis for Internet royalties, but media executives countered that rising costs and growing competition made it difficult for them to surrender Internet revenues at a time when the income from online sources was minimal and tenuous. Executives for the media conglomerates seemed to be speaking out of both sides of their mouths, however. To advertisers at the upfront sales events, network executives presented their companies as powerful multimedia providers, while only months before they had told the writers exactly the opposite. Although seemingly duplicitous, their position pointed to a momentous transformation of the American television industry, as it moved from the network era into the matrix era.

During the 1950s, when American television was in its infancy, executives confronted the challenge of building a durable and prosperous industry, despite the enormous capital costs of production and distribution. At the time, most agreed that television would be ten times as expensive as radio, a prospect that encouraged industry leaders and policy-makers to advocate for a centralised commercial system in hopes of realising economies of scale. By the time television took off, three networks were solidly entrenched and would remain so for more than twenty years, a system based on principles of national mass production, distribution and consumption.

With the arrival of cable, these mass-media logics were challenged, however, as the number of channels multiplied and the audience began to fragment. Advertisers helped to instigate this transition, as they sought to undermine the network monopoly and to pursue greater efficiencies in the delivery of advertising messages to targeted audiences. As television headed into the multichannel transition, the fundamental logic of the network system remained in place as programme development, scheduling and advertising practices remained largely the same. Still, audiences and their viewing behaviours were changing, and the industry began to respond.

Unlike the mass-television era when the industry churned out inoffensive mass-appeal programming, executives during the multichannel transition began to pursue groups of viewers that were passionate about particular ideas, topics and interests. These niches were constituted as much by their audiences' shared worldviews as they were by their sense of difference from other viewers. To serve these audiences, producers began to pitch programmes with 'edge', meaning both programmes that pushed up against the boundaries of mass taste and programmes that hailed their viewers as self-consciously distinct from others. These niche programmes were not for everyone. Indeed, they offended some viewers while catering to the passions of others.

Observing these changes, executives came to believe that they needed to compensate for the erosion of network ratings by investing in niche cable channels as well as mass-appeal network services. They furthermore needed to anticipate the emergence of new digital media offerings and Internet services. This led to a period of mergers and empire building during the 1990s, resulting in the formation of huge media conglomerates premised on the notion that content might be successfully exploited across a range of media. Proponents argued that successful corporations would be those that could control multiple sites of creativity and diverse modes of distribution, and could operate them in synergistic harmony.

Yet synergy was easier to imagine than to execute, largely because the various components of each conglomerate were too accustomed to operating as distinct units: as network broadcasters, cable channels, Internet portals and so forth. Moreover, line executives were compensated based on the performance of their respective divisions, not on the health of the overall corporation. In the very top echelon of the media conglomerate, synergy seemed a logical objective, but down in the trenches executives and creative talent often fought bitter battles with their corporate cousins. When the merger bubble burst shortly after the

new millennium, many executives became openly critical of the huge conglomerates, which they averred only made sense to investment bankers who pocketed
fat fees for putting them together. Consequently, the promise of synergy began
to fade as media executives more or less went back to their same old ways.
Despite such resistance, changes in the media industries continued to unfold,
driven largely by the fact that audiences and advertisers were increasingly engaging with television as part of a multimedia environment. The 2007–8 TV season
therefore proved to be something of a tipping point for the industry, a moment
of crisis when executives and creative talent were again forced to revisit the
issues of synergy and intermedia strategy. In part, they needed to recalibrate
daily practices, audience-measurement techniques and revenue-sharing formulas, but at a deeper structural level, they needed to rethink the spatial logic of
electronic media.

Both the radio and television eras in the United States were premised on the
notion of broadcasting: the dispersal of information and entertainment from a
central source to a diverse audience, limited only by the reach of electronic transmission waves. Radio did not discriminate among its listeners, indeed, as Roland
Marchand argued, it played upon the ambiguity of second-person address, beck-
oning 'you', the mass audience and 'you', the individual listener at home, while
also massaging the two into an 'us' (Marchand 1986). Advertisers paid to
become part of that circle of mutual recognition, and the most powerful among
them would underwrite the interconnection of transmitters across the country,
so that they might deliver their messages from highly centralised facilities in New
York and Hollywood to a vast networked nation. By the 1960s, each of the three
major television networks regularly drew close to 25 per cent of all television
households to their primetime schedules. Yet during the 2008 season, primetime
audiences for each of the four leading networks averaged roughly 5 per cent of
television households, only a fraction of what they had attracted during the classical era. Interestingly, daily television viewing hours remained high – in fact
higher than in the 1960s at more than four hours and thirty-nine minutes among
adults – but television was coming from more centres and flowing through more
circuits than ever before, via DVD, cable, satellite and broadband; via Telemundo, Spike, Netflix and YouTube (TVB Online 2009). It was no longer a
broadcast medium or a network medium or even a multichannel medium; television had become a matrix medium, an increasingly flexible and dynamic mode
of communication.

According to the *Oxford English Dictionary*, 'matrix' was first employed with
reference to social life during the late nineteenth century when biological
metaphors spawned conceptions of human societies as comprised of complex,
dynamic and interconnected elements. In the 1960s, managerial experts began

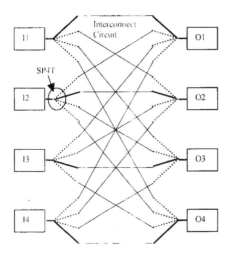

This diagram features a simple matrix switch, which is designed to allow multiple inputs, outputs and pathways for the flow of electrical impulses

to invoke the term with respect to flexible organisational structures as opposed to linear or hierarchical institutions. This emphasis on complexity and flexibility was seemingly picked up by the telecommunications industry as it developed the matrix switch, which is an array of circuits laid out in a grid so that paths can be established between any input port and any output port. A matrix switch can furthermore provide full bandwidth to multiple transmissions. When confronted with traffic congestion, it allows signals to be broken down and rerouted, only to be reassembled at their destination. These basic principles of electronic design prevailed during the late twentieth century, but just as importantly they governed the development of vast telecommunication systems, which were often portrayed as large-scale iterations of the matrix switch: a field of paths and possibilities for multiple users.

If the classical network era was characterised by centralised production and transmission to an undifferentiated mass audience, the matrix era is characterised by interactive exchanges, multiple sites of productivity and diverse modes of interpretation and use. Although huge corporations continue to shape and influence the media environment, they can no longer presume to deliver a national mass audience at an appointed hour and they can no longer market the attention of that audience to eager advertisers at the upfront presentations each spring. For media industries, the matrix era suggests emerging new structures and practices as well as changing conceptions of advertising, which remains the single most important source of media financing. A closer look at some of the strategies pursued by media companies in response to these changes helps to clarify what it means to say that television is entering a matrix era.

It's always difficult to lay a confident finger on watershed moments of significant historical change, but the 2007–8 season seemed to offer stark evidence that the television industry was undergoing a profound transformation. CBS saw its viewership plummet by almost 30 per cent, from a 7.9 rating to a 5.6 average for the season. ABC and Fox experienced a similar slide and NBC brought up the rear with a 4.8 rating (Simons 2008). In response to its changing fortunes, NBC announced it would substantially alter its upfront sales presentation in May, transform its marketing practices and reconfigure its season schedule. Instead of a conventional fall premiere, NBC said it would introduce new series throughout the year, devoting more attention to the promotion of each new show. Instead of a twenty-three-week season anchored by autumn premieres and summer reruns, it would shift to a fifty-two-week schedule that would constantly be adapted and reinvigorated by the addition of new series. And rather than presenting the entire season schedule at the upfront market in New York, NBC executives began to travel the country consulting with advertisers about programme ideas and multiplatform content.

NBC's weak network ratings no doubt motivated this change in strategy, but company executives were also seizing the opportunity to direct attention to their best performing assets: cable and Internet enterprises. (See Box 1.1.) Remarkably, while NBC's primetime line-up was faltering, its cable channels were flourishing and even more importantly, its advertising sales remained strong, largely because it was presenting itself less as a broadcasting network and more as a multiplatform operator. As if to emphasise the point, top management at NBC mandated that every television programme must develop intermedia strategies for programming and advertising.

Among NBC's divisions, Bravo is one of the most successful practitioners of what the company now refers to as 360-degree programming. For example, *Top Chef* – a popular cooking competition presided over by head judge Tom Colicchio – features a cable show and a robust web site that extends the brand via recipes, games, blogs and dedicated mobile video content. Most popular is Colicchio's blog where he provides commentary on the show and related topics, and where fans can engage in online deliberation. Most of the show's judges and contestants (including both winners and losers) maintain blog sites as well. In addition to these services, the site delivers broadband video programming and promotes products such as the *Top Chef* cookbook. Bravo furthermore has a talent-management company that represents chefs whose careers take off after appearing on the show. These 'brand-extension' strategies aim to deepen the viewer experience by delivering content in a variety of formats so it is available to audiences wherever and whenever they wish to engage with it. As Bravo president Lauren Zalaznick puts it, 'Our value comes from super-serving a niche of passionate customers' (Whitney 2007). Unlike the network era of weekly primetime scheduling or even the daytime practice of stripping, *Top Chef* develops and delivers content in rolling timeframes on multiple platforms, while striving to retain a coherent brand identity.

Bravo serves one of the youngest and most affluent audiences in cable television and has scored notable success with its intermedia strategies. It targets an upscale, educated and metropolitan mindset, primarily viewers living in the top thirty television markets. It designs programmes aimed at affinity groups that organise around food, fashion, beauty, design and pop culture. Zalaznick says that women comprise some 60 per cent of the audience, but she claims that's less a matter of targeting by gender than one of building a brand around topics that attract passionate customers. In addition to Bravo, Zalaznick presides over NBC's recently acquired Oxygen channel, which describes itself as being 'on a mission to bring women (and the men who love them) the edgiest, most innovative entertainment on television'. Claiming to air more original series than any other women's channel, Oxygen promotes itself as a slightly younger and hipper version of the industry leader, Lifetime.

In 2006, NBC also acquired the i-Village web site, dedicated to 'connecting women at every stage of their lives'. Claiming 31.4 million unique visitors per month, iVillage.com touts itself as the number-one destination on the web for women seeking information about health, parenting, pregnancy, beauty, style, fitness, relationships, food and entertainment. The site's interactive features include thousands of message boards and a variety of social-networking tools, allowing women around the world to share information and advice. By assembling this collection of enterprises NBC is able to present advertisers with a matrix of media opportunities that include Bravo, Oxygen, iVillage and the *Today* show. It can package spots according to age, interest, psychographic profile and socio-economic background. It can provide access to broadcast viewers of *Today*, cable fans of the *Bad Girls Club* (2006–) and online customers with a passion for cheese. Rather than assembling a mass audience, these NBC services accumulate a very substantial base of users via the multiple circuits of matrix media.

Strategies such as multiplatforming, repurposing and cross-promotion became important tools of network news divisions during the 1990s. The most successful organisations expanded into cable and web services, spreading the cost of the newsgathering infrastructure and branding their content in multiple formats. NBC News was the most ambitious practitioner of this strategy, which not only extended its presence across the media matrix but also strengthened its core properties, helping to sustain the leadership of *NBC Nightly News* and *Today.* The news division's strategy was largely driven by a desire to control costs and secure new markets. No doubt similar concerns spurred recent changes in the entertainment division, but these more recent innovations also seem to be motivated by the fact that advertisers are now asking for more than thirty-second TV spots when they purchase commercial time. Instead, they're looking for product-placement opportunities, Internet click advertising and pre-roll ad spots on mobile video devices. As a result, NBC altered its 2008 upfront presentation, focusing less on primetime and more on the company's ability to package advertising opportunities across media (Adalian and Schneider 2008). NBC furthermore conducted a series of smaller meetings with advertisers to solicit their input regarding plans for the upcoming season. Emphasising partnership, NBC is responding to advertisers' growing desire to break out of the box that defined American network television for more than fifty years. The flexible, dynamic and horizontal qualities of these services suggest a matrix media strategy rather than a conventional network strategy.

In interviews with more than 100 senior media executives worldwide, researchers for Accenture found that between 2005 and 2008 opinions began to coalesce regarding corporate strategy in the new media environment. Almost two-thirds said that multiplatform distribution would be the key driver of future growth. New types of content were the second most commonly mentioned (24 per cent) and new geographies of operation were third (10 per cent) (Accenture 2008). These results suggest that media companies are beginning to focus on the meaningful execution of matrix strategies. Although rivalries and differences within conglomerates persist, the erosion of revenues among the discrete media divisions as well the further development of broadband and mobile delivery systems have encouraged companies to revisit the complementarities of various media platforms and the advantages of cumulative audiences.

Some television series are now viewed millions of times after they are broadcast, via Fancast, Veoh, Hulu and dedicated network sites. For example, in spring 2008, MTV's most popular show, *The Hills* (2008–), premiered to 3.7 million 'live' viewers. Within the next three days it added almost 1 million DVR viewers and over the next few weeks episodes and excerpts of the show were streamed 32 million times (Stelter, 'In the Age', 2008). Although some overlap is likely, MTV seemingly generated many more advertising opportunities outside of conventional telecasting. *The Hills* also generated other revenue streams, as it scored among the top ten downloads on iTunes and among the top five videos in the 'teen scene' television category on Amazon, where one can also buy licensed merchandise that includes books, wall calendars and soundtrack albums. On the MTV web site, one can find *The Hills* music, news, games and message boards in addition to the episodes themselves. This not only reflects changes in audience use patterns but also points to changes in the ways that programmes are conceived, financed and executed. As one executive put it, 'We have to manage for profit margin and not for ratings' (Adalian and Schneider 2007).

Mobile telecommunications is another medium of growing interest to television executives. At its 2007 upfront presentation, ESPN executives lavished attention on new programmes designed to appear exclusively via mobile devices, including *Mayne Street* (2008–) (featuring Sports Center's Kenny Mayne), a mixed martial-arts series, and POV, a compilation of clips submitted by viewers and fans. According to one ESPN executive, these mobile services are a strategic attempt to broaden and deepen the network's relationship with sports fans (Steinberg and Elliott 2008). ESPN isn't alone in its enthusiasm for mobile delivery. It's estimated that content delivered over cell phones could generate $50 billion in revenue worldwide. Alert to the music industry's success with the multibillion-dollar ringtone trade, television executives are adding mobile video services to their media matrix (Halper 2006).

With all these changes afoot, the scheduling, distribution and financing of TV programming pose significant challenges for media executives. Just as challenging are the creative decisions associated with the production of online and mobile video content. Some 75 per cent of US Internet users view online video regularly, streaming an average of eighty-five videos per month (Fulgoni 2008). Google delivers more than a third of all views, much of it amateur content. Initially the service grew popular as a site for sharing video clips from TV shows. However, the major television companies soon protested about copyright infringement and pressured YouTube staffers to remove the offending videos or share revenues derived from their exhibition online.

Interestingly, the major television companies not only complained, they soon launched services of their own, many of them quite successful. Others, such as CBS, have struck deals with YouTube that allow Google to deliver the video and charge advertisers while splitting the revenue with television networks and producers. Altogether, the major television companies as a group now deliver well over half of all advertiser-supported video streams (Garrett 2008). Their success seems in part attributable to the quality of their content. A Pew Foundation study found that 62 per cent of Internet users prefer professional video, while only 19 per cent prefer amateur material (Madden 2007). Just as importantly, advertisers are more willing to place their messages alongside professional video because they find the content more compelling and less likely to engender controversy. Rather than posing a threat, online video may represent a grand opportunity for television companies, but executives are nevertheless aware that they cannot simply recirculate broadcast programming onto the web. They must develop dedicated material that is conducive to web viewing.

The potential for online video seems enormous, as suggested by Will Ferrell's and Adam McKay's brief series about a foul-mouthed two-year-old

Table C.1 Top Video Sites, May 2008

Property	Unique viewers (000s)	Average videos per viewer
Total Internet	141,657	85.3
Google sites[1]	83,828	50.2
Fox Interactive[2]	60,760	12.8
Yahoo! sites	40,197	8.6
Microsoft sites	29,471	8.3
Time Warner	24,612	5.9
AOL	21,670	4.8
Viacom	21,260	9.7
Disney	12,385	8.7
ESPN	8,425	8.9
ABC	7,747	16.3
Hulu (NBC)	6,800	13.0

Notes
[1] Includes YouTube.
[2] Includes MySpace.

Source: comScore, 'Americans', 2008.

landlord that was streamed more than 50 million times on funnyordie.com. Within months their company added more than twenty-five employees and expanded its website into a robust buffet of comedy videos that reportedly generates more than $50 million in annual revenues (Alexa 2008; Marx 2009). Backed initially by Sequoia Capital – one of the most successful venture-capital firms in Silicon Valley – funnyordie.com soon attracted HBO as a minority partner interested in securing cable television products that could complement the online service.

A contrite Will Ferrell plays a tenant whose rent is overdue in *The Landlord*

Online producers such as Ferrell and McKay are experimenting with the emerging conventions of online video genres. In order to make their work commercially viable, they're tinkering with formats and formulas, hoping to come up with generic conventions that will bring viewers back on a regular basis. For example, even though most creatives agree that online videos should be short, successful videos range from two to seven minutes in length. Producers also debate about the frequency of episodes, the length of 'seasons' and strategies for promotion. These challenges may seem manageable, but many video ventures – some with very big budgets and strong institutional backing – have nevertheless failed miserably, such as Budweiser's bud.tv site and *Quarterlife* (2007–8), a melodrama series sponsored by Pepsi and Toyota that was directed by Marshall Herskovitz and Edward Zwick of *thirtysomething* (1987–91) fame.

Producers are also experimenting with interactive features, hoping to mine their fan bases for feedback and creative input. In May 2007, Mindshare, an advertising agency in the WPP Group, launched a series on MSN called *In the Motherhood* (ITM). Mindshare executives initially came up with the series while brainstorming with executives from Sprint and Unilever, both of which appear as prominent sponsors on the site. Billing *ITM* as a series 'for moms, by moms, and about moms', producers solicit story ideas from the audience and then set about fashioning episodes featuring Jenny McCarthy (formerly of MTV), Leah Remini (*The King of Queens*) and comedian Chelsea Handler. The production values are professional, but the budgets are modest.

In the Motherhood has a homey, 'let's put on a show' quality to it. Visitors to the site are immediately invited to write a story or to read and comment on stories that others have written. More than 1,000 script ideas are submitted for every show that is ultimately produced, and more than 13,000 fans regularly vote for the top candidates. The value of the series resides in its ability to tap the millions of stories that mothers have to tell about their lives, their children and their

In the Motherhood webisode featuring Leah Remini and Jenny McCarthy

families. The producers and the cast (all of them mothers) then bring the stories to life using the generic formulas of the domestic television comedy. Each episode runs five to seven minutes and is supported by online discussions, games and recipes, as well as interviews with the cast and outtakes from the series. By the spring of 2008, the audience had grown to more than 20 million streams per month, encouraging ABC executives to pick it up and develop *ITM* as a prime-time network offering as well.

Unlike the classical network era when three dedicated television companies exercised oligopoly control over production, distribution and exhibition, the matrix era is characterised by the formation of huge multimedia conglomerates. Although constituted more than a decade ago, these conglomerates are finally beginning to pursue the strategies and practices that are appropriate to this new media environment. Accordingly, their conception of television has changed from that of a highly centralised mode of transmission to a more flexible field of electronic media. Rather than indifferently transmitting a line-up of shows each evening, television companies now operate in an interactive, asynchronous and intermedia milieu. They build brands and render them accessible to audiences in a range of formats across rolling time horizons. Still financed primarily by advertising sales, television companies no longer rely solely on ratings as a measure of their success but rather have begun to embrace the importance of intermedia reach, as they attempt to target and accumulate audiences in a cost-efficient manner. Anxious to please advertisers who are demanding accountability and input, networks have opened their doors, infusing their clients' messages into the media matrix rather than selling them gross lots of commercial minutes.

These changes have been motivated in part by new competitors and new technologies but they are just as importantly spurred by the changing behaviours of audiences that now navigate a growing universe of entertainment, information and interactivity. No longer restricted to a menu of 'least offensive' mass-appeal programming, audiences make use of a diverse repertoire of mass, niche and micro-niche content. Accordingly, television companies are complementing their investment in capital-intensive studios with multiple modes of production and creative input. This is partially a cost-cutting assault on unionised labour, as they pursue lower-cost and non-union production opportunities, but it is also part of what Tiziana Terranova (2000: 821) refers to as a broadening out of media production into society as a whole. Citing the Italian autonomists, she observes that 'work processes have shifted from the factory to society, thereby setting in motion a truly complex machine'. The media matrix increasingly thrives in an environment where distinctions between production and consumption blur, where television seasons give way to an evergreen cavalcade of content that is made use of by audiences on flexitime schedules. It is perhaps remarkable that it took television companies so long to adapt to these changes and to acknowledge the fundamental transformations of the matrix era. One can only hope that their increasing enthusiasm portends a more open media future rather than the more ominously imagined matrix of Baudrillard (1995) and the Wachowski brothers (1999).

Bibliography

'A World of Discovery: Facts & Figures', *Globe: A Quarterly Newsletter from Discovery Communications* September 2008.

Accenture. 'Accenture Survey Finds Broad Agreement within Media and Entertainment Industry on Direction of Digital Market', company press release 5 May 2008: <newsroom.accenture.com/article_display.cfm?article_id=4674>, accessed 10 May 2008.

Adalian, Joseph and Michael Schneider. 'Strike May Force Rewrite', *Variety* 17 December 2007: 28.

Adalian, Joseph and Michael Schneider. 'Upfront Upheaval', *Variety* 31 March 2008: 14.

Alexa: <www.alexa.com/data/details/main/funnyordie.com>, accessed 12 June 2008.

Allen, Robert C. *Speaking of Soap Operas*, Chapel Hill: University of North Carolina Press, 1985.

Anderson, Chris. *The Long Tail: Why the Future of Business Is Selling Less of More*. New York: Hyperion, 2006.

Anderson, Christopher. *Hollywood TV: The Studio System in the Fifties*. Austin: University of Texas Press, 1994.

Anderson, Christopher. 'The Long Tail', *Wired* vol. 12, no. 10 (October 2004): <http://www.wired.com/wired/archive/12.10/tail.html>.

Applebaum, Simon. 'Hispanic TV Upfronts', *Mediaweek* 21 May 2007: M1–M5.

Arango, Tim. 'CBS Said to Consider Use of CNN in Reporting', *New York Times* 8 April 2008: C1.

Arsenault, Amelia H. and Manuel Castells. 'The Structure and Dynamics of Global Multi-media Business Networks,' *International Journal of Communication* vol. 2 (2008): 707–48.

Atkinson, Claire. 'What to Watch? How about a *Simpsons* Episode from 1999?' *New York Times*, 24 September 2007: C4.

Aufderheide, Patricia. *Communications Policy and the Public Interest*. New York: Guilford, 1999.

Aufderheide, Patricia. 'Public Television', *Museum of Broadcast Communication On-Line Encyclopedia*: <http://www.museum.tv/archives/etv/P/htmlP/ publictelevi.htm>, accessed 7 June 2009.

Balio, Tino, ed. *Hollywood in the Age of Television*. Boston, MA: Unwin Hyman, 1990.

Barnouw, Erik. *A History of Broadcasting in the United States* (3 volumes). New York: Oxford University Press, 1966–70.

Barnouw, Erik. *Documentary: A History of Non-fiction Films*. Oxford: Oxford University Press, 1993: 255.

Barnouw, Erik *et al*. *Conglomerates and the Media*. New York: New Press, 1997.

Baudrillard, Jean. *Simulacra and Simulation*. Ann Arbor: University of Michigan Press, 1995.

Baughman, James. *Creating American Television*. Baltimore, MD: Johns Hopkins University Press, 2007.

Becker, Ron. *Gay TV and Straight America*. New Brunswick, NJ: Rutgers University Press, 2006.

Bedell, Sally. 'Pay TV Challenges the Networks'. *New York Times* 3 April 1983: 2.1.

Benson, Thomas W. and Carolyn Anderson, *Reality Fictions: The Films of Frederick Wiseman*. Carbondale: Illinois State Press, 2002: 2.

Boddy, William. *Fifties Television*. Urbana: University of Illinois Press, 1990.

Boliek, Brooks. 'The Battle of the Titans: The Fin-Syn Fight Pitted Studios against TV Networks', *Hollywood Reporter* 23 June 2005.

Bordwell, David, Janet Staiger and Kristin Thompson. *The Classical Hollywood Cinema: Film Style & Mode of Production to 1960*. New York: Columbia University Press, 1985.

Brooks, Tim and Earle Marsh. *The Complete Directory to Primetime and Cable TV Shows*, 9th edn. New York: Ballantine Books, 2007.

Buzzard, Karen S. F. 'The Peoplemeter Wars: A Case Study of Technological Innovation and Diffusion in the Ratings Industry', *Journal of Media Economics* vol. 15, no. 4 (2002): 273–91.

Carter, Bill. 'CBS's *Survivor* Is Winner for Network: Real-life Show Pulls in Younger Viewers', *New York Times* 2 June 2000: C1.

Carter, Bill. 'TV Has New Stories to Tell, but Reality Lurks in the Wings', *New York Times* 2 October 2000: E1.

Carter, Bill. 'Late at Night, That's NBC Crowing', *New York Times* 3 November 2003: C1.

Carter, Bill. 'O'Brien to Succeed Leno on *Tonight* Show', *New York Times* 28 September 2004: C1.

Carter, Bill. *Desperate Networks*. New York: Broadway, 2007.

Carter, Bill. 'A Matrix of News Winners Buoys NBC', *New York Times* 9 March 2009: B1.

Castleman, Harry and Walter Podrazik. *Watching TV*. Syracuse, NY: Syracuse University Press, 2003.

Chan-Olmsted, Sylvia and Yungwook Kim. 'The PBS Brand versus Cable Brands: Assessing the Brand Image of Public Television in a Multi-channel Environment', *Journal of Broadcasting and Electronic Media* vol. 46 (2002): 300–21.

'CNN Deploys Video Correspondents', *CyberJournalist.Net* vol. 7 (9 February 2004), accessed 7 June 2009.

Coe, Kate. 'On the Prowl for Telegenic Experts', *Chronicle of Higher Education* vol. 49 (1 August 2003): C3.

comScore. 'Americans Viewed 12 Billion Videos Online in May 2008': <www.comscore.com/press/release.asp?press=2324>, accessed 14 July 2008.

comScore. 'Number of Online Videos Viewed in the US Jumps 13 Percent in March to 11.5 Billion', 12 May 2008: <www.comscore.com/press/release.asp?press=2223>, accessed 8 August 2008.

Corner, John. 'Performing the Real: Documentary Diversions', *Television & New Media* vol. 3, no. 3 (2002): 255–70.

Curtin, Michael. *Redeeming the Wasteland*. New Brunswick, NJ: Rutgers University Press, 1995.

Dann, Gabrielle. '*American Idol*: From the Selling of a Dream to the Selling of a Nation', *Mediations* vol. 1, no. 1 (2004): 15–21.

Deggans, Eric and Lynnette R. Holloway, 'The New BET', *Ebony* vol. 62, no. 12 (October 2007): 216–24.

Douglas, Susan. *Listening In*. New York: Times Books, 1999.

Downey, Kevin. 'The New World of Hispanic TV', *Broadcasting & Cable* 5 March 2007, p. 26.

Downing, John. 'The Political Economy of US Television.' *Monthly Review* vol. 42, no. 1 (May 1990): 30.

Edgerton, Gary R. and Kyle Nicholas. 'I Want My Niche TV', in *Thinking outside the Box : A Contemporary Television Genre Reader*, eds Gary R. Edgerton and Brian G. Rose. Lexington: University Press of Kentucky, 2005.

Epstein, Edward Jay. *The Big Picture*. New York: Random House, 2005.

Epstein, Michael M., Jimmie L. Reeves and Mark C. Rogers. 'Surviving "The Hit": Will *The Sopranos* Still Sing for HBO?', in *Reading The Sopranos: Hit TV from HBO*, ed. David Lavery. London: I. B. Tauris, 2006: 15–26.

Feuer, Jane, Paul Kerr and Tise Vahimagi, eds. *MTM Quality Television*. London: BFI, 1984.

Fleeson, Lucinda. 'Bureau of Missing Bureaus', *American Journalism Review* October/November 2003: <http://www.ajr.org/article.asp?id=3409>.

Fritz, Ben. 'Summer's 'Grand' Slam', *Variety* 21 April 2008: 1.

Fulgoni, Gian. 'Online Is the New Primetime', Advertising Research Foundation Annual Summit: <www.comscore.com/press/presentations.asp>, accessed 31 March 2008.

Garcia, Maria Antonia. 'New Behaviours Cannot Be Induced in the United States if the Image of the "Ethnic" Is by Definition Degrading and Discriminatory', *El Tiempo* 24 January 2007: <http://www.watchingamerica.com/eltiempo000030.shtml>.

Garrett, Diane. 'Skeins Swim in Web Stream', *Variety* 3 March 2008: 16.

Gertner, John. 'Our Ratings, Ourselves', *New York Times Magazine*, 10 April 2005: 20, 34.

Gibson, Owen. 'The Story of the Long Tail', *The Guardian* 10 July 2006.

Gitlin, Todd. *Inside Primetime*. New York: Pantheon, 1985.

Glover, Kara and Anne Rackham. 'Fin-Syn Ruling Leaves All Scorned and Some in Fear of Extinction – Effect of Federal Communication Commission's Relaxation of Financial Interest and Syndication Rules on the Entertainment/Media Industry', *Los Angeles Business Journal* 15 April 1991.

Goetzl, David. 'A Decent BET: New Programs, More Cash Boost Channel', *Broadcasting & Cable* 17 September 2007: 22–3.

Gordon, Devin. '*Entourage*: Low Ratings? Who Cares? Why We Love This Comic Joyride', *Newsweek* 2 August 2005.

Gordon, Devin. 'Part of the "*Entourage*"? *Newsweek* 22 August 2005: <http://www.newsweek.com/id/56509>.

Gray, Herman. *Watching Race*. Minneapolis: University of Minnesota Press, 2004.

Halper, Mark. 'Hollywood Comes Calling on Mobiles', *Variety* 20 February 2006: 19.

Havens, Timothy. *The Global Television Marketplace*. London: BFI: 2006.

Heffernan, Virginia. 'Hey, Adrift and Famous? Do a Celebreality Show', *New York Times* 5 July 2007: E1.

Hickey, Neil. 'Enter CNN', *Columbia Journalism Review* vol. 40, no. 4 (November/December 2001): 88.

Higgins, John M. 'Angels, Emmys and DVD: Award Haul Promises to Lift HBO Miniseries' Home-Video Sales', *Broadcasting & Cable* 27 September 2004.

Higgins, John M. 'Comcast–Disney Fight Simmers', *Broadcasting & Cable* 20 March 2006.

Hilmes, Michele. *Only Connect*. Belmont, CA: Thomson Wadsworth, 2007.

Hope, Darrell J. '*Frasier*: How the *Frasier* Directing Team Keeps Things Fresh and Deliciously Funny', *DGA Quarterly* (January 1999): 54–60.

Hornaday, Ann. 'Television: Programming for Reputation; For Profit', *New York Times* 7 November 1993: 2.37.

Horwitz, Robert Britt. *The Irony of Regulatory Reform*. New York: Oxford University Press, 1991.

Hartley, John. 'The Infotainment Debate', *The Television Genre Book*, ed. Glen Creeber. London: BFI, 2001: 120.

Jarmillo, Deborah L. 'The Family Racket: AOL Time Warner, HBO, *The Sopranos*, and the Construction of a Quality Brand', *Journal of Communication Inquiry* vol. 26, no. 1 (January 2002): 59–75.

Jenkins, Henry. *Convergence Culture*. New York: New York University Press, 2006.

Johnson, Catherine. 'Tele-branding in TVIII: The Network as Brand and the Programme as Brand', *New Review of Film and Television Studies* vol. 5, no. 1 (2007): 5–24.

Kirkpatrick, William. 'Localism in American Media, 1920-1934', PhD dissertation, University of Wisconsin, 2006.

Kompare, Derek. *Rerun Nation*. New York: Routledge, 2004.

Kraszewski, Jon. 'Country Hicks and Urban Cliques: Mediating Race, Reality, and Liberalism on MTV's *The Real World*', in *Reality TV: Remaking Television Culture*, eds Susan Murray and Laurie Ouellette. New York: New York University Press, 2004: 179–96.

Lavery, David, ed. *Reading The Sopranos: Hit TV from HBO*. London: I. B. Tauris, 2006.

Learmonth, Michael and Michael Schneider. 'Can't Stop the Music', *Variety* 27 February 2006, 1.

Learmonth, Michael. 'Univision Opens La Puerta', *Variety* 25 June 2007: 16.

Lotz, Amanda. *Redesigning Women*. Urbana: University of Illinois Press, 2006.

Lotz, Amanda. *The Television Will Be Revolutionized*. New York: New York University Press, 2007.

Lowry, Brian. 'How *Law & Order* Rewrote the Rules', *Los Angeles Times* 18 May 2003: E-1.

Lowry, Brian. 'Grazing Viewers Could Gore Cablers', *Variety* 14 August 2006: 15.

Madden, Mary. 'Online Video', 25 July 2007. Pew Internet & American Life Project: <www.pewinternet.org/Reports/2007/Online-Video.aspx>, accessed 4 June 2008.

Manly, Lorne. 'Brands Go from Props to Stars', *New York Times* 2 October 2005.

Marchand, Roland. *Advertising the American Dream: Making Way for Modernity, 1920–1940*. Berkeley: University of California Press, 1986.

Marx, Nick. 'Dying Laughing: Funnyordie.com and the Sketch Comedy Aesthetic in the Matrix Media Era', unpublished manuscript, 2009.

'Mass Production', *Encyclopædia Britannica*, 2009. *Encyclopædia Britannica*: <http://www.search.eb.com/eb/article-9106304>, accessed 6 January 2009.

Mattson, Kevin. 'Channeling History', *Dissent* vol. 52, no. 4 (Fall 2005): 69–74.

Mayer, Janet. 'Letter from Hollywood: Whatever It Takes', *New Yorker* 19 February 2007: <http://www.newyorker.com/reporting/2007/02/ 070219fa_fact_mayer?>.

Meehan, Eileen and Jackie Byars. 'Telefeminism: How Lifetime Got Its Groove', *Television and New Media* vol. 1, no. 1 (2000): 33–51.

Meehan, Eileen. *Why Television Is Not Our Fault*. Boulder, CO: Rowman and Littlefield, 2005.

Mitchell, Lisa. 'A Conversation with Lee Shallat Chemal', *DGA Monthly* vol. 1 (November 2004): <http://www.directorsguildofamerica.com/news/dgamonthly-1104/evnt_wsc-shallatchemel-1104.php3>.

Mittell, Jason. 'Narrative Complexity in Contemporary American Television', *The Velvet Light Trap* vol. 58 (Spring 2006): 29–40.

Murray, Susan. 'Reality Television (US)', *Encyclopedia of Television*, ed. Horace Newcomb, 2nd edn. New York: Routledge, 2004: 1903.

'NBC', *Television Week* 14 April 2008: 46.

'Networks Thrive Even as Viewership Dips', *Broadcasting & Cable* 29 March 2004: 28.

Newman, Michael Z. 'From Beats to Arcs: Toward a Poetics of Television Narrative', *The Velvet Light Trap* vol. 58 (Spring 2006): 16–28.

Nielsen Company. 'Nielsen Reports TV, Internet and Mobile Usage among Americans': <www.nielsen.com/media/2008/pr_080708.html>, accessed 8 July 2008.

Nielsen Media Research, 'Nielsen Media Research Reports Television's Popularity Is Still Growing': <www.nielsenmedia.com/nc/portal/site/Public/menuitem.55dc65b4a7d5adff3f6593 6147a062a0/?vgnextoid=4156527aacccd010VgnVCM100000ac0a260aRCRD>, accessed 21 September 2006.

Nielsen Media Research, 'Average US Home Now Receives a Record 104.2 TV Channels': <www.nielsenmedia.com/nc/portal/site/Public/menuitem.55dc65b4a7d5adff3f6593 6147a062a0/?vgnextoid=48839bc66a961110VgnVCM100000ac0a260aRCRD>, accessed 15 July 2008.

Nielsen Media Research, see Television Bureau of Advertising Online (TVB Online): <www.tvb.org/nav/build_frameset.asp>, accessed 8 August 2008.

Ouellette, Laurie. *Viewers like You? How Public TV Failed the People.* New York: Columbia University Press, 2002.

Poppy, Nick. 'Frederick Wiseman', *Salon.com.* <dir.salon.com/story/people/conv/2002/01/30/wiseman/index.html?source=search &aim=/people/conv>, accessed 5 January 2009.

Potter, Deborah. 'The Secrets of Fox's Success', *American Journalism Review* December 2006/January 2007: <www.ajr.org/Article.asp?id=4236>.

Raphael, Chad. 'The Political Economic Origins of Reali-TV', in *Reality TV: Remaking Television Culture*, eds Susan Murray and Laurie Ouellette. New York: New York University Press, 2004: 123–40.

Rice, Ron, ed., *Media Ownership.* Cresskill, NJ: Hampton Press, 2008.

Rincon & Associates. *Latino Television Study.* Dallas, TX. National Latino Media Coalition, 2004.

Salamon, Julie. 'History That Calls for a Bit of the Ham', *New York Times* 3 November 2002: 2.1.

Schatz, Thomas. 'Desilu, *I Love Lucy*, and the Rise of Network TV', in *Making Television: Authorship and the Production Process*, eds Robert Thompson and Gary Burns. New York: Praeger, 1993.

Schneider, Steve. 'Cable TV Notes: A Channel with a Difference', *New York Times* 16 June 1985: 28.

Seiter, Ellen and Mary Jeanne Wilson, 'Soap Opera Survival Tactics', in *Thinking outside the Box: A Contemporary Television Genre Reader*, eds Gary R. Edgerton and Brian G. Rose. Lexington: University of Kentucky Press, 2005: 136–55.

Sella, Marshall. 'The Red-State Network', *New York Times* 24 June 2001: 6.26.

Simons, John. 'The Networks' New Advertising Model', *Fortune*:
<money.cnn.com/2008/05/02/technology/upfronts.fortune/index.htm?postversion=2008050507>, accessed 5 May 2008.

Smith, Merritt Roe and Leo Marx, eds. *Does Technology Drive History?* Cambridge, MA: MIT Press, 1994.

Smith, Neil. 'The Channel That Transformed TV', *BBC News Online* 25 February 2004: <news.bbc.co.uk/1/hi/entertainment/tv_and_radio/3485916.stm>.

Smythe, Dallas W. *Dependency Road*. New York: Ablex, 1981.

Spigel, Lynn. *Make Room for TV*. Chicago, IL: University of Chicago Press, 1992.

State of the News Media:
<www.stateofthenewsmedia.org/narrative_cabletv_economics.asp?cat=4&media=5>, accessed 15 July 2008.

Steinberg, Brian. 'Ads on ABC Most Expensive at Season Bow', *Television Week* 8 October 2007: 15.

Steinberg, Jacques. 'Digital Media Brings Profits (and Tensions) to TV Studios', *New York Times* 14 May 2006: 3.1.

Steinberg, Jacques and Stuart Elliott. 'ABC Roster Is Heavy on the Already Proven', *New York Times* 13 May 2008: C6.

Stelter, Brian. 'In the Age of TiVo and Web Video, What Is Prime Time?', *New York Times* 12 May 2008: C1.

Stelter, Brian. 'Whichever Screen, People Are Watching', *New York Times* 8 July 2008: C5.

Sterling, Christopher H. and John M. Kittross. *Stay Tuned: A History of American Broadcasting*, 3rd edn. Mahwah, NJ: Lawrence Erlbaum, 2001.

Story, Louise. 'Viacom's Full-Court Press for Online Ads', *New York Times* 19 March 2007: C7.

Story, Louise. 'A Variation on the DVR, without Ad Skipping', *New York Times* 13 August 2007: C1.

Streeter, Thomas. 'The Cable Fable Revisited: Discourse, Policy, and the Making of Cable Television', *Critical Studies in Mass Communication* vol. 4, no. 2 (June 1987): 174–200.

Terranova, Tiziana. 'Producing Culture for the Digital Economy', *Social Text* 63, vol. 18, no. 2 (Summer 2000): 33–58.

Thompson, Kristin. *Storytelling in Film and Television*. Cambridge, MA: Harvard UP, 2003.

Tinker, Grant and Bud Rukeyser. *Tinker in Television: From General Sarnoff to General Electric*. New York: Simon and Schuster, 1994.

Turner, Ted. 'My Beef with Big Media: How Government Protects Big Media – And Shuts Out Upstarts like Me', *Federal Communications Law Journal* vol. 57, no. 2 (2005): 223–33.

Turow, Joseph. *Breaking up America*. Chicago, IL: University of Chicago Press, 1998.

TV by the Numbers, 'Season to Date Network TV Ratings': <tvbythenumbers.com/2007/12/18/season-to-date-broadcast-net-ratings-924-1216/2160>, accessed 12 December 2007.

TV by the Numbers, 'Top ABC Primetime Shows': <tvbythenumbers.com/2007/11/20/top-abc-primetime-shows-november-12-18/1845>, accessed 12 December 2007.

TV by the Numbers, 'Top Cable Channels': <tvbythenumbers.com/2007/11/21/weekly-top-cable-networks-november-12-18/1864>, accessed 12 December 2007.

TV by the Numbers, 'Top CBS Primetime Shows': <tvbythenumbers.com/2007/11/20/top-cbs-primetime-shows-november-12-18/1846>, accessed 12 December 2007.

TV by the Numbers, 'Top Syndicated Shows': <tvbythenumbers.com/2007/11/29/top-syndicated-shows-nov-12-18/1951>, accessed 12 December 2007.

TVB Online, 'Media Trends Track': <www.tvb.org/rcentral/MediaTrendsTrack/tvbasics/39_Consumers_Allocate.asp>, accessed 4 June 2009.

Universal McCann, see Television Bureau of Advertising Online (TVB Online): <www.tvb.org/nav/build_frameset.asp>, accessed 8 August 2008.

Wachowski, Andy and Larry Wachowski. *The Matrix*. Warner Bros. Pictures and Village Roadshow, 1999.

Wang, Jennifer Hyland. 'Convenient Fictions : The Construction of the Daytime Broadcast Audience, 1927–1960', PhD dissertation, University of Wisconsin, 2006.

Wasko, Janet. *Understanding Disney*. London: Polity, 2001.

Waxman, Sharon. 'At an Ad Industry Media Lab, Close Views of Multitasking', *New York Times* 15 May 2006: C1.

'Weekly Primetime Ratings', *Television Week* 26 November 2007: 25.

Whitney, Daisy. 'Building a Blended TV Family', *Television Week* 10 December 2007: 1.

Williams, Raymond. *Culture and Society*. New York: Columbia University Press, 1983.

Williams, Raymond. *Television*, 3rd edn. New York: Routledge, 2003.

Zook, Kristal Brent. *Color by Fox*. New York: Oxford University Press, 1999.

Index

A History of Britain 123
A&E (Arts and
    Entertainment Network)
    121–2, 128, 154, 161,
    169
  origins and brand identity
    121–2
  true-crime shows and reality
    programming 122
ABC (American Broadcasting
    Corporation) 28–30, 89
ABC/Disney 112, 115–16
  acquisition by Disney 27–9,
    97
  brand identity 65
  classical network era 7
  Disney-ABC merger 30
  NBC 28
  news 146–9
  scheduling and
    programming strategies
    62–4
  takeover by Capital Cities
    29
ABC World News 146
Accenture 179
advertising 34
  ad sales 50–3
  ad spots 51–4, 178
  advertisers 2, 39
  agency operations 45–7
  audience data 36, 59
  brand integration and
    product placement 55
  commercials 40, 54
  control over shows 8, 68, 89
  daytime television 69
  Latino audience 43–5
  mass and niche audience
    42–3, 45, 49

advertising *cont.*
  NBC and matrix media
    178–9
  niche media ads 43
  upfront market 48
AETN (A&E Television
    Networks) 121
African American audience
    43
  BET 77–8
  CW 78
  Fox 25–6
  TBS 78
  TV One 78
AGB (Audits of Great
    Britain) 39
  see also Nielsen
Airline 122
Allen, Gracie 55, 90
All-New Mickey Mouse Club,
    The 134
Ambrose, Stephen 123
AMC 84
American documentary 151
American Experience, The 150
American Idol 106, 112, 145,
    161, 168
American Justice 122
American Playhouse 150
American Splendor 136
America's Funniest Home
    Videos 95, 104, 106–7
America's Most Wanted 25
America's Talking 158
  see also MSNBC
Amos 'n' Andy 91
An American Family 104, 151,
    162
Ancier, Garth 105
ancillary markets 84, 86,
    113–14, 121, 139
  Disney 29

ancillary markets *cont.*
  ESPN 77
  Family Guy 85
  Hills, The 179
  PBS 153
  24 113–14
Anderson, Chris 119
Andy Griffith Show, The 9
Animal Planet 128, 131–2
  Animal Planet Asia 132
  Animal Planet Europe 132
  Animal Planet Latin
    America 132
anthology drama 90
Antiques Roadshow 152
AOL (America Online) 19
  merger with Time Warner
    30
Apprentice, The 105, 108, 145
Arbitron 40–1
  see also Nielsen
Are You Smarter than a Fifth
    Grader? 108
Army Wives 84
Arrested Development 112
art television 141
Arthur 152–3
Astro All Asia Networks 122
A-Team, The 95
audience
  African American 25–6, 43,
    77–8
  baby-boomers 43
  brand communities 120
  children 77, 151–2
  classical network era 7, 9,
    58–9
  daytime audience 69
  DVR audiences 172
  ESPN 77
  FNC 157
  Fox 25–6, 112

audience *cont.*
  Latino 43–5, 115
  Lifetime 77
  mass audience 17, 19, 37,
    42
  MSNBC 159–60
  NBC 48–50
  Nickelodeon 77
  Nielsen 35, 56, 59
  Oxygen 178
  UPN 26
  Viacom 23
  WB 26
  women 43, 77, 178
  youth 43, 48–9
audience research 35, 38–41
Audimeters 36, 59
  see also Nielsen
Austin City Limits 154

Babylon 5: DVD afterlife 86
Back to You 61
Bad Girls Club 178
Ball, Lucille 8–9
Barney 152
Barnouw, Erik 162
Baseball 151
Battlestar Galactica 133
  DVD afterlife 86
Bauer, Jack 112
BBC (British Broadcasting
    Corporation) 121, 123,
    129
  comparison with CNN
    155–6
  PBS 150, 152
BBC America 154
BBC Worldwide 131
BBC2 128, 151
BBQ with Bobby Flay 128
Behind the Mysteries:
    Unlocking Da Vinci's
    Code 126
Bell and Howell Close Up!
    147
Benny, Jack 90
Berle, Milton 111
BET (Black Entertainment
    Television) 77–8
  acquisition by Viacom 78

BET *cont.*
  competitors 78
  critique 78
  programme genres 78
  response to competition 78
  target demographic 78
Betamax 14
Betty La Fea 114–15
Beverly Hillbillies, The 9
Beverly Hills 90210 25, 96,
    111–12
Beyond the Da Vinci Code
    126–8
Big Brother 105, 108, 164–5
Big Story, The 159
Biggest Loser, The 166
Biker Build-Off 125
Biography 121
Biography Channel 121
Black. White 145
Bloggermann 159
Boomtown 98
Boot Camp 167
Bordwell, David 141
branding 120, 125, 133,
    137–42, 145
  cable networks 133
  CNN 160
  ESPN 77
  FNC 157
  Fox 25
  HBO 137–42
  Lifetime 77
  MSNBC 157–60
  NBC 48–50
  niche cable channels 82
  Oxygen 178
  'utility brand' 155
Bravo 103, 122, 166, 169,
    177–8
  'brand extension' strategies
    177–8
'breakfast television' 148
  see also news
Brooks, James L. 61
Brown, David 138
Bruckheimer, Jerry 65
BSkyB (British Sky
    Broadcasting) 122
FNC 158
Budweiser bud.tv 182

Burnett, Mark 107–8
Burns, George 55, 90
Burns, Ken 151

cable television 103, 110–11,
    120
  ad spots 52
  'Big Three' 128
  brand identities 82
  cable platforms 82–3
  cable programming 76–7
  demographically driven
    channels 77, 81
  general-interest channels
    76, 81
  genre channels 76–7, 81
  growth of cable 13
  income 81, 83
  information genres 153
  niche cable channels 82,
    174
  Nielsen 38–9
  original programming 76–7,
    83–4, 132–42
  premium networks 136
  programming strategy 81
  ratings 52
  rise of cable 15–19
  utopian vision 12
Californication 139
Candid Camera 104, 161
Capital Cities 29
Carnegie Commission on
    Educational Television
    149
Carter, Bill 111
Casey-Werner Company 105
cassette technology 14
CATV (Community Antenna
    Television) 15
CBC (Canadian Broadcasting
    Corporation) 129
CBS (Columbia Broadcasting
    System): brand identity
    65, 67
  classical network era 7–10
  news 146–9, 160–1
  scheduling and
    programming strategies
    50, 65–7
Survivor 107–10
Viacom 21–3

CBS News 146
  CBS Evening News 70
  CBS Reports 147
celebrity shows 160–1
Changing Rooms 105
Channel 4 150
Chapelle's Show: DVD sales
  85
Chase, David 142
Cheers 49, 62
Child, Julia 152
Children of Dune 133
cinéma vérité 151, 162
Cinemax 136
Cisco Kid, The 94
City Confidential 122
Civil War, The 151
classical network era 5–15
Clockwork Production
  Process 101
  see also sitcoms
Closer, The 84, 133
CNN (Cable News Network)
  16, 76, 154–6
  branding 160
  CNN Headline News 16,
    155
  CNNI 155
  comparison with BBC
    155–6
  global expansion 155–6
  Gulf War coverage 16, 155
  website 156
Cold Case 66
Cold Case Files 122
Combat Missions 108
Comcast 78
Comedy Central 23
  DVD market for niche
    shows 85
Communication Act of 1934
  27
*Conspiracies on Trial: The Da
  Vinci Code* 126
Contender, The 108
COPS 106–7, 161
COSMEO 130
  see also Discovery Channel
*Countdown with Keith
  Obermann* 159

Couric, Katie 148–9
CPB (Corporation for Public
  Broadcasting) 150
Cribs 77
Criminal Minds 66
Criss Angel Mindfreak 122
Crocodile Hunter, The 131
Cronkite, Walter 146
CSI: Crime Scene Investigation
  60, 65, 106
  franchise 65
  CSI: Miami 66
  CSI: NY 66
Curb Your Enthusiasm 138–9
Curtis, Bill 122
CW 26, 112
  African American viewers
    78

*Da Vinci Code – Bloodlines,
  The* 126
Da Vinci Code, The 126–8
  documentaries 126
Da Vinci Declassified 126
Da Vinci: Seeking the Truth
  126
Da Vinci's Code 126
Dallas 68, 111
Damages 84, 134
Dateline 148
David, Larry 138
DBS (direct-to-home
  broadcasting satellites) 13
Deadliest Catch 125
Deadwood 138
Deal or No Deal 61
*Decoding the Past: The
  Prophecies of Israel* 128
Demme, Jonathan 151
Desilu Studios 94
Desperate Housewives 62, 69
Dexter 139
  see also Showtime
Diller, Barry 24
direct cinema 151, 162
Dirt 134
Dirty Sexy Money 63–4
Discovery Channel 128–31
  edutainment genre 82
  international networks 129

Discovery Channel *cont.*
  Latino audience 80–1
  marketing and promotion
    130
  new networks 129–30
  'shark week' 129
  website and Internet
    acquisitions 131
Discovery Civilization 130
Discovery Group 123
Discovery Health Channel
  130
Discovery Health Network
  131, 154
Discovery Home and Leisure
  130
  see also Planet Green
Discovery Kids 129
Discovery Kids on NBC 130
Discovery Science 129
Discovery Times 130
Discovery Wings 130
Disney 98
  acquisition of ABC 27–9,
    97
  ancillary markets 29
  Disney-ABC merger 30
  media conglomerate 29
Disney Channel 134–5
  audience 134
  brand identity 134
  made-for-TV film 134
  multiplatform strategy
    134–5
  programming 134
Disney, Roy 92
Disney, Walt 92
Disneyland 29, 92
DIY (Do-It-Yourself
  Network) 153
Dog the Bounty Hunter 122
Donald Duck Presents 134
Dow Chemical Company 151
Dr. 90210 166
Dragon's Den 105
Dragon Tales 152
Drew, Robert 162
*Drive thru History: Conquest
  of America* 124
Dumont 89

DVD 40, 84–6
  afterlife 86
  Disney 29
  Family Guy 85
  The Hills 179
  PBS 153
  The Sopranos 86
  24 113–14
  viewing habits 85–6
DVR 40–1, 54–5, 86
  DVR audiences 172
  DVR penetration 86
Dynasty 68, 111

E! Entertainment Channel
  160–1
Early Show, The 148
Eco-Challenge: Adventure
  Race, The 108
Ed Sullivan Show, The 90
Eddie 162
Edgerton, Gary 123–4
Eisner, Michael 30
El Show de Cristina 79
Emergency Vets 131
Emmy Awards 84, 128, 134
Encore 136
Endemol 105
Entertainment Tonight 149, 160
Entourage 138
  see also HBO
Epstein, Michael M. 140
ER 49
Erin Media 42
ESPN 43, 76–7, 80–1, 155,
  180
  ancillary enterprises 77
  ESPN Deportes 80
  Latino audience 80
  male demographics 77
  synchronous audiences 77
Eureka 133
Everyone Loves Raymond 61
Extreme History with Roger
  Daltrey 123
Extreme Makeover 145, 166
Extreme Makeover: Home
  Edition 105
Eyes on the Prize 151

Family Guy: DVD sales 85
  fans 85–6
  see also DVD
Farscape 133
Fashion Police 161
FCC (Federal
  Communications
  Commission) 17
  cable 12, 15
  CBS 9–10
  deregulation policies 70
  FCC freeze 28
  fin-syn 20–2, 97
  Fox 25–6
Fear Factor 105
Ferrell, Will 180–2
fifth estate, the 148
  see also 60 Minutes
fin-syn (Financial Interest
  and Syndication Rules)
  20–2, 97
1st & Ten 137
  see also HBO
First 48, The 122
Five Days to Midnight 133
Flavor of Love 168
FNC (FOX News Channel)
  156–8
  audience 156–7
  branding 157
  global expansion 158
  Time Warner 157
Fontana, Tom 138
Food Network 153
48 Hours 160
48 Hours Mystery 160
4400, The 133
Fox 38
  African American viewers
  25
  audience 25–6, 112
  branding 25
  FCC 25–6
  Latino audience 80
  news 156–8
  programming strategy 25–6,
  50
  reality television 106
  studio and network merger
  30

FOX Entertainment Group
  156
Fox Reality Network 112,
  154
Fox Sports en Espanol 80
Fraggle Rock 137
franchise 65–6
Frank Herbert's Dune 133
Frasier 61, 75, 102
FreemantleMedia 168
Freke, Timothy 127
French Chef, The 152
Friends 49, 50, 69, 75
Frontline 150, 153
Fugitive, The 111
Fuller, Simon 168
funnyordie.com 181
FX Network (Fox eXtended
  Network) 103, 110,
  133–4
  brand identity 133
  original programming 84,
  133–4

Galavision 79
  see also Univision
game shows 90, 108, 167
Gates, Bill 158
GE 98, 158
Gilmore Girls: DVD sales 85
Girls Next Door, The 161
Goldbergs, The 89, 91
Goldenson, Leonard 28
Gone with the Wind 16
  see also TNT
Good Morning America 148
Google 172, 180
Grammer, Kelsey 61
Grey's Anatomy 62–3, 65, 116
Growing Up Gotti 122
Guiding Light, The 91
Guns of the World 124
Gunsmoke 102

Handler, Chelsea 182
Hard Copy 160
Hardball with Chris Matthews
  159
Hartley, John 170
Hayek, Salma 115
HBO (Home Box Office) 18,
  76, 110, 122, 135–42

HBO *cont.*
audience 135–40
branding strategy 137–9
channels 139
HBO Comedy 139
HBO Family 139
HBO Films 136
HBO Latino 139
HBO Pictures 136
HBO Signature 139
HBO Zone 139
HBO2 139
marketing campaign 140
original programming
136–9
origins 136
'quality TV' 135–6, 137–9
subscribers 137–40
Healing the Hate 128
Heaton, Patricia 61
Hendricks, John 128
Heroes 86, 111
appointment television 68
Herskovitz, Marshall 182
HGTV (Home and Garden
Television) 153
High School 151
High School Musical 134–5
sequels and spin-offs 135
see also Disney Channel
Highway Patrol 94
Hill Street Blues 49
Hills, The 179
Hilmes, Michele 7
Hilton, Paris 165
Hispanic Television Index 44
see also Nielsen
History Channel 81, 121–8
branding and
merchandising 125
criticism 124
History International 124
programming strategy 124
Hitchhiker, The 137
Hitler's Skull 123
Hollywood studios and
networks 9, 13, 20, 27,
92, 99, 100
Disney's acquisition of
ABC 29
Paramount and ABC 28

Horizon 151
House M.D. 133
House of Payne 78
Hudlin, Reginald 78
Huntley-Brinkley Report 146

I Led Three Lives 94
I Love Lucy 9
I Want a Famous Face 166
Ice Road Truckers 125
Imagine Television 112
*In Crisis: Behind a Presidential
Commitment* 147
In Living Color 25, 112
In Search of the Holy Grail
126
independent television
producers 94
independent television
stations 24
WGN 13, 15
independent television
studios 96, 99
infotainment programmes
148–9
Inside Edition 149
Internight 158
*Investigating History: The
Holy Grail* 126
Investigation Discovery 130
see also Discovery Channel
Irwin, Steve 132
ITM (In the Motherhood) 182
*It's Always Sunny in
Philadelphia* 134
ITV 150
iVillage.com 178
Ivory Wars 129

Jack Benny Show, The 91
Jayne Mansfield's Death Car
123
Jazz 151
Jennings, Peter 146
Jericho 86, 111
Jerry Springer Show, The 106,
149
Joe Millionaire 106, 112, 167
Johnson, Robert 78

Kid Nation 61–2
Kids Incorporated 134
Kinney Services 17
Klauber, Edward 146
Kraft Television Theatre 89
Krause, Peter 63

L Word, The 110, 139
La Fea Mas Belle 114–15
L.A. Heat 133
*Laguna Beach: The Real
Orange County* 164
Larry Sanders Show, The 110,
137
*Late Night with Conan
O'Brien* 149
*Late Night with David
Letterman* 70, 149
Latino audience 43–5
Discovery 80–1
Nielsen 44
sports coverage 80
Telemundo 43, 71, 79, 115
telenovelas 79, 114–15
Televisa 43, 79
Univision 43, 79
Lauer, Matt 70
Law & Order 102–3
episode structure 103
*Law & Order: Criminal
Intent* 103, 122, 133
*Law & Order: Special
Victims Unit* 103
*Legend Detectives: The
Mystery of Rennes-le-
Chateau* 126
*Legend Hunters: The Holy
Grail – The Real Story*
126
Leigh, Richard 127
Levinson, Barry 138
Lifetime 77
branding 77
niche cable channel 82
original programming 83
women's audience 77
'long tail' model 119
LOP (Least Offensive
Programming) 7, 37, 59

Lost 69, 85–6, 111, 113
  appointment television 68
Lost Tomb of Jesus, The 126
Lotte 115
Lotz, Amanda 31, 120
Lou Grant 62
  see also spin-offs

Mad Men 84
Maday, Charles 124
Maddow, Rachel 159–60
made-for-TV film 92
'majors' 59, 120
makeover shows 145, 166–7
  American egalitarianism
    167
Marchand, Roland 175
Maria Full of Grace 136
Married with Children 24, 112
Mary Tyler Moore Show, The
    94
Masterpiece Theater 150
matrix media 11, 175–83
  The Hills 179
  matrix era 183
  matrix switch 176
  NBC 177–8
matrix TV 113, 116, 175
Matson, Kevin 125
Mayne Street 180
McCarthy, Jenny 182
McCarthy, Joseph 147
McKay, Adam 180–2
media conglomeration and
    synergy 28–31, 173–5
media mergers 30
Meehan, Eileen 36
Meerkat Manor 131, 142
Melrose Place 112
Men who Killed Kennedy, The
    123
Metromedia 24
Mickey Mouse Club, The 134
Microsoft 158–60
Military History Channel 123
Mindshare 182
Minow, Newton 146
Missouri River: A Journey, The
    123

Mister Roger's Neighborhood
    152
mobile telecommunications
    180
  ESPN 180
Monday Night Football 72
Monk 93, 103, 133
Monster Garage 125
Monster House 125
Moore, Mary Tyler 94
Moore, Michael 151
Morning Show, The 148
Morris, Errol 151
Movie Channel, The 18, 136
MOW (movie of the week)
    92
MSN 182
MSNBC 158–60
  audience 159–60
  branding 157–60
  Internet and portal 159–60
  talk shows 159
  Time Warner 157
MSOs (multiple-system
    operators) 18
  Disney's acquisition of
    ABC 29
  Viacom 21–2
MTM Productions (Mary
    Tyler Moore) 94
MTV (Music Television) 18,
    21, 43, 76–7
  global expansion 22
  The Hills 179
  Latino audience 80
  matrix media 179
MTV en Español 80
multichannel transition 31,
    174
multimedia environment 175
mun2 79
  see also Telemundo
Murdoch, Rupert 24–5,
    156–7
Murrow, Edward 146–7
MyNetworkTV 115
Mystery! 150
Mystery Science Theater 3000
    133

narrowcasting 120, 142, 157
National Amusements 22
National Film Unit of New
    Zealand 129
Nature 151
NBC (National Broadcasting
    Company)
  branding 48–50
  'brand extension' strategies
    177
  classical network era 5, 8,
    14
  CNBC 71
  matrix media 178–9
  MSNBC 71, 158–60
  news 70–1, 146–9
  quality programming and
    youth audience 49
  talk shows 69–70, 148–9
  Telemundo acquisition 71
  Weather Channel 71
NBC Nightly News 70, 178
NBC Universal 115
network oligopoly 3, 12, 24, 31
network studios 98
networks and Hollywood
    studios 27
  Disney's acquisition of
    ABC 29
  Paramount and ABC 28
new media 12, 130, 159, 179,
    183
news 145–61
  audience 71
  cable networks 145, 154–61
  celebrity shows 160–1
  confessional talk shows 149
  CBS 146–9
  CNN 154–6
  daytime talk shows 70, 145,
    149, 154, 165–7
  documentaries 147, 150–1,
    162
  entertainment news
    magazines 149, 154,
    160–1
  FNC 156–8
  infotainment 148–9

news *cont.*
  late-night talk shows 70, 149
  local news 74
  morning talk shows 69–70,
    148–9
  MSNBC 71, 158–60
  multiplatforming,
    repurposing and cross-
    promotion in network
    news 178
  NBC 70–1, 146–9
  network news 146–9
  news channels and
    narrowcasting 120
  news magazines 147–9
  nightly news 70, 146
  PBS 150
News Corp 24–6, 28, 98
  FNC 156
News Hole, The 159
News with Brian Williams,
  The 158
Newshour with Jim Lehrer 150
niche network 120
niche producers 125
Nicholas, Kyle 123–4
Nickelodeon 18, 21, 77
  programming strategy and
    scheduling 77
Nielsen 2, 35–6, 38–40, 42,
  56, 59
  C3 ratings 40
  data collection 36, 39–41
  Latino audience 44
  monopoly 36
  timeshifted viewing 40–1, 54
Nintendo 172
Nip/Tuck 110, 133–4, 139, 166
Nixon, Richard 147
Not Necessarily the News 137
Noticiero Univision 79
Nova 151

O&O stations ('owned and
  operated') 10, 24–6
Obermann, Keith 159–60
off-network reruns 9, 15, 20,
  52, 74–7, 84
On Location 137

One Hundred Years of Terror
  124
online video: content 172
  genres 182
  video ventures 182
  viral video 181–2
Oprah Winfrey Show, The 53,
  145, 149, 154, 165
Orangutan Island 132
O'Reilly, Bill 157
  MSNBC 159–60
O'Reilly Factor, The 157, 159
Osbourne, Ozzy 165
Osbournes, The 145, 165
Outdoor Wisconsin 150
OWN (Oprah Winfrey
  Network) 131, 154
  see also Discovery Channel
Oxford Scientific Film 132
Oxygen Network 77, 154
  brand identity 178
Oz 138

package unit system 99
Paley, William 7–8, 146
Panorama 148
Paramount Television 93
Paramount Theatres 28
Party of Five 112
Past Life Investigation 124
Payne, Tyler 78
PBS (Public Broadcasting
  Service) 131, 149–54
  ancillary sales 152–3
  British imports 150, 152
  children's programming
    151–2
  competition from cable
    153–4
  criticism 153
  documentary 150–1, 162
  educational 151–2
  'how-to-do' programmes 152
  merchandising 152–3
  news 150
  programme genres 150–3
  stations 150
  website 153
people meter 39
  see also Nielsen

Phil Donahue Show, The 145,
  149
pilot episode 99–100
Pimp My Ride 77
pitches 99
Planet Earth 129
Planet Green 130
Pop Idol 168
  see also American Idol
post-network television 145
POV 151
PPM (Portable People
  Meter) 40–1
  see also Nielsen
Price Is Right, The 167
Primary 147, 162
Primetime Live 148, 161
Prison Break 93, 111, 113
Private Practice 62–3
  see also spin-offs
product placement:
  classical network era 55
  24 and Ford 113
production studios 98
programming strategy 50, 59,
  61–3, 65, 69
  block programming 64
  cold roll 62
  counterprogramme 62
  hot switch 62
  lead-out 62
  Nickelodeon 77
  tentpole 63
  see also scheduling
Psych 93, 133
Pushing Daisies 62–3
  see also programming
    strategy, scheduling
push-pull technology 11
PVR (Personal Video
  Recorder) 40
  see also DVR

Quarterlife 182
  see also online video
Queer as Folk 110, 139
Queer Duck 139
Queer Eye for the Straight Guy
  145, 166
quiz show scandals 89

Rachel Maddow Show, The
  159
radio: advertisers 175
  audiences 42
  licensing and regulation 6
  localism 6
  radio networking 5–6
Radio One 78
radio soap operas 90–1
Raising the Mammoth 129
Ralls, Karen 127
Raphael, Chad 106
ratings 34–5, 37–8, 50, 52
  C3 ratings 40
  decline in network ratings
    177
  network ratings and niche
    cable channels 174
  ratings of TV commercials
    172
  see also Nielsen
RCA (Radio Corporation of
  America) 5, 8, 14
Real World, The 77, 106, 145,
  161–5
reality television 104–7, 145,
  161–5
  A&E 122
  CBS 107
  cinéma vérité and direct
    cinema 145, 161–5
  Fox 106, 112
  Fox Reality Network 112
  game shows 90, 108
  network reality television
    107
Rebel Billionaire, The 168
Redstone, Sumner 22
Reeves, Jimmie L. 140
Remini, Leah 182
Rescue Me 110, 133–4, 139
Restaurant, The 108
Rhimes, Shonda 63
Rhoda 62
  see also spin-offs
Riches, The 134
Richie, Nicole 165
Road Rules 164
Rock of Love 168
Rogers, Mark C. 140

Ross, Steve 17
Rouch, Jean 162

Sabado Gigante 79
Sakharov, Alik 140
Saturday Night at the Movies
  92
Saving Grace 133
Sawyer, Diane 70
Schama, Simon 123
scheduling 35, 60–9
  appointment television 67–8
  independent stations 74
  Nickelodeon 77
  24 112–13
Sci-Fi Channel 133
  brand identity 133
  original programming 133
  transmedia narratives 133
Seacrest, Ryan 161
Seahunt 94
*Secret Bible: Knights Templar –
  Warriors of God, The* 126
See It Now 147–8
Seinfeld 69, 75
Selling of the Pentagon, The 147
Sesame Street 151–2
  international franchise 151
Sex and the City 138
  DVD sales 85
Shield, The 103, 110, 113,
  133–4, 139, 142
Showtime 21, 110, 136, 139
  niche network 139
  programming strategy 139
Simple Life, The 145, 165
Simpsons, The 25, 112
Singing Detective, The 141
sitcoms 91
  sitcom production 101
Six Feet Under 63, 110, 138
60 Minutes 71, 148
Sleeper Cell 139
SNC (Satellite News
  Channel) 155
  see also CNN
Snoop Dogg's Father Hood 161
soap operas 68–9, 91
  audience 69
  daytime television 69
  primetime soaps 68, 111

Sony Corporation 14
Sony Entertainment
  Television 116
Sopranos, The 62, 110, 122,
  139–42
  aesthetics 141–2
  American Dream 139, 141
  audience 140
  DVD sales 85–6
  episode structure 140
  marketing campaign 140
  narrative complexity 140
South Park: DVD sales 85
spin-offs 62–3
Spirit of Enterprise, The 123
sponsors 8
  classical network era 55
  ITM 182
  multiple sponsorship,
    magazine format 55, 89
  PBS 150, 152
  See It Now 147
  Survivor 107, 110
sports coverage 71–3
  AFL 72
  Latino audience 80
  NFL 72
  WWS 73
Sprint 182
St. Elsewhere 49
Stargate Atlantis 133
Stargate SG-1 133
Stephen J. Cannell
  Productions 94–5
*Steven Spielberg Presents:
  Taken* 133
Strauss, Carolyn 138
Studio 52 90
Sunday Night Movie 92
Survival Anglia 132
Survivor 104–5, 107–9, 164
  controversy 109–10
  Survivor: Cook Islands
    109–10
Swan, The 166
Sweeny, Anne 134
syndication: affiliate and
  independent stations
  74–6

syndication *cont.*
  barter sales 53
  classical network era 8–10
  CSI 66
  Disney 29
  feature-film syndication 16
  fin-syn 20–2, 97
  HBO 139
  independent producers and
    syndication 94
  Law & Order 103
  network-era syndication
    99–100
  off-network series 75–6
  The Sopranos and A&E 122

Tales from the Crypt 137
talk shows: confessional 149
  daytime 69, 145, 154,
    165–7
  late-night 70, 149
  morning 69–70, 148–9
Tandem Productions 96
Taxicab Confessions 137
TBS 76
  African American 78
Telecommunications Act of
    1996 27–8
telefilm 8–9, 20, 92
Telefutura 79
  see also Univision
Telemundo 43, 71, 79, 115
  programming strategy 79
  target demographic 79
Telemundo Television Studio
    115
telenovelas 114–15
  primetime telenovelas 79
Televisa 43, 79
television documentary: ABC
    147
  CBS 147
  cinéma vérité and direct
    cinema 151, 162
  independent TV
    documentary 147
  NBC 147
  PBS 150–1
television financing 98, 100
deficit financing 100

television manufacturers 14
television production 89, 100
  network production 102
television seasons 83, 112–13
television stations 53
  affiliates 74
  CW and Fox affiliates 74
  independent stations 74
  local stations 73–6
  scheduling strategies of
    independent stations 74
television studios and
    Hollywood 91–2
Templar Code, The 126
Temptation Island 106, 167
Texaco Star Theater, The 89, 90
Texas Monthly Talks 150
That's Clever 128
30 Days 139
  see also FX
Thirtysomething 182
This Old House 152
Thompson, Kristin 141
Time Inc. 136
  HBO 136
  merger with Warner Bros.
    136
Time-Life 13, 18, 136, 162
Time Warner 18–19, 136
timeshifted viewing 40–1
  see also Nielsen
Tinker, Grant 48, 94
Titicut Follies 151, 163
TiVo 40, 42, 54
TLC (The Learning Channel)
    129
TNT (Turner Network
    Television) 16, 103, 133
  brand identity 133
  original programming 84,
    133
Today 69, 70, 148–9, 178
Tonight 70, 149
*Tonight and Saturday Night
    Live* 90
Top Chef, The 177–8
  'brand extension strategies'
    177
  multiple platforms 178
Trading Spaces 105, 145

TriStar 136
Tr3s 80
  see also MTV en Espanol
Tudors, The 139
Turnaround, The 128
Turner, Ted 15–17, 19, 97,
    154–5, 157
  attempt to buy CBS 17
  MGM film-library purchase
    16
TV One 78
  programming strategy 78
  target demographic 78
Twentieth Century 147
20th Century-Fox Television
    24, 93, 112
24 112–14
  appointment television 68
  criticism 114
  DVD and ancillary sales
    113–14
  schedule 112–13
21 Jump Street 95
Twin Peaks 141

Ugly Betty 65, 114–16
  import to South America
    116
UHF (Ultra High Frequency)
    13, 15, 24, 28–9
Unilever 182
Universal-MCA 92–3
Univision 43, 79
  competitors 78
  primetime telenovelas 79
  programming strategy 79
  target demographic 79
UPN (United Paramount
    Network) 23, 26
  African American viewers
    26
  CW 26
  merger with WB 26
  programming strategy 26
USA (USA Network) 103,
    132–3
  brand identity 132–3
  original programming 133

variety shows 90

vaudeville 6
VCR 39–40, 84, 173
Verleibt in Berlin 115
vertical integration 7, 98
VH-1 168
VHF (Very High Frequency)
    28
Viacom 18, 30–1, 78, 87, 98
    conglomeration 22–3
    purchase of Blockbuster
        Video 22
    purchase of CBS 22–3
    relationship with CBS 21–3
    takeover of Paramount
        Pictures 22
Victory at Sea 147
Victory Garden 152
video games: video games
    and television 172
Vietnam: A Television History
    151
Vin Di Bona Productions 95

Walking with Dinosaurs 129
War, The 151
Warner Amex 18, 21
Warner Brothers Presents 92
Warner Communication
    International 17–18
    see also MSOs
Wayans, Keenan Ivory 25
WB (Warner Bros.) 26, 92–3
    African American viewers
        26

WB *cont.*
    CW 26
    merger with UPN 26
    programming strategy 26
WCTG 15
    see also WTBS
WE 77
Weakest Link, The 108
Weaver, Pat 69
webisodes 112, 182
Weeds 139
Weiner, Matthew 84
Welcome to Pooh Corner 134
Welfare 151
Weller/Grossman Productions
    126–8
Werner, Tom 105
Westinghouse 155
WETA 150
WGA (Writers Guild of
    America) strike 115–16,
    161, 172–3
    intermedia rights 173
    video and website revenue 173
WGBH 150–2, 154
WGN 13, 15, 19
What's My Line? 167
Wheel of Fortune 53
When Animals Attack! 106
White Paper 147
White, Paul 146
Who Wants to Be a Millionaire
    104–7
Who Wants to Marry a Multi-
    Millionaire? 106

Wife Swap 145
Williams, Brian 158
Williams, Raymond 38
Winfrey, Oprah 78, 131, 166
Wiseguy 95
Wiseman, Frederick 151,
    154, 162–3
Without Breasts There Is No
    Paradise 115
WNET 150–1, 162
    see also PBS
Women and Me 137
World's Wildest Police Videos
    106
WTBS 15, 155
    superstation to general-
        interest cable network
        76
WWS (The Wide World of
    Sports) 73

Yanki, No! 147, 162
Yesterday 136
Yo Soy Bea 115
Yo soy Betty la fea 115
Young, Gig 92
YouTube 2, 172–3, 180
Yugoslavia: Death of a Nation
    129

Zalznick, Lauren 177–8
Ziv, Fred 92
Zuiker, Anthony 65
Zwick, Edward 182